CONSPIRATORS AND POETS

CONSPIRATORS AND POETS

By

D. J. ENRIGHT

1966

CHATTO & WINDUS

LONDON

Published by
Chatto & Windus Ltd
40 William IV Street
London W.C.2.

*

Clarke, Irwin & Co. Ltd
Toronto

Printed in Great Britain by
T. & A. Constable Ltd
Hopetoun Street, Edinburgh

3. *Pleb.* Your name, sir, truly.

Cin. Truly, my name is Cinna.

1. *Pleb.* Tear him to pieces! He's a
        conspirator.

Cin. I am Cinna the poet, I am Cinna the poet.

4. *Pleb.* Tear him for his bad verses, tear
        him for his bad verses.

Cin. I am not Cinna the conspirator.

1. *Pleb.* It is no matter, his name's Cinna;
        pluck but his name out of his heart,
        and turn him going.

3. *Pleb.* Tear him, tear him!

CONTENTS

CONTENTS

Author's Note

The majority of the essays and reviews here collected were originally written (they have since been revised in varying degrees) for weekly or monthly publications of a not specifically scholarly nature. Some of these pieces can scarcely be called 'literary criticism', I should think. Some of them might be described as 'light'; many are certainly short, and could be taken to bear out, in a particular case, a rash generalization occurring in one of them, that most people do not have more than two thousand words' worth to say on most topics.

I should like to thank several of the editors concerned, and notably Karl Miller of the *New Statesman*, for editorial amendments which, however resented at the time, seem to have perpetuated themselves here, and also to thank Melvin J. Lasky of *Encounter* for the gift of a title whose apt frivolousness ought to dispel any possible misconception of the nature of the essay in question, or of the author's disposition.

For permission to reprint I am obliged to the editors of the following journals: *New Statesman, Encounter, Essays in Criticism, The Spectator, The Times Literary Supplement, International Literary Annual No.* 3 (John Calder), *The New York Review of Books, Holiday* (New York), *Quadrant* (Hobart), and *The Bulletin* (Sydney).

Singapore, 1965

I

The Rise of the Criticocracy

'Master,' said Lin Chen, 'I have but one son. For what profession
I shall prepare him?'
'Let him be trained as a judge of letters,' replied the Master, 'for
such grow increasingly wise. The same cannot be said of poets.'

(*Tao Tschung Yu*)

On leaving the Far East some nine years ago I found myself,
for a combination of reasons, unemployed, and in no
position to turn up the nose at an Assistant Lectureship (bottom
of the scale) advertised as vacant in a British colonial university
in the fairly far West. In the course of the interview in London,
a gentleman on the Selection Board remarked after scrutinizing
my application: 'You used to write literary criticism, I see. . . .
Of recent years you appear to have written only poetry and
novels.' I mumbled something about thinking there had been
rather too much criticism of late so perhaps some of us could lay
off it for a while. 'Ha!' said the gentleman sternly, 'Novels and
poetry are all very well, but they're no use to a university. What
a university wants is literary criticism.' Luckily another job
came up soon after.

Like a university, what George Watson wants is literary
criticism. The real stuff, with its own technical terminology
and imbued with the historical sense. His book *The Literary
Critics*—'the first history of English criticism by a British scholar
since Saintsbury's, which is now over fifty years old'—indicates
how sadly English criticism from Philip Sidney to Boris Ford
Inc. has failed to meet his requirements.

Let us first look at these two large desiderations. 'Rhetoric is
dead.' (Long live Rhetoric! I fear.) And the technical terms in

13

current use—'ambiguity', 'irony', etc.—'do not compensate for a loss which for two hundred years has rendered English criticism less exact but more available'. We must all agree that, other things being equal (or even a little less than equal?), 'availability' is a considerable advantage: Leavis's *Revaluation* comes to mind as a notably available work, and much of *The Common Pursuit*, both of them even more available now, in paper-back. But our anxiety about the concomitant loss of 'exactitude' will only be allayed when we realize that for Mr Watson, apparently, this virtue is something which derives from the employment of such words as 'paralipsis' and 'litotes'.

Secondly, the historical sense. Mr Watson argues that the curious reactions listed in Richards's *Practical Criticism* simply go to show that 'unhistorical reading is bad reading', that is to say, the writers of the protocols couldn't be expected to cope with poems 'torn from their historical context'. This is a death-blow to those of us who teach English literature abroad, who strive to expound works torn even from their geographical context, their climatical and botanical and every other context. (Except the merely human.) But I, at any rate, am still left with the feeling that the lesson of the protocols is a much simpler one, and with the suspicion that the historical sense is the sort of thing which is indispensable to the sort of person who, through a natural dislike for it, is not going to read much literature anyway.

Quite early on Mr Watson alludes to the 'access of doubt' and the 'flood of warnings against critical arrogance' which occurred in the 1950's. But it does not suit his book to investigate this phenomenon at all closely, since his contention is that the history of descriptive criticism is 'one of progress in a very simple sense'. But simple in what sense? Nobody, he tells us with an awe-inspiring assurance, can doubt this.

The average schoolboy of today is probably capable of analysing more closely and more accurately than Dryden or any of Dryden's contemporaries, and the ordinary reviewer often enjoys a similar unearned advantage over the greatest of English critics before the twentieth century.

One thought which this statement suggests is that the average schoolboy must be getting a very bad literary education then, and would be better left to his own devices than to the vices of his educators. Another is that, even in the shabby world of the ordinary reviewer, an unearned advantage is not an advantage.

So criticism is getting better and better. A lot of us will admit that creative writing isn't getting better and better: at the best it gets different. If this radical discrepancy between criticism and creation is a fact, then it at once accounts for the precedence, in prestige and probably in quantity, which criticism now takes over creation. Write a poem and the odds are it won't be as good as *Absalom and Achitophel*. Compose a critical paper and the chances are in favour of its being better than anything in *An Essay of Dramatic Poesy*. It is also likelier to gain you promotion, whether you are a university lecturer or a schoolboy—or, if you are unemployed, a job. Is it any wonder that some of us have been visited with religious doubts of late years, disquieted by an arrogance all the more unseemly in an activity which apparently is growing easier every day?

Mind you, at one point it almost seems as if Mr Watson believes in the unremitting advancement of literature too. He praises as 'richly historical' Dryden's comment on Chaucer (more specifically, on his lame versification): 'He liv'd in the infancy of our poetry, and . . . nothing is brought to perfection at the first. We must be children before we grow men.' But it is the tinge of historicity in the comment, not the comment itself, not what Dryden *says*, which takes his fancy. Mr Watson's distaste for poets and their doings makes itself felt throughout. Creative writing comes a disreputable second to critical description of creative writing. Consequently Pope, who had the temerity to dress criticism in the rags of verse, is severely ticked off. 'Let such teach others who themselves excel' is a 'ridiculous demand'. It is *wrong*, but it can scarcely be called 'ridiculous', seeing how large a proportion of the critics dealt with in Mr Watson's book are also 'creative writers' of some stature. Then of 'Ten censure wrong for one who writes amiss', Mr Watson remarks, 'the claim seems absurd': the poet was just covering up for himself. It is all an 'indecent, puppyish cleverness', and the *Essay on Criticism* is 'the work of a cheeky young poet'. This is certainly a refreshing reaction to the *Essay*, though all the same it might be felt that the cheek is on the other foot.

Poets are incorrigible amateurs. Mr Watson prefers a more professional sort of person—like a critic. But then, to our surprise, it transpires that he doesn't think much of our critics, either. One by one they are promisingly introduced and quickly found wanting. 'It is clear that, with Addison, something important has happened to English criticism', but a few pages later Addison is dismissed as 'ambitious but complacent'. Then comes Johnson, a poor poet ('even the eagerness of the twentieth century . . . has not found a great deal to praise in the verse-satires'), but something much more important—'the true father of historical criticism in English'. Unfortunately Johnson possessed a 'theory of literary excellence which we are obliged to snatch at as he runs'. (Critics should have the decency to stand and deliver.) There is much commendation of Johnson, but still far too much niggling.

> The comment is just: but, as so often in Johnson, there is an absolute failure to reconcile theory and practice. . . . The diagnosis is admirably just, but in his conclusion Johnson fumbles and fails.

So what? We are more interested in Johnson's diagnosis than in his conclusions: it is his diagnosis that stimulates and helps us to establish our own conclusions. When the practical critic is

as intelligent and feeling as Johnson, so much the better if the
theoretical critic in him merely fumbles.

Next on the list is Wordsworth, briefly. He suffered from an
inability to theorize. Even so, it might have been made clear to
the readers of this Penguin book that Wordsworth's *Preface* will
be read, and will be meaningful, long after the book and my
cantankerous comments on it have been utterly forgotten. To
that average schoolboy Wordsworth may seem a dreary old
square: but he was also a sincere, committed man; and, whether
or not he was blessed with the historical sense, he had a sense of
his own time. Coleridge comes off better, 'supreme among the
English critics' in fact. But it is as a thinker that Mr Watson
prizes him, and not for his actual thoughts. Mr Watson claims
that we find Coleridge's descriptive criticism disappointing
because we have divorced it from its theoretical foundations.
Yet a little later he himself tells us that 'his achievement is brilliant
but sporadic, and offers no single example worthy to be advanced
as a model'. So perhaps, despite appearances, Coleridge has not
turned out to be, what Mr Watson wanted him to be, the kind
of practitioner who presents us with the 'key' to poetry (when
what we needed was help with a poem).

'There is no coherent theory of poetry in Arnold's criticism.'
And the 'oddity' of it is that 'while we are repeatedly enjoined
to choose "the best, the really excellent" and to adopt "a high
standard and a strict judgment" and to eschew "the historic
estimate and the personal estimate", we never see Arnold doing
any of these things himself'. Which may be vivacious, but is so
untrue that we are not surprised when the poor man is written off
as a young Sohrab slain by old Dr Rustum of Rugby—a demonstration by Mr Watson of the historical sense at work, perhaps.

And so to the twentieth century. 'There are plenty of passages
in *The Sacred Wood* and even later . . . that make us wonder
what a delicately intuitive historian of literature was lost in Eliot.'
Come to that, there are passages in *Emma*, that make us wonder

what a delicately intuitive headmistress was lost in Jane Austen. But Eliot receives admiration, and several shrewd thrusts. Leavis too is admired, from a safe distance. Though—a climax of bathos—'we may despair of a lucid account of central doctrine from a critic who has always shown himself indifferent to the study of linguistics . . .'. The critics who come off best are De Quincey, Henry James (in the book's best chapter) and Empson. But commonly Mr Watson's standards are so high as to be practically invisible. Only God could satisfy him for long, and God has other things to do.

The Literary Critics is, as I hope I have indicated, a stimulating book. But it is likely to bewilder and mislead the uninformed or innocent reader. It is stimulating to those who have already thought a good deal about the practice of criticism and its present state. And to them it will be stimulating in that, through its very efforts to reach a quasi-popular public, it displays with a shocking clarity certain attitudes and assumptions which the cognoscenti prefer to leave unexamined among themselves. In popular terminology, Mr Watson has shot some neat goals, into his own net.

Incidentally, Lin Chen's promising son eventually became a literary historian, and one of the most respected and well-to-do inhabitants of the land of Han. There is no record, though, as to whether his works ever appeared in paper-back.

Articles of Use

Perhaps, before we grapple with our rather unnatural subject, a brief nature note will be in place. Observation confirms that, from a very early stage, the young bird backs hurriedly to the edge: such desperate urgency in so immature a creature is deeply moving. Truly, it is a rare bird who fouls his own nest. We should not be surprised that there is but little open protest against the mountainous molehills of criticism which increasingly usurp the literary scene and even threaten to blot it out. For such complaints would only come from literary critics and could come only from critics not themselves 'creative writers' if humiliating suspicions were to be avoided. Yet a certain disquiet seems to be felt, and to have been felt for some time. In *The Literary Critics* George Watson alluded in passing to an 'access of doubt' occurring in the 1950's. And when Randall Jarrell christened the same decade 'The Age of Criticism', he was drawing attention to yet another depressing aspect of our super-market culture: on display, and apparently well patronized, a generous counter of criticism; in a back room, a heap of obsolete lines, poetry and novels and the like.

Norman Podhoretz isn't worried by the current 'popularity' of criticism,[1] and he meets Mr Jarrell's fear lest young men should give their time to explicating other people's poems instead of writing their own by quoting Arnold. 'Is it true that Johnson had better have gone on producing more *Irenes* instead of writing his *Lives of the Poets* . . .?' Obviously *that* isn't true, but when Mr Podhoretz calls this 'the best possible retort' he is falling below his usual level of intelligence, or of fair play. What we suffer

[1] *Doings and Undoings*. Hart-Davis.

from is not a plethora of *Lives of the Poets*, but a density of non-Johnsons. The mass production of so-called criticism, 'autonomous' criticism, the dissemination of factitious discriminations and niggling non-opinions—this is far more pernicious than any flood of plain bad verse. For one thing, practically nobody will read the latter, whereas students read the former, and instead of the poetry or fiction it is nominally concerned with. Criticism is creating taste, true enough, but it is creating a taste for more criticism—and the more of it you read, the less obliged you feel (despite the warnings of the masters) to form an opinion of your own.

What probably lies behind Mr Podhoretz's seeming serenity is the thought that a lot of good 'articles' appear in magazines, especially perhaps in America, and many of them are written by people who pride themselves more on their poems or novels than on their articles—and, Mr Podhoretz feels, pride themselves improperly. It is understandable that Mr Podhoretz should find this exasperating, since he is a writer of articles himself (so wide-ranging and so personally involved that he is at once removed from that class of critics for whom my opening remarks were intended), he edits *Commentary*, a magazine printing articles of a praiseworthy standard of meaningfulness, and (as far as I know) he is not an exponent of that sort of writing which has arrogated to itself the epithet 'creative'. Perhaps the best possible retort to Mr Podhoretz is that, just as there are not many critics like Johnson, so there are not all that many article-writers like Mr Podhoretz.

It is difficult to review his collection of articles, or even to describe it, except by picking a not-quite-real quarrel with him, by exaggerating a tendency in him which he is usually too perceptive to allow to get out of control. One might sum up that tendency, at the risk of looking sillier than Mr Podhoretz ever could, as combining an excessive respect for current events and issues (well, sometimes they are sort of important!) with an excessive disrespect for 'imagination' (true, it is the kind of thing

that people who possess nothing else are frequently credited with).
At the outset Mr Podhoretz gives fair warning that most of
these essays originated in the appearance of a new book 'that
seemed to me to raise important issues of one kind or another;
and almost always it was the issues rather than the book itself
that I really cared about'. He seems to believe that the only
alternative to this would be tantamount to regarding literature
as an end in itself, as if there were no third way, however difficult
it might be to expound. It appears to me that the weakness in
Mr Podhoretz's healthy-sounding approach is that his handling
of general issues, joined with a breezy willingness not to bother
too much with specific books or authors or only with those which
happen to lie on his desk at the moment, provokes the reader
into irritatedly thinking of all the exceptions to Mr Podhoretz's
rule and suspecting that the one thing they don't do is prove it.
An instance is the essay written in 1957 on the apparent repudia-
tion of liberalism by 'the young generation' and their unearned
poise, sobriety, prudence and (in a word) 'maturity'. This sizeable and ingeniously constructed edifice of theory rests only on
a few small facts selected from a moment of time. What Mr
Podhoretz is undertaking here is an elaborate and sophisticated
version of 'the greatest novel I have read this week'.

This lively interest in 'issues' can trick Mr Podhoretz into
finding much more in a book than is there: the issues are imported,
and then devalued by their surroundings. The comment that *The
Ginger Man* is 'a book that comes out of a moment in history
when the old world has died and the new one about to be born
may never struggle its way out of the womb' is likely to evoke
a different response from the one Mr Podhoretz is expecting.
And his assertion that 'only a man who had been affected by
Marx and Trotsky down to the core would have been capable
of writing *Barbary Shore*' and that this novel is 'a pathology of
the modern spirit' will only make many people feel that in that
case they neither wish nor need to hear anything more about

Marx or Trotsky or the modern spirit. When you are talking of books then you must talk of writing, and literary judgment (dread term!) cannot be pretermitted. Otherwise what you are offering is sociology without case histories, economics without statistics, or politics without anything other than politics. A case cannot be argued respectably without producing respectable witnesses.

The journalist at least writes about something real, whereas 'imaginative' writers often occupy themselves with something which is merely imaginary, sheerly arbitrary, not to be found in 'the world out there'. Admittedly the most powerful argument for the utilitarian view of art has always been the insipid preciosity of the aesthetes. 'In the end,' says Mr Podhoretz,

> A Fable leaves us wondering whether the time will ever come again when a writer will be able to dismiss politics in favour of the Large Considerations without sounding like a chill echo from a dead world.

Well, yes, we have all suffered both from Large Considerations and from No Considerations At All. But to believe that there must be something in a work of art which will preserve it against the sheer fugacity of politics and the mutability of the social and cultural scene—this is not the same as dismissing politics as 'an obscene farce'. There was always a middle path between utility and aestheticism, and those have trodden it whose works have survived—survived quite notable social changes: the invention of gunpowder, the French Revolution, Marx, Freud, even maybe the supermarket. And how? Because—here comes some shameful banality!—because of their permanently valid and tellingly communicated insights into the condition of being human. (After all, however political situations vary, you get much the same behaviour going on within the political situation.) It seems as if the character of that middle path, where art and nature go miraculously hand in hand, can only be defined in terms of its exponents, and best described by—but what am I saying?—by literary critics, real ones of course. Yet perhaps we shouldn't be too scared of those banalities, those large-sounding considerations: Mr Podhoretz himself cheerfully informs us that what Edmund Wilson stands for is 'faith in the importance of the things of the spirit and the responsibility that rests with writers and thinkers to maintain that faith'.

It is because Mr Podhoretz too stands for this that one is distressed to see what starts as a healthy scepticism towards 'imagination' (conceived as the belaurelled or bedizened enemy of intelligence) drifting dangerously near to an attack on any sort of writing which can't be fitted into his brave new art-category of 'the magazine article'. He argues that today our sense of beauty is involved with the sense of usefulness. We go in for the 'practical'—Scandinavian chairs, stainless steel, foam rubber—and the reason why we are unhappy with 'the traditional literary forms' (as he calls poetry and fiction) is that they don't strike us as 'practical', designed for 'use', whereas

> a magazine article by its nature satisfies that initial condition and so is free to assimilate as many 'useless', 'non-functional' elements as it pleases. It is free, in other words, to become a work of art.

It is often the case that my students find literary-critical articles very practical—and seemingly find the traditional literary forms not designed for use—when it comes to writing essays and examinations. Mr Podhoretz concludes thus:

> Certainly the rigid distinction between the creative and the critical has contributed to the growth of a feeling that the creative is 'useless'. Curiously enough, the very concept of imagination as a special faculty—and of novels and poetry as mysteriously unique species of discourse subject to strange laws of their own—itself implies that art is of no use to life in the world.

One would like to know who is responsible for that 'rigid distinction', whose exactly this 'very concept of imagination' is, what the word 'special' means (imagination *is* something special, something specially human), and what is intended by the expression 'strange laws of their own' (they *are* rather strange, seeing that, although they must exist since those who break them are punished, they don't seem amenable to satisfactory codification). Otherwise one is touched by this evidence of an editor's respect for his craft, while maybe failing to see quite why magazine articles *need* such an eloquent defence. It would have been enough for Mr Podhoretz simply to say: whatever is read, is right.

Yet, speaking of the occasional rhetoric in Robert Warshow's article on the Rosenbergs, Mr Podhoretz explains that 'the heart has discovered something and the mind springs like a panther to formulate its meaning'. How imaginative!—and perhaps by 'heart' he means what others mean by 'imagination'. His own heart is definitely in the right place, even if not quite in literature. There are excellent pieces here on Fitzgerald, Faulkner and Kerouac, but what I found most impressive was the last section, 'The World Out There'—essays on Gallipoli, on the Irish potato famine and on Hannah Arendt on Eichmann—which (it is after all a long book) I had firmly intended to skip. It doesn't matter that in much of *Doings and Undoings* Mr Podhoretz is not being a literary critic; because he is being something else eminently worth being, something conveniently indicated by his final comment on the theory of Jewish 'complicity' in the destruction of the Jews:

> Murderers with the power to murder descended upon a defenceless people and murdered a large part of it. What else is there to say?

The burden of my initial discontent with the ruck of literary critics is that they are (and quite contentedly) being nothing.

Randall Jarrell's heart most certainly is in literature—and if it is not quite broken, it is very sad indeed.[1] His collection of

---

[1] *A Sad Heart at the Supermarket*. Eyre & Spottiswoode.

'essays and fables' begins with the story of Alexander the Great asking Diogenes if there was anything he could do for the philosopher. 'Yes, you can get out of my light.' The contemporary American reaction to this anecdote, according to Mr Jarrell, is one of simple incredulity: why on earth would a top government official bother to call on a down-at-heel egghead? Mr Jarrell describes the same situations that Mr Podhoretz has summoned up. People who wouldn't hang a Kandinsky on their walls are quite ready to buy it in the form of a sports shirt or swimming trunks or, better still, a chair. The chair is useful. 'The great new art form of our age, the one that will take anything we put in it, is the chair.' The chair, and the magazine article.

Poetry, Wordsworth proclaimed, gives pleasure, which is why a description in verse will be read a hundred times where a description in prose is read once. But not any longer, adds Mr Jarrell: today the prose will be read a thousand times where the verse is read once. To most of us verse is 'so uncongenial, so exhaustively artificial' that a man could make his fortune, Mr Jarrell suggests, by entirely eliminating from American culture all traces of verse of any sort. This is much what Mr Podhoretz says, but in a very different spirit, for he is celebrating the magazine article, whereas Mr Jarrell is lamenting the passing of something which he contends can never be replaced. The 'imaginative' writer is no longer able to console himself with hopes of posterity, for he feels that the future, if there is one, will be like the present but worse. True, he still retains an audience of sorts, he is still read by a kind of happy few: the critics—but 'Better to sing my songs to a wolf pack on the Seeonee than to a professor on the *Sewanee!*' One wonders whether Mr Podhoretz will continue to rate Mr Jarrell's articles higher than his fiction. . . .

If only Mr Jarrell's values could be found in company with Mr Podhoretz's cheerfulness! Prophets of doom serve only to bring doom a little closer, and possibly Mr Podhoretz's belief in people, if less well documented than Mr Jarrell's despair, is of more utility at a time when despair seems merely sterile or worse, a personal luxury which other people, less affluent, may conceivably have to pay for. Then too, give a dog a bad name and—soon he won't read you at all, not your verse, not your fiction and not even your magazine articles. . . . But Mr Jarrell isn't really a prophet of doom if you take what he says together with the way he says it. He quotes marvellously, he deploys a sprightly wit, as when referring to consumer culture and 'the great chain of buying'; and, while in the act of mourning the disappearance of the common reading public, he shows himself so splendidly apt in discussing literature with that very public— introducing Kipling or an anthology of stories or describing how a poem of Robert Frost's adds up and what it adds up to—that you can hardly convince yourself that it really doesn't exist at all. It can't (can it?) be solely a superb act of the imagination on Mr Jarrell's part.

In their different ways, Mr Podhoretz's indirectly and Mr Jarrell's directly, both these books tend to bear out my preamble. Literary critics are parasites, if not the parasites of parasites. At the same time it must be confessed that both books contain a certain amount of what has to be called literary criticism. We are obliged to suppose that they belong to that class of exceptions which prove the rule, the two of them appearing, rather exceptionally, on the same day.

Thirty Years On: Reflections on the Reprinting of *Scrutiny*, 1963

Has the reception of *Scrutiny* Reprinted thrown any new light on the 'reputation' of the magazine and of its chief editor? *Scrutiny* has always had more than one reputation, of course, and its reputation in the teaching field has differed notably from the reputation held or bestowed by the press in general, whether the academic press or the London literary press. Indeed, the points of resemblance between the two have been as few as those between the critic and teacher F. R. Leavis as known to teachers and students of English literature (perhaps I had better confine myself to foreign students, for I do not wish to step outside my personal experience in these notes) and the Dr Leavis of Downing of the London literati and (alas) some cosy home academic circles. By the former class he is recognized, read and respected as someone who has committed himself to judgments strong enough, meaningful enough and sufficiently well supported to be of help to them (and foreign students cannot be expected to gasp over the finicking and falsely fine points of another sort of critic). To the latter, he is the dyspeptic Doctor, a near-Dickensian caricature, though more sinning than sinned against.

Leavis's animadversions on the 'two Cambridges' and on the comprehensive hostility and 'habit of discrimination' against *Scrutiny* of the metropolitan press have of course drawn the old charge of paranoia from the reviewers of the reprint. Yet the very reception of the re-issue might seem in its characteristically contemporary and watered-down way to bear out Leavis's beliefs. With a few honourable exceptions (and those, it seems,

chiefly from outside the academic world) the reviewers have
come both to praise *Scrutiny* (rather consciously) and to bury it
as well. As Alan Brien put it in *The Spectator* of 1 November
1963 (and he may well have been thinking especially of the two
articles printed in the preceding issue of the same periodical):
'Despite all the tributes and wreaths piled on the magazine's
grave by these and other reviewers, I was left with a feeling of
niggling reluctance to make a warm, generous gesture of gratitude.'

But there is a difference between the quasi-reasonable attitude
of these latter-day reviewers and the attitude which prevailed
among their counterparts during the 'thirties and the 'forties.
The former derives not so much from outraged feelings, vested
interest, fear and jealousy, as from a degree of putative sophistication, self-complacency and indeed self-conceit which in turn are
born out of ease, affluence, success, the intellectual side of the
expanding welfare state. The 'sixties is indeed a very different sort
of time from the 'thirties, and I shall return to this theme later.

The reviewers of the reprint have of course praised—and
sometimes praised generously, so generously that it is barely
possible to reconcile their reservations with their commendations.
Sometimes too they have praised where their own withers could
never have been wrung, though even if the music criticism of
Wilfrid Mellers is in that way a safe choice for commemorative
literary reviewers, one still welcomes their praise, for it is right
and it is long overdue. (Q. D. Leavis comes in for favourable
mention, too, as an 'astringent and serious reviewer'—perhaps
of books neither written, nor written about, nor taught, by the
current assessors.) They are right, too, in mentioning the increasing proportion of marginal (even perhaps scholarly) material
in the later numbers of the magazine, though this could also be
taken as a tribute to the sheer amount of basic work done in the
earlier numbers and its sheer effectiveness: the times were changing, and popularization was already afoot elsewhere, with
varying success, as for instance in the *Pelican Guide to English*

Literature. In some cases, it must be granted, mere aggression was replacing needful demolition. At the same time it should be noted that the complaint about *Scrutiny* losing its liveliness over the years and contracting its range of subject-matter has been voiced in magazines which never had very much liveliness to lose and whose greater range has therefore been a matter of greater boredom and for greater regret.

Another common criticism or complaint relates to Leavis's disciples and pupils, or some of them. There was always some sort of critical authority behind the strictures, however severe of the senior contributors to the review—says the writer of the *Times Literary Supplement* 'front' of 1 November, a decently balanced and warm-hearted account—but 'this was not always true of the "juniors". Scanning again these well-remembered volumes, one cannot absolve all contributors from the charge of unnecessary offensiveness.' Frank Kermode in the *New Statesman* of 25 October puts it more strongly though less persuasively in speaking of the 'tones of authoritative anger and self-regard from epigoni with nothing authoritative to communicate beyond their conviction that although the world has much to learn from *Scrutiny*, a *Scrutiny* man has nothing to learn from the world'.

It would be wrong to dismiss these complaints, whatever their provenance. At least I should myself find it impossible (out of personal experience) to do so. Leavis's admirers have not always heeded his insistence that 'a judgment is personal or it is nothing; you cannot take over someone else's'. It remains to add that the phenomenon of attempting to live on unearned (and therefore unreal) capital has by no means been reserved to followers of Leavis, and that the motives of those who rally to a banner, however noble the cause may be, have always been mixed and never exclusively of the highest kind. The bigger the dog, the more numerous his fleas. If there had been university schools of English in Samuel Johnson's time—and I must admit that Leavis has always struck me as bearing a more immediate kinship to

Johnson than to Arnold[1]—then think what droves of little Johnsons there would have been! None of them remembered today, none of them surviving even as sticks for others to beat their master with.

What is to be deplored in these reviews is not so much what is said—the truth of the complaints I have listed is fairly obvious, and so is the limitedness of its significance—as the tone in which it has been said. The articles in *The Spectator* are the worst offenders in this respect, and one wonders why the paper felt it necessary to print two pieces which are unanimous in their patronizing attitude.[2] (The *New Statesman* was clearly deliberate in its printing of two articles, the one an appraisement by an English professional and the other a touching personal tribute from a South African non-professional.) We will pass over in silence C. B. Cox's unfortunate description of Dr Leavis turning up to give his seminars 'in an old dressing-gown that revealed his bare chest': he must be bitterly regretting it, if only because it raises a doubt as to whether he ever attended a seminar given by Dr Leavis. But he follows up with this:

> At first I was very disappointed, for he proved without the necessary talents to lead a seminar. He asked questions followed by silences, and most of the hour was taken up by a feverish monologue,

---

[1] The admirer of Leavis will feel able to apply to him some of the observations he has himself made on Johnson: not only '. . . the traditional notion of the arbitrary Great Cham of criticism, narrow, dogmatic and intolerant', but also, 'Johnson is not invariably just or complete; but the judgment—and he never fails to judge—is always stated with classical force and point, and based beyond question on strong first-hand impressions. He addresses himself deliberately and disinterestedly to what is in front of him; he consults his experience with unequivocal directness and always has the courage of it' (*Scrutiny*, Summer 1944).

[2] Obviously the diagnosis made by H. A. Mason in 1947 (in the second number of *The Critic*) is not yet entirely out of date: 'The Leavis case is fortunately the rare one of the obnoxious character holding on until in the course of time it has become apparent that he is a great man and must be admitted, however reluctantly, into the fold, if only to avert scandal.'

full of his reminiscences of past disputes. But just occasionally he would make a point about some line in Blake or Hopkins which, now so many competent lectures have faded from my mind, I remember vividly. . . .

It sounds like nothing so much as a conscientious and worried head of department struggling to compose a fair-minded confidential report on a somewhat disappointing junior member of his staff. So perhaps I may be permitted to introduce my own memories, which go back further than Mr Cox's, and tell me that Leavis was one of the very few teachers I came across who actively and deeply *wanted* his pupils to follow what he was saying and treated them as something approaching equals, without a hint of condescension. Perhaps that is what today is called 'feverish'. At all events I consider myself extremely lucky to have had as tutors both Leavis and James Smith, for Professor—as he now is—Smith had the gift of bringing out the most gauche of pupils by deceiving them into thinking that they were teaching him and that he was grateful for it.

Mr Cox's subsequent remarks, in which he strives to give this bare-chested devil his due, merely have the effect of discrediting Mr Cox even further:

> He forced students to abandon received opinions, and to make a personal response to the words on the page. This highly sensitive response to words marks the unique quality of *Scrutiny* criticism. Today it is a scandal that a large percentage of teachers of English, at all levels, still have no personal appreciation of great literature. . . .

'Scandal' seems hardly the right word. Maybe there was great virtue in that old dressing-gown. . . . But—and this is certainly a scandal—Mr Cox's tone is very wrong. Admittedly he is a university teacher of English and joint editor of a critical journal and joint author of a book of essays in Practical Criticism. But the dissimilarities between Mr Cox and Dr Leavis are, to put it gently (and in accordance with Mr Cox's demand that 'this tone ought never to be heard again in literary dispute'), more striking than the resemblances.

The second *Spectator* article, by J. B. Bamborough, is a good deal more sophisticated in manner, much more judicious in tone, but rather more incorrect in substance. Mr Bamborough's contention is that Leavis—and history will prove as much—is a follower, not a leader, 'and what may seem to us now important and vital differences between his work and that of others may seem in fifty years' time so subtle and tenuous as to be insignificant . . .'. Yes, history is cruel—but it is cruel to hangers-on, to inert disciples, and to careerists and opportunists. And it is a peculiar type of historian (though after all one has observed before the strange lack of relationship between historians and history) who can predict that (say) *Revaluation* and *The Great Tradition* and a healthy number of essays by the same author will not be found among the few critical documents of our time to survive. If these do not live in history, what on earth will? Who are those 'others' to whom Mr Bamborough refers, and what are their works? Where else is 'the splendid passion giving life to Dr Leavis's own pronouncements'—to quote from *The Times Literary Supplement* article—'a passion reminiscent, at times of the best passages of Milton's pamphleteering'?

Mr Bamborough sets up as himself an historian in describing Leavis as essentially a Victorian in the general ethos of his work, or even a Romantic: 'from the point of view of the historian he could truthfully be described as a disciple of Arnold—or, indeed, of Shelley'. For Mr Bamborough is concerned with 'principles' and 'critical standards', which means that he can go on to inform us that Leavis's *New Bearings in English Poetry* and *Revaluation* 'are in fact the application of principles and insights derived from Eliot and Richards'. (The later work, however, derives from Henry James and D. H. Lawrence.) How come that Aristotle has been left out of this cloud of origins? Only someone obsessed with critical principles in the void could fail to see how utterly distinct is the mass of Leavis's writing from that of Eliot and Richards and so on.

Mr Bamborough gives the game away when he speaks of 'Leavis's conspicuous failure to state an aesthetic in support of his draconian judgments'. (Compare this with George Watson's dictum in his recent book, *The Literary Critics*: 'We may despair of a lucid account of central doctrine from a critic who has always shown himself indifferent to the study of linguistics . . .'.) 'Conspicuous failure'—well, 'conspicuous' at least is the right word. And who, incidentally, are those critics who have scored a conspicuous *success* in stating their aesthetic? (Even Mr Watson fails to track them down.) When Leavis does get round to stating his aesthetic, if he does, then we shall know that he has really retired from literary criticism. And if smugness about the present state of criticism could be shaken by anything at all then it would surely be shaken by a moment's cool consideration of these pronouncements of Mr Bamborough and Mr Watson and what they imply. Any idiot can state an aesthetic, and many do. What is the right word for those who, without (incidentally) stating their own aesthetic, reproach others with not having done so?[1]

To return to this popular charge of paranoia.[2] It would be

---

[1] What is amusing in those who level the reproach at Leavis is their innocent assumption that the question of stating an aesthetic or expounding central doctrine has never occurred to him. Yet (if this were needed) his essay on 'Literary Criticism and Philosophy' appeared in *Scrutiny* for June 1937 and has been available in *The Common Pursuit* since 1952: '. . . I can only reply that I think I have gone as far in explicitness as I could profitably attempt to go. . . . In fact, though I am very much aware of the short-comings of my work, I feel that by my own methods I have attained a relative precision that makes this summarizing seem intolerably clumsy and inadequate. . . .'

[2] The paranoia is not all on one side. In *The Listener* of 7 November Graham Hough says, 'It is hard to write justly about the value of *Scrutiny* when its real achievement is subject to so much posthumous inflation. Readers of the correspondence columns in literary journals will have observed the process going on for some years now.' True, the correspondence columns do from time to time carry protests against the stock gibing at *Scrutiny* which goes on elsewhere in the journals.

dishonest of me not to confess my own feeling, that Leavis has at times engaged in breaking butterflies on wheels—and then gone on to break the broken remains. This has gained for the objects of his anger a sympathy which otherwise they would not have enjoyed. But who can be wise, amazed, temperate and furious, loyal and neutral, at the same time? When men have been treated as outcasts, they can hardly be expected to show the dispassionate sobriety of the law-abiding citizen. To say this is not to bring an accusation of persecution-mania—a condition which is, precisely, a delusion. And I think that today's younger generation are badly placed to gauge the temper of the period in which Leavis achieved maturity as a critic and undertook his most important work as a teacher and an editor. 'History' may set us right about this in due course: the difficulty is for the 'sixties to imagine the conditions which prevailed in a period so near in time as the 'thirties.

Life was hard then, in all sorts of ways. It was hard for 'scholarship boys' to get scholarships enough to enable them to go up to the university. It was hard to get published. It was difficult to start a magazine, and difficult to keep it going. It was hard to find a post. Some experienced remarkable difficulty in obtaining promotion in their professions, or even security: in the 'Retrospect' appended to the reprint of *Scrutiny* Leavis mentions that it was not until he was 'well on into his fifties' that he at last achieved a full University Lectureship.[1] Today a lot of us are Professors, and most of us at any rate contrive to become full Lecturers well before our fifties. Professor Kermode, incidentally, remarks of *Scrutiny* that 'merely to appear in those pages, it seems, was to found a reputation'. Yes, but what sort of reputation? Paranoia does not loom large in my own make-up—I confess at once to a sense of having done rather better for myself in life than I deserve—so I can assure Professor Kermode,

[1] 'For the first half-dozen years of *Scrutiny* I had no post and no salary, and was hard put to it to make a living' (*Listener,* 1 November 1956).

without any personal bitterness, that for a candidate for home university posts immediately after the war—let alone earlier—to have appeared in the pages of *Scrutiny* was considerably more disadvantageous than to have appeared in no pages at all. Some of us went abroad in the first case—and whether we afterwards regretted it is a another matter—simply because foreign universities were less particular or (perhaps through backwardness) less prejudiced against *Scrutiny's* minor fry. What it was like in the 'thirties and early 'forties I can only imagine—but I *can* imagine.

That the Establishment of today is so much more tolerant, or nervous, or splintered, or amorphous, may in part be the result of the hard and telling knocks which *Scrutiny* gave the Establishment of its time. Today nothing succeeds like satire, as the history of the Angry Young Men so aptly indicates. Voices crying in the wilderness are soon after to be heard echoing through the corridors of powers. And the academic arena is more often given over to exhibitions of grunt-and-groan than to genuine battle. In the age of affluence and atomic anxiety the missionary spirit seems hard to come by and hard to hold. Today *Scrutiny* would receive a grant from some foundation or other, it would even be able to pay its contributors, probably. But whether anything really like *Scrutiny* would last for long these days is a more doubtful question.

The generation to which the present writer belongs has a foot in each of these two worlds, and there is small excuse for *us* if we forget the conditions, the atmosphere, in which the Leavises lived and worked during their formative and perhaps their greatest years. You *had* to be devoted, you had to be tough, to survive in any serious and minority-supported endeavour in those days. 'Profound conviction, conviction displayed, argued and articulated, is peculiarly disturbing', as William Walsh has said[1]—at any time. Certainly sweetness did not always go with

[1] 'A Sharp Unaccommodating Voice: the Criticism of F. R. Leavis', *A Human Idiom*, 1965

light, then. The ensuing hardships, whether social or moral or financial, brought out the best in men: they also imposed their penalties and left their scars. There were giants in those days, and the life of giants is rarely one of placid happiness. We need them, though, from time to time, so perhaps we should try a little harder to bear up under their sufferings.

My last three paragraphs indicate why (or indicate one reason why) the pontifical, judicious, wreath-bearing sort of 'assessment'—for example, 'If Leavis remains an Awful Example, like Rhymer (who is only remembered for his boob about *Othello*), a grave injustice will have been done'—strikes one as indecently ignorant as well as incongruous, so much less real and to the point than Alan Brien's simple recall of 'the feeling of release I experienced when I first met *Scrutiny*' or Dan Jacobson's account in the *New Statesman* of 'the feeling of curiously personal gratitude which I have, and I know others have, to Dr Leavis and his magazine', and of the way he used *Scrutiny* as 'a kind of home university'.

As for the paranoia and its consequences. . . . Even if granted, this is a narrowly temporary and marginal objection. And an objection which, by the way, one hears much less about overseas, where the climate is unfavourable to imported fashions, where personalities and 'personalities' count for so much less, and where Leavis is known as the author of certain cogent and illuminating books and essays—the author of work which (to use a Leavisism) is 'there', very definitely so, and likely to remain there for a long time to come.

Hands White and Calm: on Cyril Connolly

CYRIL CONNOLLY is an introvert on a grand scale. With a whole-heartedness which only Etonian breeding could render tolerable, he has devoted the bulk of his writing to himself. And, if we leave aside the cryptic references to love, he has been concerned with one aspect of himself: the 'promising writer' who failed to deliver.

From his examination of self-failure Mr Connolly draws various deductions which he relates to the general literary failure of the last thirty years. Some of his conclusions are true, for he is intelligent, he has a sharp tongue which he is not afraid to use. Others have no general validity, for Mr Connolly is only one human being and not God. In other words, Mr Connolly is sometimes a shrewd, substantial critic of the ways of the literary world; sometimes he is merely an ingenious contriver of alibis for Mr Connolly. Blame, too, should begin at home; and occasionally it should stay there.

What vitiates his analysis of the general sterility, and what best explains his own, is what we must call his sub-Flaubertianism. He is obsessed with 'style'. He *knows*, very well, that 'style is . . . the relation in art between form and content', but he continues to behave as if style were art itself and the whole of art. In Parts I and II of *Enemies of Promise* (now a Penguin Modern Classic) he recommends a language combining the graces of the Mandarin with the force and rapidity of the colloquial. (A blend, perhaps, of Etonian and State school English?) This solution sounds very feasible, but it rests on the assumption that style is something which you concoct in advance and then spread over your subject-

37

matter. Part III, which is meant to exemplify the solution, indicates how false the assumption is. For this section of the book, largely an account of the author's schooldays, varies as the subject dictates between light Mandarin (public school slang) and heavy Mandarin (classical quotations, public schoolboy's journal). As the subject dictates. And Mr Connolly's real trouble (if I may be so rude, and so inartistic as to begin with a conclusion) has been a deficiency of subject-matter. A 'promising writer' who remains promising is often that: intelligent, well educated, witty, a skilled phrasemaker (like Mr Connolly himself, with his 'seeking a womb with a view' and 'cultivating the chairmanities'), but lacking subject-matter. Such a writer may well, by a natural self-deception, see his difficulty as one of 'style': language has let him down: a 'literary' explanation is found for a literary failure.

Mr Connolly has something sensible to say about each of the 'enemies of promise', broadcasting, advertising, journalism, the killers with kindness. On, for instance, the insidious pleasure afforded by journalism of 'being paid on the nail, and more especially of being praised on the nail'. But however lively his exposure of these enemies, there is usually something to be said on the other side; his diagnosis isn't wholly convincing; the fault is not altogether in our stars or our editors or our wives. 'It is the two-thousand word look which betrays journalism', says Mr Connolly, for a critic needs the greater length which only a few quarterlies can offer. But surely we can admit that most long articles in the critical heavies are not especially life-giving (however helpful they may be in making an academic living) and that most of us don't have more than two thousand words' worth to say on most topics. The brevity of journalism can be a godsend both to the writer (who is forced to think clearly) and to the reader (who doesn't have to put up with scholarly padding and evasions). How many of our large tomes about The Novel tell us as much about the subject as Lawrence's short piece on 'Why the Novel Matters'?

Mr Connolly's 'Georgian Boyhood' features as the fiercest of the enemies of promise. A fairly personal enemy, since not everyone of his generation was condemned to Eton. Life there is —or was—lived at such a pitch that the rest of one's allotted span seemed a long, sad anti-climax. When Mr Connolly left, 'I was, in fact, as promising as the Emperor Tiberius retiring to Capri. I knew all about power and popularity, success and failure, beauty and time. . . .' No wonder the fees have always been so high. We notice, however, that Mr Connolly was prone to these experiences of anti-climax long before he entered Eton. To receive and unroll the bundle of *Comic Cuts, Magnet, Gem*, was 'my thrill of the week', but 'even then I am depressed by the knowledge that nothing I shall find inside will come up to the sensation of opening them'. (No, I don't think this shows how sound a literary critic he was at that early age.) It was at Eton that he decided that 'all was vanity', a finding confirmed by his favourite authors, the Greek lyric poets, Horace, Voltaire, Verlaine, God, and so on. Were these the only authors on the Etonian syllabus, or was the young Cyril drawn to them by some predisposition?

Circling round, we find ourselves back at the question of 'language'. One result of his Etonian education was that linguistically Mr Connolly lost on both the swings and the roundabouts: 'I didn't see how one could well write in English, and my Greek and Latin were still not good enough.' Is he parodying the parodies of Waugh and Huxley, or is he serious? Apparently the latter, since a similar confession is made in *The Rock Pool*, an early tussle in faintly fictionalized form with the preoccupations of his later work. Naylor, the failed author, failed hero, reflects that he failed to write his book

> partly because he found he could only write in one language . . . the style that is common to mandarin academic circles given over to clique life and introspection. This dead literary English . . .

blocked any approach to a new vernacular. In addition a heavy vein of Yellow Book preciousness appeared; he became not quite himself when he wrote. . . .

The Rock Pool is an account of failed artists and sexual eccentrics on the French Riviera, more humane than Waugh-like, but still (one would have thought) fairly devastating. The 'artists' are *Punch* caricatures, and the sexual eccentrics run to expatriate form. Yet it transpires at the end that the novel is seriously intended to denounce 'the clumsy capitalist world that exalts money-making and poisons leisure, that suppresses talent, starves its artists, and persecutes its sexual dissenters . . .'. And Naylor, a feeble, ridiculous and distasteful creature, discloses himself as Cyril Connolly lamenting at the age of thirty his own lost promise —lost, or assassinated by the aforementioned enemies of promise. Retrospectively we note that this was Palinurus's maiden voyage round his rock pool, and that later expeditions uncovered nothing essentially new.

'Brilliant but unsound.' Mr Connolly appears to have fallen in love with this early self-description. 'Whom the gods wish to destroy they first call promising.' He can be a very charming and amusing masochist, talking of himself (see p. 122 in the Penguin *Enemies of Promise*) in rather the same way as Auden used to talk about other people. *Enemies of Promise* does have claims to be a 'modern classic'. *The Unquiet Grave*, however, seems to me largely a tedious and pretentious exercise in well-read masochism, sick with the 'virus of good taste', a prolonged indulgence in a half-hearted death-wish. It gives the game away. Palinurus tells us, 'he would like to have written *Les Fleurs du Mal* or the *Saison en Enfer* without being Rimbaud or Baudelaire, that is without undergoing their mental suffering and without being diseased and poor'. A gentleman first and an artist afterwards—was that another Etonian lesson never to be escaped from? Or was it 'Saint Flaubert' as quoted on the first page of *The Unquiet Grave*:

'*L'art est un luxe; il veut des mains blanches et calmes*'? Really Mr
Connolly was in no position to ask the cultivated reader of
Horizon whether he or she could honestly say 'that you would
rather have your child turn into Baudelaire than Lord Nuffield'.
Palinurus agrees with Flaubert that '*à mesure que l'humanité se
perfectionne, l'homme se dégrade*'. In his mouth this is not so much
an admonition as an enervated acknowledgement of defeat, the
measure of his Flaubertianism, and a ripe expression of that
'futilitarianism' (promising coinage!) which Mr Connolly traces
to 'a passionate belief in art, coupled with a contempt for the
subjects about which art is made'. That is, for life, with its soiled
and twitching hands.

This is the root of the failure. Wordsworth's *Preface* is tendentious, muddled, boring, priggish and pompous; but it is the
voice of a man with real passions and real beliefs about real life.
Mr Connolly's long 'preface' to his unwritten work has all the
minor graces which Wordsworth lacks and none of Wordsworth's gracelessness; but it is cold and sterile, not a cure but a
post-mortem, not a personal struggle but a general capitulation.

'When the time came for my Oxford viva, I was older than
the rocks and my eyelids were definitely a little weary.' As
'Where Engels Fears to Tread' shows, Mr Connolly is a splendid
parodist, and a good practical critic, when he can take several
steps back from himself and stay put. When he can stop being
so fearfully *conscious* about writing, and style and language, and
how 'the health of a writer should not be too good', as if one
needed a medical certificate to write, and so on. He has the saving
wit of English aestheticism, though it doesn't save enough. He
is a latter-day Oscar Wilde, damped down by good social and
political sentiments, a hard gem-like flame with irresolute
ambitions to drive a turbine. I suppose he himself, if not his
writings, could be termed a 'modern classic', at any rate a classic
case, of the more romantic sort.

Once below a Time

DYLAN THOMAS, who died in 1953 at the age of 39, was a writer. His reputation rests on *Under Milk Wood*, an entertaining and touching 'Play for Voices' ('Isn't life a terrible thing, thank God?'), and on twelve or fourteen highly individual and energetic poems (simple in theme, verging on the sentimental) and a large number of brilliant lines. It seems likely that posterity will accord Thomas (I shall take the liberty of referring to him by his surname) a status similar to that of Beddoes.

Thomas should not be confused with that far more famous phenomenon known as 'Dylan'. 'Dylan' is the equivocal hero of this album[1] of old cuttings (from *Adam International Review, Encounter, Yale Literary Magazine*, etc.) which throws new darkness on no end of unreal questions. 'Dylan' is here very thoroughly documented. He was, we gather: 'the Villonesque king of the vagabonds' (Introduction) as well as 'a sort of Roi d'Ys' and 'an explosive mixture of Rimbaud and Verlaine' (John Davenport); 'a Promethean keeper of fire and secrets' though, at the same time somehow, 'a rare heedless fornicator of language' (Theodore Roethke); a 'wonderful baby' (Richard Eberhart), and 'no piner for Fanny Brawnes' (Geoffrey Moore), indeed 'a Donne to Christopher Fry's Marlowe' (John Graddon); 'a sort of Peter Pan and William rolled into one' (Ralph Wishart), but less like William since 'he was very manly, athletic, and a great runner, though there was something wrong with his reflexes and he never learned to fight; which was a great pity in one so extremely aggressive and pugnacious' (Roy Campbell), notwithstanding

[1] *Dylan Thomas: The Legend and the Poet.* A Collection of Biographical and Critical Essays. Edited by E. W. Tedlock.

which handicap, he 'struck a blow for basic humanity, and died of the fight' (Introduction).

Pamela Hansford Johnson tells us how in earlier years she wrote poems in collaboration with Thomas, each of them supplying alternate lines. Daniel Jones used to do the same, and adds that 'some of the poems are very, very beautiful' and he still has 200 of them. (Publishers please note.) Perhaps this procedure left its mark: Thomas appears to have conceived his poems very largely line by line, so that they break out at all points in all directions and the consequent eduction of an 'argument' is more a matter of goodwill than conviction. The effect of his working method ('a phrase at a time . . . I am a patient man')—for he was all the same a very deliberate artist—was to breed further images out of images already too easily arrived at. 'Unconscious' where he should rather have been conscious, he seems to have been conscious where this was of little relevance to the sort of writing he had committed himself to. We hear a lot about his *hwyl*, his marvellous spontaneity and flow; but some of us may feel that much of his verse is laboured and unwieldy, that the way he says a thing is out of all proportion to what he is saying.

There being but little argument to get a grip on, commentators have generally resorted to the interpretation of his 'symbols', which (such is the nature of symbols, or of commentators) turn out to be chiefly 'sexual'. The long interpretative essay by David Aivaz provokes the reflection that, whatever you intend to do with Thomas's poetry, you shouldn't 'interpret' it. When one has been instructed that 'head' is a male sexual symbol, that 'maid and head' is a pun on 'maidenhead', that 'cockshut eye' is both female sexual symbol and the mind's eye, or (by Marshall W. Stearns) that 'the conceivable image of a gusher spouting to a divining rod lends itself to a sexual interpretation', the poem has lost most of its charm and more of its interest. How odd that in this age of precision instruments in literary criticism it is still supposed that to call something a symbol is to make a meaningful statement! After all—as someone has probably said—a sexual symbol's only a sexual symbol, whereas a good cigar's a smoke.

One of the more amusing pieces is by Augustus John who claims that Thomas was possessed by 'the Lord of Laughter, the Elemental *Clown*'. It is true that Thomas had a rich sense of humour. But next to Mr Eliot he has attracted the most unhumorous admirers ever. He couldn't afford—I mean in the financial sense, as a family man—to laugh at *them*. Unhappily, as a poet (and John Davenport says that 'the only work which had the faintest importance in his eyes was the making of poetry'), he couldn't afford not to laugh at them. Perhaps the saddest pages in this sad compilation are those which describe a performance Thomas underwent at the University of Utah. Professor Brewster Ghiselin 'and his following' (I quote the co-ed reporter) are putting the poet through his paces:

Ghiselin: But, on the other hand, isn't it possible to narrow and fix a meaning to the exclusion of richer levels of meaning?

Thomas: Oh God, isn't an education wonderful!

Ghiselin: I shall be silent from now on.

Thomas: No, I mean it as a compliment. You say things so well, and I'm ashamed to be flippant and go down the side-alleys. . . .

The Elemental Clown just remembered in time that he couldn't afford to laugh at his masters. . . .

Student:Why do you write poetry, Mr Thomas?

Thomas: Because I have the time. Because I have to live too; (*mumbled*) I don't know why. It is very slow work, however. Only five poems published in the last six years. . . . And it's work! Oh God, it's awful! . . . I write some very bad poems.

We are told that Thomas won a uniquely large audience for

poetry. Better for him had he had no audience at all than the kind whose admiration no sensible man could find other than grotesque or else impertinent, the kind who salivate aesthetically to the sound of jargon which Thomas as a poet was under the necessity of avoiding. (I'm not thinking of the WEA-type audience: their breeding is far better, but they can't pay so handsomely.) What could he do, in the face of this, for he was a sensitive man, but get drunk and try to stay drunk? And of course act the buffoon—for, as Karl Shapiro points out, 'all the literary world loves a buffoon'. There are almost as many stories about Thomas as about ex-king Farouk—the last of the capital-p Pashas, the last of the capital-p Poets—and the wonder is that Thomas lasted as long as he did.

His death was the occasion for a general leave-taking of senses, even on the part of normally reasonable people, a large-scale collapse of common sense and common decency. Richard Eberhart tells us that 'it is not time to tell the truth, maybe it is never time'. He then starts to tell us the truth, even so, because 'one should tell the truth', but then decides that 'one cannot tell the truth. It would be too harsh, too unbelievable; too rich, too deep, too wild and too strange.' This particular truth, when one eventually gets to it, seems to be that Thomas astounded a whole lot of people in America and then went off with Eberhart's naval officer's raincoat which was never seen again. (In much of this obituary writing it is curiously difficult to know whether Thomas is being celebrated or arraigned.) William Jay Smith remembers that 'once in the midst of a dinner-party, when the conversation had turned to literary topics, he broke in. "There's nothing so beautiful," he said, and his hand shot up, "as a lark rising from a field. That's what we . . . we . . .". He left the sentence for us to complete.' Francis Scarfe declares that Thomas's philosophy is 'an advance on the pretty pantheism of Words-worth', and Edith Sitwell that 'his poems appear, at first sight, strange. But if you heard a tree speak to you in its own language, its own voice, would not that, too, appear strange to you?' In a piece portentous even by local standards, George Barker gives us to know that 'the pathologist's opinion that he died "of a brain ailment of unknown origin" simply illustrates the undisguised intervention of the powers of darkness in our affairs: for this is one of their greatest as it is their latest triumph. With this sleight-of-hand assassination such powers now openly operate among us.' And with a nice effect of irony, Marshall W. Stearns remarks that 'little is known of Thomas's life; he is Welsh and was born in Swansea in 1914'.

Assuming they ought to have been reprinted, then these items really should have been dated. Many of them are sadly dated. It's a bit much at this point in time to have André Breton and Freud waved about your head as brave new critical weapons. The editor claims to have represented the chief objections against Thomas's work, but he doesn't hide his own sympathies; the objections occupy some 20 pages out of a total of 280. Best of the critical criticism is Geoffrey Grigson's essay on 'the slide into idiot romance'; and points of various interest are to be found in the contributions of Lawrence Durrell, Hugh Gordon Porteus, Henry Gibson and Karl Shapiro.

The effect of this book, in which friend after friend bears witness to Thomas's gaiety, humour and charm, is to depress unbearably. Apparently the editor intended to distinguish between the Legend and the Poet. He has merely confused them further. What the publisher intended I can't imagine—unless to promulgate a dreadful warning against the literary world. The old lady was not so far out who remembered Thomas at seven as the 'Bubbles' of the painting (here ascribed to Joshua Reynolds. Ah, scholarship, scholarship!). He was a Bubbles who fell among literary touts, publicity hounds, non-writing writers agog to bring a writer down, and 'acceptable compromises'. The compromises were simple: instead of writing he was to talk; instead of working he was to drink; instead of being a poet and a person

ONCE BELOW A TIME

he was to be a 'character'—and how acceptable they were events soon proved. If his poems don't, then the *Letters to Vernon Watkins* will show us fairly clearly what there was in Thomas to be wasted. This present volume mostly itemizes the wasting or sickens us with high-sounding and false explanations of it. The vultures who fed on him alive still feed on him dead.

Robert Graves and the Decline of Modernism[1]

'I had been sent there on a Command staff-course along with thirty
or forty rigidly regimental brother-officers who detested me because
I was not one of them, and whom I detested because they were not
one of me. . . .'

Robert Graves: *Mrs Fisher, or The Future of Humour*, 1928)

I MUST at once apologise for bringing you here tonight merely
to listen to a talk, and moreover to listen to a talk merely about
poetry. About a commodity in large supply and short demand
whose social value is problematical at the best. And I am not
even going to talk about poetry at its best. I abase myself for
failing to slant my inaugural lecture to local needs and interests;
I realize that I cannot expect to be offered a commission in the
Cultural Brigade on the strength of it.

But it seems impossible to avoid altogether the pressing
question—'How is a culture built up?' So let us, by way of
propitiation, make a short and modest proposal. A culture is
built up by people listening to music and composing it; reading
books and writing them; looking at pictures and painting them;
observing life and living it. Now, using the word 'culture' in its
widest sense (and its sense grows wider day by day), we must
admit that the cultures of the old world were *extremely* cultural—
in the sense of being very distinctive, very idiosyncratic, very
different from one another. Today the most distinctive national
cultures are those which involve cannibalism, head-shrinking or

[1] An inaugural lecture given by the Johore Professor of English in the
University of Singapore, 17 November 1960. An 'Historical Note' on the
reactions of the Singapore Government and succeeding events can be found
in *Essays in Criticism*, Vol. XI, No. 3, pp. 319-20.

other forms of human sacrifice. Alas, it sometimes seems that the most striking national elements are also that nation's most deplorable mannerisms. I had compiled a list of examples, but on second thoughts I won't read it out. Enough to say that in these days 'national culture' is chiefly something for the tourists from abroad: the real life of the country goes on somewhere else. The world is growing smaller, and therefore more homogeneous, and the cultures of individual countries are bound to draw closer together than they used to be. A few years ago I had an argument with Edward Seidensticker, a distinguished American specialist in Japanese literature. He maintained that the Japanese could not have any real modern poetry (in the Western sense) because they had not had a Western-style seventeenth century. That is, T. S. Eliot created modern Western poetry on the authority of the seventeenth century: and that legitimacy is not available to the Japanese. My answer was (not very seriously) that the Japanese had *our* seventeenth century, and (more seriously) that they had our twentieth century, and (most seriously) that anyway the Japanese had had a distinctively modern poetry for some time already and good luck to them.

In the new countries—Singapore, Malaya, Ghana and so forth—you will often be told in an envious tone that England is blessed with a firm and long-established culture. Yet when we look at England, culturally, as it is at this moment, are we so impressed by its solidity and assurance? We are not. Which is not to invite jeremiads about poor sick England, or poor old broken-down Europe. Things aren't what they were, of course: they never were. My point is that there is a danger in being so *conscious* about culture; culture is not an orchid, true culture does not have 'the look of flowers that are looked at'. It more nearly resembles the asphodel, that Elysian flower, beloved of literary souls, but as Robert Graves describes it: 'a hardy, tall, tough, unscented and commercially valueless plant'.[1]

[1] Introduction to *The Common Asphodel*, 1949.

I am not setting up shop as a prophet. I only wished to suggest that at this point in time it would be as ridiculous to institute a sarong-culture, complete with pantun competitions and so forth, as to bring back the Maypole and the Morris dancers in England just because the present monarch happens to be called Elizabeth. The important thing for Singapore and Malaya is to remain culturally *open*. Who can decide in advance which seeds will fall on barren ground and which will grow? Arising from this is a further consideration: please don't think that I am advocating legalized pornography if I suggest that there is a trace of 'yellow' in most works of culture. (As in most of us.) Art doesn't begin in a test-tube, it doesn't take its origin in good sentiments and clean-shaven upstanding young thoughts. It begins

. . . where all the ladders start,
In the foul rag-and-bone shop of the heart.[1]

Art is not good manners and proper behaviour: to obtain art you cannot use the same methods of discipline and control by which you encourage these social amenities. To obtain art, to build up a culture, you must leave people free to make their own mistakes, to suffer and discover, to come to terms with the foul rag-and-bone shop of their own hearts and whatever else, less foul, more fair, their own hearts may contain or be capable of. It is an old-fashioned view, but I persist in thinking that the greater part of a people's culture lies in the art which those people produce and consume. I say 'old-fashioned', because these days we are for ever being told that actually 'culture' is a much wider conception altogether, which comprises things altogether more important, such as whether people eat with the right hand or the left, whether they carry their babies on their backs, their hips, their fronts or their heads, and so forth. If we allow my old-fashioned view, then we should remark that a woman who has

[1] W. B. Yeats, 'The Circus Animals' Desertion', *Last Poems*, 1940.

been sterilized will not produce a baby. An artist who has been successfully psycho-analysed will not produce any more art. A society which has been thoroughly swept and garnished, brought to a high degree of spiritual hygiene, will not produce any art. Remove all the 'dirt' from a human being, and you will be left with an invertebrate. The boundary between 'cleaning up' and 'brain-washing' is very uncertain. For that reason, and although I am not addicted to juke-boxes, I deplore their banning from Singapore. Singapore, we hope and believe, is a real place inhabited by real people. We hope that they will continue to be real people, more active and independent than before, less narrow in their interests. We do not wish to see life here decline into an interminable Sunday-school meeting.

Shakespeare spoke of 'Art made tongue-tied by Authority'.[1] Authority, when it is kindly, achieves that end by fighting our battles for us, by providing us not only with social welfare—no one can decently object to that—but also with spiritual welfare. That is, by imposing subjects upon the artists and bestowing prescribed, as it were rediffused, art upon the audience. This has its advantages, of course. A successfully totalitarian state affords the most civilized society you can have: it is civilized because, temporarily at any rate, its citizens are essentially dead. Authority must leave us to fight our battles for ourselves, especially our personal battles (and that is what culture is: personal)—Authority must leave us to fight even that deadly battle over whether or not to enter a place of entertainment wherein lurks a juke-box, and whether or not to slip a coin into the machine.

This serves to bring me to the announced subject of my talk: a poet who, though he is not of the world's greatest, has always insisted on fighting his own battles. Perhaps, after all, my theme is not utterly irrelevant to here and now.

Robert Graves, who attained his sixty-fifth birthday a few months ago, has been publishing poems for over forty years.

[1] Sonnet LXVI.

His first *Collected Poems* came out in 1927. The second, in 1938, drew on nineteen earlier volumes. A revised *Collected Poems* came out in 1948, and another in 1959. This last was the occasion for a fairly general celebration of a poet who had hitherto been largely ignored—at least, by serious people. It seems that the supposedly Georgian versifier of the nineteen-twenties has now become a sort of father-figure (albeit a not wholly respectable father) to the younger practitioners of the art. Indeed—to advance a more cogent witness to success—I hear that Buffalo University has just offered him U.S. $30,000 for his complete manuscripts.

How did this happen? It is not so much that Graves has changed (though I think his work has improved, and he has improved his work in another way by throwing a good deal of it out), as that the times have changed. When an art is in the doldrums, the outsider, the lone wolf, comes into his own; it may even happen that he—and only he—can help that art to get moving again. As you can trace in the work of one poet, Yeats, the decline of late romanticism and the rise of modernism, a résumé of poetic history between 1880 and 1940, so in the history of Graves's reputation you can trace the rise of modernism and its present decline. Graves's rise coincides with its decline. He was always outside movements; and now that—despite the various contrivings of reviewers, critics and other interested persons—there are no real movements to get into, the contemporary poet turns to Graves for encouragement and advice. Whether he will get what passes as advice is another matter.

In a broadcast several years ago Graves said:

> I have known three generations of John Smiths. The type breeds true. John Smith II and III went to the same school, university and learned profession as John Smith I. Yet John Smith I wrote pseudo-Swinburne; John Smith II wrote pseudo-Brooke; and John Smith III is now writing pseudo-Eliot. But unless John Smith can write John Smith, however unfashionable the result, why does he bother

to write at all? Surely one Swinburne, one Brooke, and one Eliot are enough in any age?[1]

I suppose even the more sceptical of us still feel that the young novice will be more intelligently occupied writing pseudo-Eliot than pseudo-Swinburne or pseudo-Brooke, but we shall hardly expect very much from that sort of intelligence alone, for creatively it is likely to be just as sterile and sterilizing as the simple-mindedness which draws people to copy Swinburne or Brooke. (There is a point where extreme sophistication and extreme naïvety meet and become in effect indistinguishable. Some of us may experience an odd preference for the latter, but the former is more conducive to a successful career.) In the thirties, in the forties, that remark of Graves would be considered reactionary in the extreme. It will be so considered by many people today: to me it seems liberal and liberalizing. And incidentally, the worst one can say of Graves in this connection is that at time he writes pseudo-Graves.

It should not be thought that, modernism having fairly obviously lost its nerve, Graves is being wise after the event, or getting his own back on a movement from which he was excluded. In a recent talk to the University of Michigan he remarked, 'In the present confused state of literature, I probably rank as a traditionalist; but not as one who opposes innovations in poetic technique.'[2] One might agree with the first part of that statement, except that the term 'traditionalist' has no definite meaning. The second part is undoubtedly true. In the early twenties Graves dismissed Swinburne quite effectively and differentiated between Brooke and Wilfred Owen. In *A Survey of Modernist Poetry* (1926) he dealt sympathetically, even protectively, with E. E. Cummings (while remarking that this poetry

---

1 'The Poet and his Public', printed in *The Crowning Privilege*, 1955.
2 'Preface to a Reading of New Poems at the University of Michigan', *Steps*, 1958.

was 'clearly more important as a sign of local irritation in the poetic body than as a model for tradition'), he wrote appreciatively (though not uncritically) of Eliot, and he distinguished between the genuinely original and therefore 'indecorous' modernist like Hopkins and the faked modernism, the decorous sheep-like sentimentality disguised in wolfish accents, of a writer like Carl Sandburg. His attitude has been consistent: Graves was never a reactionary, never a revolutionary (it is only now that he *seems*, such is our current decorousness, to be revolutionary). In *A Survey of Modernist Poetry* he explained himself clearly enough: 'Real poets . . . do not pursue innovation for its own sake: they are conservative in their methods so long as these ensure the proper security and delivery of the poem.'

There is nothing exceptionable about that. If you desire to enter a room, you open the door and walk in: a conservative but effective means of achieving your purpose. You only climb through the window or drop down the chimney if for some reason you cannot open the door. Graves's comment might strike the uninformed reader as a commonplace; anyone who knows what goes on in the literary world of today will realize how near-revolutionary it is. And it was earlier in the nineteen-twenties that he wrote something which he could well have written yesterday:

> Poets appear spasmodically, write their best poetry at uncertain intervals, owe nothing to schools and, in so far as they are behaving poetically, steer well clear of politics. Schools are formed by the fakers who try to formalize the magic of the true poets; and the history of such set forms as the sonnet, the Spenserian stanza and the heroic couplet is of no greater importance to the student of poetry than is the history of numismatics to the student of finance.
>
> Poetry is not a science but an act of faith. Mountains are moved by it against all the rules laid down by the professors of dynamics—only for short distances, admittedly; still, beyond dispute, moved. The one possible test of the legitimacy of this or that technical

method is the practical question: 'Did the mountain stir?' Yet the same mountain will never move twice at the same word of command.[1]

I am well aware that there is more to be said on this subject, much of it on the other side. The trouble is that *that* has now been said so often, has hardened into 'doctrine'. It is *this* that needs to be said—or repeated—at the present time. Four years ago, in an article in the London Magazine,[2] John Wain remarked on how much more modern *The Waste Land* was than anything being written in 1956. 'After all,' he added, 'to write even a pastiche of early Eliot requires some verbal disciplines which had not been required by Victorian poetic fashions. . . .' Wain spoke as himself a writer, a poet and critic, 'a batsman going out to the wicket as fifth or sixth man, to follow a succession of giants who have all made centuries.' It is true that Wain was attacking current reviewing, which no doubt can always do with it; I would have thought criticism a more deserving target, but Wain seems to admire current criticism. And he was repeating, apparently, what F. R. Leavis has said for many years: that a good deal of talent fails to develop because of the absence of critical standards. But Wain's outburst (a highly respectable sort of outburst, by the way) seemed to me to have an oddly sinister side to it. His point appeared to be not merely that talent should be guided by criticism, but that creative writing needs to be ruled by critical theory and even grows out of it:

> The fact is that a grip on contemporary literary history is a necessity for anyone wishing to know what can usefully be done *next*. The time has gone by when a writer could just soldier on. Given the initial spark, there has to be some idea of the chart we are sailing by. Otherwise we are back in the position Mr Eliot was trying to combat in *Tradition and the Individual Talent*. . . .

1 'Observations on Poetry (1922-1925)', *The Common Asphodel*.
2 November 1956, Vol. 3, No. 11.

I then argued that the current preoccupation with 'tradition' —as if it were a sort of vitamin pill for writers—could only foster a self-conscious willed verse; that Eliot's *Tradition and the Individual Talent*, undeniable as was its topical and localized value and despite its permanent interest as a point of view, should not be prescribed as a chart for young writers to sail by or as a recipe for literary success; that as for writers having a grip on literary history, it seemed to me that literary history had a policeman's grip on writers; and that 'soldiering on' struck me as a far apter description of the writer's prospect than the picture evoked by Wain's remarks—of the writer sitting in a control tower planning his life's work with guidebooks and maps and pins. It is true that the past can help us—I hope I don't seem to be preaching the gospel of the illiterate *naïf*—but the past cannot help us *that* much. If it could, there would be no need for a present; indeed, there would be no present. Wain replied adroitly, more in sorrow than in anger: I hadn't understood him, I was objecting to excessive respect being paid to what I considered obsolete criticism 'such as Mr Eliot's(!)'—he'd caught me spitting in church there; and he was sorry not to have my support but would continue to make his brave if solitary protest.

What has happened—or failed to happen—during the four years since that interchange has only confirmed me in my feelings. It would seem that those who claim to have the greatest respect for literature are really crypto-worshippers of the machine: they debase art by treating it as a minor branch of technology. If you read the right authors, in the right spirit, and follow the other directions, then you won't go far wrong. 'The time has gone by when a writer could just soldier on. . . .' Yes, that is the true voice of Authority speaking—'Art made tongue-tied by Authority'—even though this particular incarnation of Authority is dressed respectably in cap and gown. Perhaps it is a fact of human nature that in all spheres of activity the young rebels of yesterday, whether men or ideas, make up the Establishment of today. If so, there is only one thing we can do about it: recognize the fact, and not deceive ourselves, through scruples, that it is otherwise. Robert Graves has a poem called *In Broken Images*, which may have to do with this opposition between 'soldiering on' and methodology:

> He is quick, thinking in clear images;
> I am slow, thinking in broken images.
>
> He becomes dull, trusting to his clear images;
> I become sharp, mistrusting my broken images.
>
> Trusting his images, he assumes their relevance;
> Mistrusting my images, I question their relevance.
>
> Assuming their relevance, he assumes the fact;
> Questioning their relevance, I question the fact.
>
> When the fact fails him, he questions his senses;
> When the fact fails me, I approve my senses.
>
> He continues quick and dull in his clear images;
> I continue slow and sharp in my broken images.
>
> He in a new confusion of his understanding;
> I in a new understanding of my confusion.[1]

Remembering how modernism began, with what sheer necessity and abused by what vested interests, it is natural that we should feel reluctant to criticize it in any of its parts. But movements are born and die—they must die, in that sense, if literature is to go on. No movement, no style, can be kept artificially alive: it can only be preserved as pastiche. It is symptomatic that a recent reviewer in the *New Statesman*, a young man, should attack the world of letters for supposedly no longer paying enough attention to Pound. His implication was that the British were returning to their native element: a sort of eternal Georgianism. I cannot say where English poets are going: I only hope they are going somewhere. And not in Pound's direction:

---

[1] *Collected Poems*, 1959, p. 94.

English poets have surely learnt what they can from him by now, and there is plenty about Pound which they ought not to learn. To hold up certain English and American writers of the younger generation as truly contemporary because they write Pound-pastiche, pseudo-Pound, is to commit nonsense. To be contemporary now, whatever it may be positively, is pretty obviously *not* to be modernist; and the gallant knights of Pound, seeing themselves as progressives, are merely reactionary in a conventional way. No, we *don't* learn from history, do we? The wheel turns in spite of all the critical blocks we put under it. I am not denying that the way it turns may not please us, or that it may take a turn for the worse. But I am sure that it *must* turn, that it is in the nature of human needs and literary responses that change should take place; and that change cannot be calculated in advance, cannot be 'worked' from such old recipes as 'read Laforgue and Corbière', or whatever. (I take this as an example because at the very time when one critic was complaining that So-and-So would have written a better review of Philip Larkin's poems if the reviewer had read Laforgue and Corbière, another critic was complaining that Larkin would have written better poems if he had read Laforgue and Corbière. This nagging and niggling is what Eliot's insistence on the 'historical sense' has come to in our time.)

That I should be making such heavy weather of this point— unless it merely reveals a predilection in me for heavy weather —is an indication that our own age, though much more self-conscious and sophisticated in literary matters (how primitive Dr Johnson looks by the side of our critics!), is not discernibly more intelligent than earlier ages. The dark gods still rule in those places where art, minor as well as major, is born. (No doubt it is from them that culture's yellow tinge comes.) I prefer the dark gods to Graves's 'White Goddess': she sounds like a cross between a shrewish wife and a military dictator, they at least govern by majority rule—or misrule.

White goddesses or dark gods—Graves knows that it is from them that real poetry comes, whether one calls that poetry 'romantic' or 'classical', 'modernist' or 'traditionalist'. Contemporary critics often speak of poetry—of the writing of poetry—as an 'ordering of experience', which makes the poet sound like a sergeant drilling some raw recruits. Really this is only one step less cosy than those Victorian paintings which show the poet cocking his ear to catch the well-bred whispers of a visiting angel. What happens usually, I suspect, is a good deal less orderly, less domestic, than this. Behind the creation of much art is the horrified effort to win a degree of order (so much is correct), of mere comprehensibility, out of the surrounding anarchy; to secure a modicum of temporary mercy from the midst of cruelty, to tame one small beast in a jungle of wild beastliness. 'Poetry . . . is not the expression of personality,' Eliot wrote in that same essay, 'but an escape from personality.' Perhaps that was an appropriate way of putting it in 1917. Today, one would rather say, perhaps, that poetry is not the expression of personality—who wants to *express* it?—but the preservation of it against those forces which in their different ways, whether savage or kindly, are out to kill it. Poetry is written on a battle-field, not in a library, not in the imaginary museum crammed with all the cultural objects of the past which you must have fingered carefully one by one, the theory has it, if you wish to be more than minor and provincial these days.

Graves is not—what there is a risk of his being thought simply because he is obviously no *fauve*, and not given to the verbal melodramatics of Dylan Thomas or (if I may spit in church again) the brilliant sensationalism of *The Waste Land*—Graves is not genteel, tame, castrated.

> Children are dumb to say how hot the day is,
> How hot the scent is of the summer rose,
> How dreadful the black wastes of evening sky,
> How dreadful the tall soldiers drumming by.

But we have speech, to chill the angry day,
And speech, to dull the rose's cruel scent.
We spell away the overhanging night,
We spell away the soldiers and the fright.

There's a cool web of language winds us in,
Retreat from too much joy or too much fear:
We grow sea-green at last and coldly die
In brininess and volubility.

But if we let our tongues lose self-possession,
Throwing off language and its watery clasp
Before our death, instead of when death comes,
Facing the wide glare of the children's day,
Facing the rose, the dark sky and the drums,
We shall go mad no doubt and die that way.[1]

This is a long way from Eliot's chilly division between 'the mind which creates' and 'the man who suffers', from his desire to escape from the self into something putatively grander—the mind of Europe, the Church, Tradition, Royalism or whatever it may be.

If we let our tongues lose self-possession,
Throwing off language and its watery clasp . . .
We shall go mad no doubt and die that way. . . .

It isn't those who make the most noise who are nearest to madness. And the neighbourhood of madness, and the sober consciousness of it, is what leads to poetry. Not a preoccupation with some sort of Tradition, not the proud possession of a theory of literature, and certainly not the ambition to cut a figure in the literary-cum-social world. It is, to put it baldly, a late manifestation of the instinct to survive—the poet is the man who has most accurately gauged the odds—and to survive with some honour. As for the reading of poetry, Graves described that

[1] 'The Cool Web', *Collected Poems*, p. 56.

rather baldly thirty-five years ago, when he compared a poetry anthology to 'a well-stocked medicine chest against all ordinary mental disorders'[1]—an agreeably modest way of making a reasonably large claim.

I have often wondered what the term 'a poet's poet' meant. Perhaps simply a poet, like Graves, with no definable 'message', no 'unifying philosophy', no marketable gimmick. A unifying philosophy in a poet is a very valuable thing—from the point of view of the research worker or the lecturer. In other respects, it is a less unambiguous blessing. A philosophy, what is properly termed a philosophy, is more precisely expounded in prose, and more precisely understood. A philosophy can be used in poetry, of course—but that poetry will not thereby be superior to the kind of poetry which is used by the poet, in lieu of a philosophy, because the sort of exploration which it allows, which it *is*, seems to him more to the point, more 'live', than any sort of philosophical writing could be. Because it is 'the thing itself', rather than 'a thing about a thing'.

'My stutter, my cough, my unfinished sentences', Graves says in a poem, 'Denote an inveterate physical reluctance / To use the metaphysical idiom.'[2] In prose he has defined poetry as 'sense; good sense; penetrating, often heart-rending sense.'[3] This poet's poet is engaged in working towards a philosophy which is never reached, in the subduing of small confusion after small confusion through exorcism or celebration, each confusion of a different kind and needing to be faced in a different way, and each confusion so real, so distinct, so much itself, that the conclusion—I mean the grand conclusion which is to conclude every confusion, those that have not yet manifested themselves as well as those which have—this grand conclusion not only cannot be

[1] *Poetic Unreason*, 1925.
[2] 'The Second-Fated', *Collected Poems*, p. 315.
[3] 'Legitimate Criticism of Poetry: A Talk for Mount Holyoke College, 6 February, 1957', *Steps*.

visualized but can only seem a disastrous immorality, a throwing up of the sponge.

> He in a new confusion of his understanding;
> I in a new understanding of my confusion.

One valid criticism of Graves, I think, is that he is too much the poet. That is, he tends to set himself to clear up confusions which don't really exist. He applies that technique of his, so ready to hand, to situations not warranting its employment. More simply, some of his poems have no subject: he writes without needing to write. He can even operate as a poet of the Commonplace Book, a Keepsake versifier. The Clark Lectures (which he gave during 1954-1955 and then printed under the title *The Crowning Privilege*) offer a convincing explanation of this not uncommon phenomenon. A poet, he there says, craves the sheer excitement of writing a poem. Hence he puts himself 'into a receptive posture' and awaits the visitation of the Muse. But the visitation thus contrived is 'not of the Goddess but of one of those idle, foolish, earthbound spirits that hover around the planchette board, or the pillows of sick men'. Graves adds that though a poet knows in his heart which are necessary poems and which are unnecessary, 'too often he tries to fool himself that all are necessary'. This is not a mortal sin, however: 'the unnecessary ones drop out, the necessary ones remain'. Elsewhere, in a poem, he comments wryly, 'We are not Virgils, but one night in twenty.'[1] At any rate, Graves's unnecessary poems are unpretentious; they will harm no one; and time will soon dispose of them if the poet himself does not.

While on this aspect of his work, I should say something about his prose, part of which I suspect is also unnecessary. I am not referring to his novels (which seem to me intelligent, enjoyable and a remarkably clean way of making a living out of words), but to his poetic mythology of the White Goddess and to much

---

[1] 'Virgil the Sorcerer', *Collected Poems, 1914-26*; not reprinted.

of his Clark Lectures. Of the former I think Karl Miller has offered a convincing explanation, or extenuation, in remarking that 'Graves's poetry becomes the place where make-believe is known for what it is. . . . And it almost seems as if the cleaner his verse becomes and the more "man-like" his subject-matter, the higher the slag of make-believe piles up in his prose.'[1] The Clark Lectures contain some shrewd comment on particular poets (Dylan Thomas, for instance) and on poetry in general, such as:

> Personally, I expect poems to say what they mean in the simplest and most economical way; even if the thought they contain is complex. I do not mind exalted language in poetry any more than I mind low language, but rhetoric disgusts me.

The objection to these lectures, in which Graves lists a number of things which a true poet is not, is that he displays himself as something which a true poet is not—a nagging old woman. Again, there is a sort of extenuation: the lectures were given at Cambridge, and he must have felt that he was on enemy ground, that he was entrapped in an imaginary museum, if not a real one. It was from Cambridge that, as an inveterate non-museumite, he was doomed to minority.

Graves once remarked that the only kind of lecture you could give about poetry was what Cummings called a non-lecture; and the Clark Lectures are really un-criticism. In 1926 Graves wrote:

> It was surely a critic who first pointed out the distinction between subject-matter and form, and from this began to philosophise on form; as it is surely criticism which has always stood between poetry and the plain reader, made possible the writing of so much false poetry and, by giving undue prominence to theory, robbed the reader of his power to distinguish between what is false and what is true.[2]

[1] *The Spectator*, No. 6832, 5 June 1959.   [2] *A Survey of Modernist Poetry.*

Graves there offers a good definition of *bad* criticism, and also, one notes, a good definition of much current kudos-winning criticism.

I had better add—the occasion being what it is—that I am not opposed to the teaching, as such, of literature. Nor am I assailing practical criticism, which seems to me the real criticism and essentially unassailable. F. R. Leavis is the outstanding practical critic of our times: his cogency results from the fact that what he says is backed up by the text. He puts questions—the right questions—to the text and the text makes answer. My own objection is to those critics who make statements and then seek justification in the text, or indeed scorn to seek justification at all. The theoreticians—to use a polite term; to use a franker one— —the manipulators of gimmicks.

I want to close by reading three poems by Graves, each illustrative of a prominent aspect of his work. First, because of its subject, a poem about love—'love, the near-honourable malady'—called *With Her Lips Only*. The theme is not remarkable, by no means out-of-the-way; the treatment is characteristic; the simplicity, the downright tone, and the neatness (urgent lover followed by urgent husband, the children appealed to on each occasion, a sequence of acts of non-love):

> This honest wife, challenged at dusk
> At the garden gate, under a moon perhaps,
> In scent of honeysuckle, dared to deny
> Love to an urgent lover: with her lips only,
> Not with her heart. It was no assignation;
> Taken aback, what could she say else?
> For the children's sake, the lie was venial;
> 'For the children's sake,' she argued with her conscience.
>
> Yet a mortal lie must follow before dawn:
> Challenged as usual in her own bed,
> She protests love to an urgent husband,
> Not with her heart but with her lips only;

'For the children's sake,' she argues with her conscience,
'For the children'—turning suddenly cold towards them.[1]

The second demonstrates how little artiness there is in this poet's make-up. Like the china plate, he wants to be used, to 'soldier on', not to be stuck on a shelf in a museum:

From a crowded barrow in a street-market
The plate was ransomed for a few coppers,
Was brought gleefully home, given a place
On a commanding shelf.

'Quite a museum-piece,' an expert cries
(Eyeing it through the ready pocket-lens)—
As though a glass case would be less sepulchral
Than the barrow-hearse!

For weeks this plate retells the history
Whenever an eye runs in that direction:
'Near perdition I was, in a street-market
With rags and old shoes.'

'A few coppers' —here once again
The purchaser's proud hand lifts down
The bargain, displays the pot-bank sign
Scrawled raggedly underneath.

Enough, permit the treasure to forget
The emotion of that providential purchase,
Becoming a good citizen of the house
Like its fellow-crockery.

Let it dispense sandwiches at a party
And not be noticed in the drunken buzz,
Or little cakes at afternoon tea
When cakes are in demand.

Let it regain a lost habit of life,
Foreseeing death in honourable breakage
Somewhere between the kitchen and the shelf
To be sincerely mourned.[2]

[1] *Collected Poems*, p. 151. [2] 'The China Plate', *Collected Poems*, p. 141.

The last is one of his quasi-allegorical pieces; I mean the sort of poem which has an obvious, logical, contained meaning and at the same time carries the suggestion of another significance. You don't feel that the poem was written for the sake of the allegory, and if you don't want allegory, fair enough, you can ignore it and still be left with a perfectly legitimate poem. This is called *Beauty in Trouble*:

> Beauty in trouble flees to the good angel
>   On whom she can rely
> To pay her cab-fare, run a steaming bath,
>   Poultice her bruised eye;
> Will not at first, whether for shame or caution,
>   Her difficulty disclose;
> Until he draws a cheque book from his plumage,
>   Asking her how much she owes;
>
> (Breakfast in bed: coffee and marmalade,
>   Toast, eggs, orange-juice,
> After a long, sound sleep—the first since when?—
>   And no word of abuse).
>
> Loves him less only than her saint-like mother,
>   Promises to repay
> His loans and most seraphic thoughtfulness
>   A million-fold one day.
>
> Beauty grows plump, renews her broken courage
>   And, borrowing ink and pen,
> Writes a news-letter to the evil angel
>   (Her first gay act since when?):
> The fiend who beats, betrays and sponges on her,
>   Persuades her white is black,
> Flaunts vespertilian wing and cloven hoof;
>   And soon will fetch her back.
>
> Virtue, good angel, is its own reward:
>   Your dollars were well spent.
> But would you to the marriage of true minds
>   Admit impediment?[1]

[1] *Collected Poems*, p. 242.

That poem is about Beauty, a pretty girl attracted despite herself to a bad man. And, or, perhaps, about Beauty—Art, that is—which must consort with Evil, which apparently cannot find inspiration in Good alone. If so, it is added testimony that art will not thrive in any society which is run in the style of a children's nursery, whether the role of nanny is taken by a set of well-read dons or by a government department. Robert Graves is a rare writer who, throughout a long working life, has neither succumbed to any sort of nanny nor set up as some sort of nanny himself.

The Novel and Politics

IRVING HOWE'S *Politics and the Novel*, a New Left Book, strikes me as peculiarly exasperating and provoking. But it certainly does provoke the reader into establishing whether or not he agrees with what it says. The sideshows of undeniable intelligence put us on our honour, we cannot refuse the sometimes obscure challenge.

Mr Howe's critical variations are always interesting and often illuminating. It is his theme that seems somehow perverse. As if his way of reading a novel is radically different from what one had (perhaps wrongly) supposed to be the usual way. Is he at heart more interested in Politics than in the Novel? To put it like that means nothing—for what *is* the Novel that one should be exclusively interested in it, *tout court*? In any case, the critic of 'political novels' will need to be interested in politics, presumably. No, it is nearer the point to suggest, not that Mr Howe is merely interested in ideology, but that he is imbued with an uninhibited, unquestioning respect for ideology. He attaches too much weight to what people say they mean. The serious novelist, the serious political novelist even, will attach weight to what people mean they mean.

The critic simplifies, the critic of the critic simplifies further. I have distorted Mr Howe's attitude in thus isolating it. He is not naïve. He admits at the outset that conflict is inevitable: 'the novel tries to confront experience in its immediacy and closeness, while ideology is by its nature general and inclusive'. But from this conflict, he says, the political novel 'takes on the aura of high drama'. The ideology is to be—ever so respectfully—subsumed. But Mr Howe doesn't like to see ideology too completely

THE NOVEL AND POLITICS

subsumed. His objection to *The Secret Agent* is that Conrad is being grimly flippant about anarchists and revolutionists. Conrad is playing with loaded dice. But Mr Howe seems to me to be implying that ideology is a pure phenomenon, pure and absolute and unalterable. And isn't it clear by now that shades of the prison-house and the gas chamber soon begin to close upon the growing ideology? Like Conrad's art, ideologies are 'loaded', loaded and re-loaded. It is not surprising that Mr Howe should find Conrad's irony 'heavy', for he himself is innocent of this subversive quality of mind.

One of the supreme challenges for the political novelist is 'to make ideas or ideologies come to life . . . even more, to create the illusion that they have a kind of independent motion. . . '. One assents uneasily, and the uneasiness grows. Is it a question of ideas or ideologies coming to life, just like that? Or is it a question of them yielding to another, prior sort of life, human life? For perhaps the political novelist's challenge is to make sure that, in his novel, the ideas or ideologies become *dead*. If so, then to talk afterwards of such novels in political terms is not to clarify but to undo the novelist's work, merely to resort to one of those 'imitation-botanical' classifications, as Lawrence called them. One should add that a critic of Mr Howe's intelligence will not be altogether damned even by his classifications.

'The political novel turns characteristically to an apolitical temptation.' Perhaps that is well said: one cannot be sure of the tone in which Mr Howe pronounces the final word. It seems that he will permit, even advocate, a degree of succumbing to this temptation—a sort of fairly advanced petting. Some of us would rather have the novel go the whole hog, some of us would feel it a duty to do so rather than an indulgence. And especially in the mid-twentieth century, when political behaviour is pushing out all other kinds of behaviour. There is a grim, unintended humour in that phrase 'apolitical temptation'. One hopes that such things linger on in the shady corners of our world, like sexual pleasure in Orwell's Oceania. As puritanical ideology tightens and extends its grip, only by virtue of his vices shall the human individual survive.

Again and again one stops short in front of Mr Howe's assertions—often illogically, no doubt, like a burnt child dreading a reading-lamp. 'Politics rakes our passions as nothing else.' Who is that 'us'? Very well, you and I and the Laotian peasant. Politics rakes us. But does politics rake our *passions*, and rake them continuously? In the name of whatever might still be holy, do we have to lick the hand which is suffocating us? Quoting Orwell's remark that all revolutions are failures though not the same failure, Mr Howe reminds us that some have been successful. He instances the French Revolution, which 'opened Europe to political freedom'. Maybe it did that. Maybe something else would have done that. The French Revolution—and at least there is no maybe here—put paid to a lot of people in the course of opening them to political freedom. But Mr Howe has a wholehearted respect for History. He trusts History. Whatever was, was right. Some of us may feel uncertain as to what did happen, let alone as to how we should attribute moral rectitude. It is consistent in Mr Howe to complain of Conrad's seedy caricatures: the anarchists and revolutionists of History were serious persons. But how do we know that? What reason do we have—real, not ideological, reason—for supposing that Conrad wasn't essentially right? Just because History says so. But whose History? And at what stage are we obliged to believe History, since History is still expounding herself?

Perhaps, when she gets to the end of her long, long sentence, History will have undermined those revolutionists far more thoroughly than Conrad 'undermines the dramatic integrity of his book' by representing them as 'knaves or fools'. 'The central event of our century remains the Russian Revolution.' A stirring, if banal, pronouncement. Even so, for many individuals the central event of their century is still love, or God, or cinema-going, or Beethoven, or their offspring, or the horses. . . . The serious novelist doesn't concern himself with the 'central event' of a century—any more than the poet, writing *sub specie aeternitatis* though he may be, confines himself to descriptions of the Creation. And perhaps Mr Howe's appetites are best satisfied by the formal historians, the authorities on 'central events'.

The chapter on Dostoevsky is excellent; and there is good stuff in Mr Howe's accounts of *Nostromo* and *La Condition Humaine* in particular. Yet it may still be felt that less than a whole truth (and less than a novel half-truth) lies in his statement that the San Tomé mine, as symbol, 'forces the reader to see private drama as public struggle, to recognize that not the least tragic aspect of individual life is the fatality with which it melts away in the stream of history'. The characters thus become 'emblems' or 'agents' or 'representatives', and the novel is denovelized, reduced to the comparatively crude abstract propositions with which the writer may have begun. In the case of the artist, his end is definitely not in his beginning.

Henry James 'had no larger view of politics as a collective mode of action. He had a sense of the revolutionaries but not of the revolutionary movement.' So much the better. Political movements, whether 'revolutionary' or something else, force their sense upon us—and perhaps only a sense of politicians can save us from destruction by that force. Mr Howe is divided on the subject of Malraux. 'Sometimes Malraux is able to reach a deeper human vision than Trotsky. . . . In other respects Malraux is far inferior to Trotsky. . . .' It is hard to see what is being compared with what, unless Mr Howe is simply saying that Trotsky is a better historian of the Russian Revolution than Malraux, while Malraux is a better novelist of the Chinese revolution of 1927 than Trotsky. Perhaps this is the case, for Mr Howe remarks that 'Malraux has a rather poor because uncultivated sense of historical movement'. Well, the sound of cracking human bones which accompanies historical movement may well distract the observer's attention from the direction in which History is moving. The scene in which Katov gives his cyanide to a fellow-prisoner is very fine, lacking, one would have said, any particular ideological significance, even the significance that 'ideology, being pure and selfless, transcends itself to become something better than itself'—for what has ideology to do with this at all? Then—for Mr Howe is continually casting ideology to the winds with one hand and plucking it back with the other— we are told that 'Kyo's Marxism, as embodied in Katov, helps modern man to find a proper way of dying'. One is left with a string of questions as to what exactly helps who exactly to die properly, and at the end another question: Isn't the function of the novel to teach us how to *live* properly?—a task more arduous and more to the point.

In *Darkness at Noon* Koestler is a truly political novelist, writing consciously, ideologically, against an ideology. But here Mr Howe's complaint is that ideology has not been sufficiently subsumed. Koestler 'is like a stricken Midas yearning for the bread of life yet, with every touch, turning experience into the useless gold of ideology'. Again, a very perceptive comment. But between the excessive ideology of *Darkness at Noon* and the insufficient ideology of *The Secret Agent* one wonders where on earth the happy mean can be, or whether in truth Mr Howe wants neither to have his cake nor to eat it. For at times his arguments are nimble and sophisticated, the movements of a brilliant mind. Then suddenly, with the same air of close thinking, a truism or false profundity is presented for acclamation or note.

In the course of a moving appreciation of *1984*, Mr Howe tells us that no one has yet been able 'to provide a satisfactory explanation for that systematic excess in destroying human values which is a central trait of totalitarianism'. Perhaps there is no satisfactory explanation. We may have to put up with a rather dissatisfying, even rather hurtful, one. And it hardly needs a great novelist, let alone a great political novelist, to point to the old

THE NOVEL AND POLITICS

Adam in us, to the satisfactions of power and the pleasure of destroying. No need to adduce Milton or Shakespeare, for there are the ballads, sagas, fairy tales, nursery rhymes, myths. . . . Alas, it seems that Mr Howe prefers political explanations of human phenomena to human explanations not only of political but even of human phenomena. This is surprising only in a literary critic. For literature—poor thing!—having been wellnigh invalidated recently by Freudian psychology, is now being rendered redundant by politicology. Gone is the old romantic conception of it as a storehouse of the wisdom of the ages. There are countries in the world, dominated by politics, where people are only just finding out (unless they are failing to find out) that men sometimes tell lies.

But perhaps *Politics and the Novel* is a brilliant, true and original book throughout—really New and really Left—and this review of it merely an exhibition of mild lunacy. After all, Mr Howe at any rate keeps his balance pretty well—a precarious balance between the demands of ideology and the claims of art. It is just that his scrupulousness seems a little ridiculous, more than a little pathetic, in the world of today. Perhaps the only trouble with this book is that, professing to deal with central, urgent and public issues, it is so *academic*. As the scholar puts the final touches to his Ph.D. thesis, the thugs kick down the door.

II

All in the Saga: a Biography of Rupert Brooke

'Indeed, why keep anything? Well, I *might* turn out to be eminent and biographiable. If so, let them know the poor truths. Rather pathetic this.'

(*Rupert Brooke to Dudley Ward shortly before his death*)

WE cannot be sorry that Rupert Brooke died young. Had he lived longer, probably Christopher Hassall's biography of him would have been shorter. It would have been a little less lengthy had Mr Hassall not chosen to begin his story in 1520, and to pause in 1783, when John Reeve, a tenant farmer who married into the quality, took his wife's surname and thus 'prevented the name of Rupert Reeve from being enrolled among the English poets'. It would have been shorter had Mr Hassall cut down on Brooke's early letters and other writings, with their schoolboy cynicism and fabricated 'decadence'. It would have been shorter had Mr Hassall spared the detailed descriptions of the town of Rugby in 1880 (and, come to that, of the school of the same name), or of King's College, and the stock reconstruction of an undergraduate's life, including his bed-maker and her picturesque sayings, 'This place fair *eats* dusters'. Mr Hassall's story is full of names, there were great names in those days, and Brooke knew most of them: he was born into Bloomsbury, and he had to fight to get out. But even so, there are too many names dropping too thick and fast.

Now it was Dent looking in to discuss the music of *The Silent Woman* (the Marlowe Dramatic Society's next venture), now Ronald Firbank, leaning against the chimney piece and looking witty, and now it was the poet Flecker, looking swarthy, who had dropped from Caius. It was maddening.

It still is. And Mr Hassall is so unrelentingly straight-faced, so solemn about it all, even when negotiating a light touch:

> People in the streets of Rugby looked round as he passed. He was not so unambitious as to be sorry that he was not inconspicuous. In fact he was very ambitious, so why not be top in looks as well as Greek?

This and much else in the book reads like a send-up of the sound-track to a British Council film about the English way of life in some never-never heyday, and with its cosy cultivatedness and private jokes it is likely to turn the stomach of anyone not born around that time into that class. Yet perhaps there is some good in the story. It demonstrates—supposing demonstration was necessary—that to be born with a silver spoon in one's mouth doesn't ensure immunity against emotional indigestion of a drastic kind; and it even inspires a new sympathy for Brooke. Whom the gods love die young: or may hardly start to live, even.

Certainly Brooke went on being young for some time—for nearly twenty-eight years. In intellectual matters this book shows him to have been more intelligent than we may have thought. He was the bright young man rather of an ebbing tide than of a new wave, but he was bright and often very perceptive—much more so than his friend Edward Marsh—about literature. In friendship of a temperate kind he was at his happiest, lively and charming, but if the friendship took on a deeper tinge he began to falter. His relationships with women, when they passed beyond friendship, are marked (according to Mr Hassall's material, though not according to his explicit comments) by a mixture of condescension (a woman is always 'child' to him) and resentment rising to near-hysterical grievance. He is at once the worldly-wise elder brother and the love-hungry child.

Mr Hassall's exercises in literary criticism are fortunately few; he considers 'Seaside' a poem of 'subtlety and curious beauty'. This *is* a biography, a full-length one and the first, and however ready one might be to leave Brooke's bones in peace, it has to be discussed as such. One cannot fall back on the excuse that the life helps to elucidate the poems, for the poems require no elucidation. Simply, the poems proceed side by side with the life. Neither does the life need much explication, for it was, in spite of the good looks, the prizes won, the admiration, the influential friends and the opportunities (in 1910 he was offered a lectureship in English at Newcastle 'as a preliminary step to a Chair at a University', but preferred to continue working for a Fellowship at King's)—in spite of all this, it was a story of a not uncommon kind, perhaps, if we are to talk of cases, a rather simple and standard case. Unhappily the gods are many and jealous and tend each to harry another's favourite.

Mrs Brooke was a strong character, unlike her husband, and a Guardian of the Poor and a Justice of the Peace. Rupert called her 'the Ranee', not only because of their dubious kinship with the Rajah of Sarawak. Her first child was a son, her second child a girl who died in infancy, and she was 'desperately wishing for another daughter' when Rupert was born. He was aware of her disappointment, and the presence of feminine qualities in his character (as he supposed) together with his physical grace seems to have led him to over-assert his masculinity. Not that anyone, by this account, ever accused him of effeminacy. He was popular with women as with men, and Hassall recounts his three love affairs, more particularly the 'passionate misadventure', as the blurb calls, it, 'which gives him almost tragic stature'. The relationship with Ka Cox at times approached comedy or even farce. He wrote her long emotional letters, a curious mixture of arrogance and sermonizing and abject need. He begs her to come to him and heal him, she is reluctant (she is in love with Henry Lamb, the painter), and when at last she offers to come, he loses his nerve. For one thing, how is he going to square this with the Ranee?

His nervous breakdown, he tells Ka, is 'all mixed up with this chastity'. Again and again he talks of being 'dirty', 'the dirty abyss I am now', and demands of her a 'fierce and militant cleanness'. In Salzburg in early 1912, according to Mr Hassall, 'these two close friends began living together as lovers'. As lovers—or as if they were lovers, but not quite? For in a letter to Cathleen Nesbitt in 1913 he writes, and it must be of Ka, that

> She was too wise, and something in her heart too strong, for her to give herself to me, because she loved and pitied me in that way; nor did I love her little enough to want it given—in that way.

Poor Ka! If it was a tragedy, then it was her tragedy rather than his. Just as she came to realize that she was in love with Rupert and didn't need to be bullied into loving him, Rupert decided that he couldn't love her, and turned his affections (or at any rate his epistolary affections) to another girl. To Frances Cornford he wrote, 'I can't ever marry her (Ka), because of the great evil she did me.' And in later letters to Ka he spoke of the great evil they did each other and, somewhat unchivalrously if well-intentionedly, of how 'I thought at one time I'd only learnt bad from you. . . .' What was this great evil? The harmless 'mother-comfort' she gave him during his illness, drawing his head to her heart for a moment, the subject of that ridiculous and unpleasant sonnet, 'A Memory'? Here perhaps (for it seems the poetry throws light on the life rather than the other way about) we might look to the sonnet 'Success':

> I think if you had loved me when I wanted . . .
> If earth had seen Earth's lordliest wild limbs tamed,
> Shaken, and trapped, and shivering, for *my* touch—
> Myself should I have slain? or that foul you?

A perfectionist demands a woman's whole love, and stops loving her as soon as she offers it. Brooke was, very consciously, a man of honour.

Then, in love (or making as if in love) with Cathleen Nesbitt, he begs her to give up the stage ('I'd better state, before going further, that as a matter of fact I loathe women acting in public') and to 'love good and keep away from the evil things of the world, for my sake and for your sake and for our sake'. At about the same time he writes to Denis Browne,

> Friendship is always exciting and yet always safe. There is no lust in it, and therefore no poison. It is cleaner than love, and older; for children and very old people have friends, but they do not love . . . I will not love, and I will not be loved.

Fairly clearly Mr Hassall has not told the whole story. I don't think this is the aggrieved complaint of a unsatisfied prurience. To most of us Brooke's personal life is a matter of complete indifference. But if we are to read a 550-page biography, a large part of it devoted to Brooke's relationship with Ka Cox and two other women and densely documented with repetitious extracts from correspondence, then we don't expect to suffer, in addition, a genteel vagueness at the centre of it. Mr Hassall should have told us either more or less. As far as the present writer is concerned, less would have done very nicely.

By 1914 Brooke had given up his bohemian velleities and some of his advanced friends, and had shifted from his early anti-Victorianism (such as it was) to an attitude as stoutly Victorian as the great Queen herself, though where she was not amused he was filled with disgust of an intensity which this biography doesn't account for, which therefore we can only describe as 'pathological'. He was sick, so the world was sick; he was dirty, so his friends were dirty. And thus he welcomed the war, it was his escape from 'dirtiness' (Mr Hassall puts it more grandly: 'he discovered a Cause that never while he lived grew dim or faltered from perfection'), it was his chance to turn away 'from a world grown old and cold and weary,' from

> the sick hearts that honour could not move
> And half-men, and their dirty songs and dreary,
> And all the little emptiness of love!

'War knows no power.' He would be safer there than among women,

> Safe though all safety's lost, safe where men fall;
> And if these poor limbs die, safest of all.

Those famous sonnets! There is nothing new to be said of the connection between personal inadequacies or difficulties and high-minded militarism, but it is still a little alarming to find Brooke writing to Cathleen Nesbitt that 'the central purpose of my life, the aim and end of it, now, the thing God wants of me, is to get good at beating Germans', and complaining to Raverat that 'there's a sort of ghastly apathy over half the country. And I really think large numbers of male people don't want to die. Which is odd.' Perhaps it's just as well that Brooke isn't living at this hour!

The last pages of this book recount the beginnings and the development of the myth, how the memory of Brooke was transferred (in Mr Hassall's phrase) 'from the private to the national plane'. However incongruous one finds the First Lord of the Admiralty's valediction and its reference to Brooke's 'classic symmetry of mind and body', and despite the many sickening individual manifestations (and the comic one, the proposal that the clock at Grantchester should be permanently halted at ten to three), it is hardly possible not to be moved by this process of myth-making, for legends are not created without reason, without need. 'He was slain by bright Phoebus' shaft,' wrote D. H. Lawrence, 'it was in keeping with his general sunniness—it was the real climax of his pose. . . . Bright Phoebus smote him down. It is all in the saga.'

'A specimen so beautifully producible,' Henry James called

him. And perhaps Rupert Brooke's real achievement was to provide or nucleate some sort of consolation—and consolation is real if it works—for the bereaved and inarticulate. His achievement in poetry is slight: he was a graceful writer of light verse, and his light verses are few. As for his life—or so this biography leaves one feeling—it is rather as if his Shelleyan appearance obliged him to strive to be all the things he wasn't by nature. To be a bohemian, a rebel, a socialist, a ladies' man, even perhaps a poet, when in his heart of hearts he was really a scoutmaster, a housemaster, a Justice of the Peace.

Wilfred Owen

'My subject is War . . .'

'I am held peer by the Georgians.' In what (rather oddly) is
the first book devoted to Wilfred Owen,[1] Mr Welland remarks
on the paradox in this 'ecstatic' announcement 'at the very time
at which he was engaged upon the composition of poetry
markedly different from and far more important than anything
the Georgians produced'. Nowadays, when every poetic suckling
has wisdom enough to know exactly where he is going, it does
sound paradoxical, a queer thing to say. For it seems that the
Welfare State extends to poetry, artistically though not yet
economically: if you read the right books in the right spirit and
follow the other directions, you won't go far wrong. This Poetic
Welfare, I suspect, rests on the assumption that a firmly based
and highly developed literary criticism is bound to produce a
firmly based and highly developed literary creation. (I will pass
over the other assumption, that the literary criticism we have
at the moment can be properly so described.) One may venture
that the theory owes a good deal to Eliot's *Tradition and the
Individual Talent*, or to an over-simple reading of that document.
No poet . . . has his complete meaning alone. His significance,
his appreciation is the appreciation of his relation to the dead
poets.' So once you have managed to appreciate your own
relation to the dead poets, you are reasonably assured of being a
significant poet. Similarly, 'the existing monuments form an
ideal order among themselves, which is modified by the introduction of the new (the really new) work of art among them'.
So you establish this ideal order (or take over somebody else's

[1] *Wilfred Owen: A Critical Study*, by D. S. R. Welland.

establishment), look through it for a suitable niche, slide into it, and hey presto a sort of General Post ensues. As long, that is, as you've remembered to escape from emotion and extinguish your personality. The procedure whereby one creates poetry is as fully documented as was the alchemists' prescription for turning base metals into gold; and just about as successful. I exaggerate, of course, but not very much. The contemporary world of letters is very sophisticated, as well as rather simple-minded. Perhaps that is the case (the proportions varying) with all worlds of letters. But an impression remains of novelty in the present situation—when poets have such a terror of being left to their own devices that an outsider might begin to suspect that they haven't any devices of their own. It seems a paradoxical end to a liberation.

To return to the paradox of Owen. What a pleasing and healthy paradox! Would we encountered such paradoxes today! Owen wrote better than he knew: our poets write a good deal less well than they know. Owen was no literary intellectual. I mean, he had to find his own way, it was not 'charted' for him: and in finding his own way, he found himself. I am not defending ignorance: Owen was certainly not ignorant. I am not attacking knowledge, but knowingness. Owen hadn't mapped out his course; perhaps (as Mr Welland remarks) he hadn't even read Grierson's *Donne*. He merely wrote real poetry—the poetry demanded of him by his talents, his personality and his experience. He wrote it, not in any imaginary museum, but in—and about—a real battlefield. Similarly, there is nothing really 'enigmatic' about his statement, 'Above all I am not concerned with Poetry'. Surely the only response to that assurance is: Thank God! One of our current concerns is how to save poetry from the people who *are* concerned with it—like nursemaids bustling about a sickly portentous test-tube baby. Mr Welland comes near to apologizing for Owen's pronouncements, when it would be more appropriate to draw a few timely lessons from them: for instance, that professional literary men, whose pride is involved in agonizing re-appraisals, in movements and retrenchments, often make curiously amateurish poets. However unfair that may be.

But this is a good book. It doesn't propose any radical re-valuations, but its valuation is sound. Much of what it says has often been thought and perhaps expressed, though not in book-form. Owen's reputation is as secure as most literary reputations can be: if he is disliked or found boring it will be for those same reasons for which Mr Welland and his other admirers admire him. There will always be some who consider his pity sentimental and his realism inartistic, and they are not likely to be affected by Mr Welland's argument that Owen had to subordinate 'his predilections for a beautiful world to his sense of realism' or by his distinction between pity as a 'passive principle', an attitude to death, and pity as an 'active principle', an attitude to life which embraces practical views on the preservation of it. The best use for this study is indicated on the wrapper: it is 'intended for the general reader as a critical companion to the standard edition of Owen's poems'.

There could have been more criticism in the book, though. Particularly of 'Strange Meeting', which is open to criticism and merits it; something should be said about those odd and clumsy double negatives, 'None will break ranks, though nations trek from progress' and 'To miss the march of this retreating world', and about the poetical 'chariot-wheels', so different from the splendidly simple expression of more profound ideas in 'fore-heads of men have bled where no wounds were' and 'I am the enemy you killed, my friend'. Mr Welland has been engaged with Owen a long time (readers of V. de S. Pinto's *Crisis in English Poetry* will remember the tantalizing reference to an unpublished thesis), and it is strange to notice a certain defensiveness in his tone. This may be due to an awareness of that contemporary slickness which cannot but find Owen's poetry barren terrain, hardly worth the triangulation. It could also derive from a slight uneasiness about Owen's pacifism—the moral kind, not the politic brand—now as unfashionable as being influenced in one's youth by Keats, and as lost a cause as humanism itself. Whatever the considerations, it hardly needs explaining that the War writers' attacks on organized militaristic religion were not inspired by anything 'irreverent, godless and blasphemous' in them. Obviously enough, they had remarked some discrepancy between warmongering bishops and Christ on the Cross.

But one should not overstress this slight hesitancy in Mr Welland's handling of Owen's views. He speaks out clearly on a more important point, where Owen irretrievably offends some contemporary susceptibilities.

> That Owen thought of these poems primarily as propaganda is clear not only from the tenor of the whole Preface but also from his Table of Contents . . . each poem was intended to further the central object of inspiring loathing for the bestialities of war.

The theory which insists that a poem is an artifact (what else could it be?), a thing in itself, sounds highly respectable but in effect is often little more than the old aestheticism donnified. Pure form, as Sextus Propertius Pound observed, has its value. A poem of that sort cannot be proved wrong: because it is not 'about' anything. It cannot easily be charged with sentimentality: because it is careful to contain no sentiments. That a tough-looking aestheticism should find a welcome in the British mid-twentieth century is not surprising. It is just rather sad. Poetry without a subject soon degenerates into verbal onanism. Owen certainly had a subject.

> I heard the sighs of men, that have no skill
> To speak of their distress, no, nor the will!

And if he thought of his work as 'propaganda', are we in a position to feel superior?

A study of Owen's manuscripts has enabled Mr Welland to suggest some emendations to the texts as at present accepted. In the line 'My head hangs weighed with snow' ('The End'), Mr Welland tells us, the word 'everlasting' preceded 'snow' in all three manuscripts but was struck out in the latest. Since the poet obviously wanted a word there to make up the ten syllables, he recommends that the adjective be retained. I would say that since we are not conscious of any unhappiness in the line's shortness, it should be left as it is. Owen very probably struck out 'everlasting' because of its banality; and it may be felt—perhaps Owen felt it—that the curtness of the line as it stands is admirably right for 'white Age'. But 'burst' is an undoubted improvement on 'burnt' in 'Music and roses burnt through crimson slaughter' ('Conscious'). And the substitution of 'deathly' for 'deadly' in 'Exposure' (a major poem) seems to me a major emendation—

> Sudden successive flights of bullets streak the silence.
> Less deadly than the air that shudders black with snow . . .

simply because it is more just. The air is not deadlier than the bullets: it could be more deathly. And Mr Welland seems right in suggesting that 'Of tired, outstripped Five-Nines that dropped behind', in the earlier of the two manuscripts of 'Dulce et Decorum Est', should replace 'Of gas-shells dropping softly behind' (Blunden's edition), which would never have satisfied Owen's ear.[1] The only major emendation Mr Welland claims, for good reasons given, concerns the two poems 'The Calls' and 'And I must go', which he considers one poem. Almost certainly he is right, for the last line of the second piece reads in manuscript as 'And *this time* I must go' (my italics)—that is, 'the sighs of men' are the one call he cannot disregard. The fact remains, though,

---

[1] However, Mr C. D. St. Leger writes from Cape Town to express a preference, based on personal experience, for the Blunden reading and its suggestion of 'the lobbed "dropping softly" and pop of the gas shell . . . falling with the short rhythm of Chinese water torture'. He adds, 'Do not let them substitute a vulgar "crump" for that eeriness.'

that the pieces can be read as two separate poems on a similar theme; and then the fine 'And I must go' is left untouched by that slight glibness which Mr Welland remarks in the metre but which affects 'The Calls' alone.

Mr Welland fears that to speak of Owen as a 'War poet' may give a wrong impression. True, the term can have the limiting effect of 'devotional poet'. And more comparison with Siegfried Sassoon, who is a War poet, might have made the point clear. Yet we do think of Owen as a War poet, in a way we don't think of Robert Graves, say. The War was his great subject: he wrote about war as no one else did, perhaps as no one else ever will. He is a *War poet*, with both words stressed.

The Truth Told

The case of Wilfred Owen has something in common with that of Robert Graves. Owen has hardly been neglected, but there have been times when he has not received the attention and the esteem he deserves. At present his reputation stands high. D. S. R. Welland's critical study, the first book devoted to Owen, appeared in 1960, reprints of Edmund Blunden's edition of the poems were called for in 1960, 1961 and 1963, the poems have achieved the status of a set text in the Modern Literature paper of the Cambridge Overseas Higher School Certificate, and some of them alternate with the Mass for the Dead in Benjamin Britten's recent *War Requiem*. Now, in 1963, a new edition, the third, has come from C. Day Lewis.

This handsome new edition includes twenty hitherto un-collected poems and shows some thirty-two textual changes from the previous edition of Edmund Blunden. Of the new poems, mostly juvenilia, three at least are worthy additions to the canon: 'The Letter', a vernacular piece like 'The Chances', in which a soldier is hit while writing to his wife to assure her of his safety (an unsubtle but not unlikely situation); 'Maundy Thursday', where the poet kisses not the crucifix but 'the warm live hand that held the thing'; and a very odd piece, 'The Imbecile'. Perhaps to these one should add 'To— ', a poem whose gay and energetic rhythms and cheerfulness of tone distinguish it sharply from the tushery that dare not speak its name. As for the others, no doubt the Owen enthusiast will be glad to have them: the effect on those coming to him for the first time could be to muffle somewhat this poet's explosiveness.

Most of the textual changes are minor or affect minor poems, and they are generally justified by the manuscripts or by poetic preferability or by both. Some of the more significant changes should be mentioned here. 'Deathly' replaces and improves on 'deadly' in the fourth stanza of 'Exposure'. The (as it seems to me) limping eighth line of 'Dulce et Decorum Est', 'Of gas-shells dropping softly behind', is emended to 'Of tired, outstripped Five-Nines that dropped behind'. 'And everywhere/Music and roses burnt through crimson slaughter' is now 'And here and there/Music and roses burst through crimson slaughter', which makes 'Conscious' a better poem than it was. In 'Music', 'life's symphony' sits more easily in its context than did 'life's sympathy', and the sixth line of 'The Chances' benefits from the acquisition of an extra negative: 'There ain't *no* more nor five things as can 'appen'. All these changes accord with the conclusions Mr Welland drew from his study of the manuscripts.

Mr Day Lewis is, I think, right in not adopting Mr Welland's tentative proposal that in 'The End' the word 'everlasting' should be inserted before 'snow': 'My head hangs weighed with snow': for Owen struck out the word, its only service was to fill out the line, and the sparseness of the line is more effective than otherwise. Some readers may regret that Mr Day Lewis follows Mr Welland in printing 'The Calls' and 'And I must go' as one poem, in that the second part is superior to and now weakened by the first, but external and internal evidence both support the emendation as conforming to Owen's intention.

There are two occasions on which I personally would dissent

from Mr Day Lewis. In that fine line of the fine last stanza of
'Insensibility'—'To pity and whatever moans in man'—he has
substituted 'mourns', a preference which he shares with Siegfried
Sassoon, although the manuscript cancels 'mourns' in favour of
'moans'. Almost certainly Owen struck out 'mourns' because he
had this word (where 'moans' clearly wouldn't be as apt) two
lines later: 'Whatever mourns when many leave these shores':
and he didn't want to repeat it. Mr Welland has pointed out
that the combination moan/mourn occurs in 'Strange Meeting'
and mean/moan/men in 'The Snow', and it seems wrong to
interfere with the rare music of the sequence mean/immune/
moans/man/mourns/many. Then, though it is more difficult to
fix one's preference here, there is the substitution of 'patient' for
'silent', again at an impressive juncture, in the penultimate line
of 'Anthem for Doomed Youth': 'Their flowers the tenderness
of silent minds'. The manuscript is indecisive, Sassoon preferred
'patient' (which was probably his suggestion in the first place), and
it is true, as Mr Day Lewis says, that 'patient' carries on the
alliteration of the previous line. But 'silent' sounds forward to the
'slow' of the following line and, a weightier consideration, there
is a splendid solemnity in the way it chimes with 'minds' and
with the poem's closing word: 'And each slow dusk a drawing-
down of blinds'.

But these variations from Blunden's text are recorded in the
notes, along with some early drafts which are interesting in
showing how Owen customarily (and in the little time at his
disposal) moved from the limitingly personal towards the
universal, from the amateurishly clumsy towards the seemingly
simple, and from the literary circumlocution towards the fresh
and directly demanded word. If it comes as a shock to find
'Strange Meeting' at the beginning instead of the end, this is
partly because one is so used to Blunden's arrangement. Owen's
own Preface is in the right place, and Blunden's Memoir is
reprinted in an appendix: the book would have been distinctly

poorer without it, many of Owen's admirers have come to think of it as an integral part of the *Poems*. Some of us may regret the dropping of Frank Nicholson's brief note, in which mention was made of the photographs of war wounds which Owen was collecting: the footnote to 'A Terre', quoting a reference in a letter of Owen's to the retouching of a photographic representation of a dying officer, is now rather cryptic. At the same time, the poetry is the thing, we don't want it cluttered up. Mr Day Lewis does not go in for irrelevant scholarship, and his new introduction contains some new information.

In this introduction Mr Day Lewis remarks that Owen's early letters to his sister and younger brothers show 'quaint touches of pontificating and lecturing relieved by a levity which is often slightly condescending. We get the impression of a serious, clever but *naïf* youth, a little smug, a little "old-fashioned". . . .' This impression is confirmed in a recent book, the first part of a projected trilogy, by Harold Owen, one of those younger brothers.[1]

Though pinned to the figure of Wilfred Owen, these memoirs can stand on their own feet as the story of an interesting family and a description from inside of a particular period in English social history. Among other things it is an account of parents struggling to bring up their children decently in a context of genteel poverty and near-slums and uncongenial employment. There is a touch of *Sons and Lovers* about it. The mother, strongly and narrowly religious, was used to better things; the father, a born sailor and very much a man's man, found himself condemned to work on the railways.

Wilfred was his mother's favourite.

My father's love for his first-born was extremely real and a lovely thing, but the passionate determination of my mother that all of Wilfred should be hers alone embittered my father's love for

[1] *Journey from Obscurity*. I. Childhood.

him and explained the cold and antagonistic attitude he took, not so much towards Wilfred, but more towards his future ambitions and endeavours.

It was problem enough to secure an education, even a poorish one, for Wilfred, the bright child of the family. Where Harold was concerned, only his physical needs could be provided for: he was his father's boy. From the little one had hitherto gathered about the poet's family life one would have supposed he had never known his father.

Despite his determined efforts to yield the limelight to Wilfred, the author emerges as himself the most attractive character in this early instalment of the family history. Wilfred, despite the efforts of the author, features as something of a prig, always ready to believe the worst of his younger brother and to put him right in language which poor Harold could hardly be expected to understand. But Wilfred's behaviour is not too difficult to account for. From an early age he was conscious that there was something inside him which he had to express, and that he had little time to express it in. Harold liked to find new ways home from school, to explore the town in leisurely fashion, but Wilfred would rush back to his current preoccupation. 'The dread that lack of time or death itself would prevent him from doing all he must do was starting to ride him.'

Wilfred was conscious of a deficiency in other facilities too. Circumstances denied him 'if not his boyhood, at least his boyishness'. His seeming self-conceit was the only defence he could put up against a world so hostile to his unfolding nature and to those gifts of which he alone was dimly yet steadily aware. This was the enforced harshness of attitude of the 'scholarship boy' who hasn't much prospect of getting a scholarship, and the remorseless self-absorption and chilly pedantry of the child who knows in his bones that he has precious little time to learn his lessons. Those big words with which Wilfred sought to browbeat little Harold were dear to him as a talisman, as signposts out of the world in which he lived and into the world in which he sensed he must work, and his use of them as weapons may well have been exacerbated by a feeling of disloyalty towards his family. Harold Owen insists that the priggishness was only apparent, not real. 'Wilfred lacked always the only basis upon which a prig can be formed—self-satisfaction. From infancy, through boyhood and during manhood, dissatisfaction with himself remained inherent in him.'

The first volume of *Journey from Obscurity* is not so sad a book as these reflections would imply. There were good times as well as bad, there was the art school which Harold revelled in as well as the many schools he very properly loathed, and despite its dividedness the family still preserved a strong underlying sense of unity. Though in parts a little slow, the book contains some outstandingly fresh and lucid evocations, especially of family holidays and outings, and the account of the first stirrings of sexual feeling has a rare sweetness about it not easy to parallel in literature of any sort. The jacket alludes to the 'embryo painter' in the family: Harold Owen has proved himself a considerable writer.

'Even then', writes Mr Owen of his brother,

> I think he was aware that his role was more to expose the need for pity and tenderness, and himself to remain the vehicle for doing so, than be the administrator of practical action. This trait of always being the vehicle and never the actor was to remain a marked characteristic throughout his life.

Had Owen survived the War, then perhaps, as Mr Day Lewis suggests, his indignation would have been turned against social injustice. One thing seems certain. Much of the early verse collected in this new edition is as heavily derivative—from Keats or from the 'nineties—as it could well be, until suddenly a line emerges which could only have been written by Owen. His subject was War, but War did not *make* him a poet, and peace, what we call peace, would not have unmade him.

A Haste for Wisdom: the Poetry of D. H. Lawrence

THERE are two views of D. H. Lawrence's poetry, and the twain rarely meet in public. The one has it that the poetry is vitiated by formlessness and the absence of 'serious regard for rhythms'. The other maintains that it has 'organic' or 'expressive' form and its rhythms convey (in Lawrence's own words) 'the insurgent naked throb of the instant moment'. The former view has been put forward by R. P. Blackmur, by James Reeves (rather oddly, in introducing a selection of the poems) and more recently, in *The Critical Quarterly*, by Henry Gifford. The latter view has been voiced by A. Alvarez and (more guardedly, in answer to Mr Gifford) by Gāmini Salgādo, and is propounded at length by Vivian de Sola Pinto, its prime champion, in the introduction to the new *Complete Poems of D. H. Lawrence*.[1]

If it is a question of joining one side or the other, then the choice is not difficult. The argument in favour may fail to account for the poor verse to be found fairly abundantly in this collection, but the argument against simply ignores the unique and not infrequent successes. If these poems are lacking in craftsmanship, then so much the worse for craftsmanship. It might be felt, too, that the conception of poetry and poetic possibilities implied by the pro-Lawrence argument is considerably more congenial than the aesthetic (the word is wholly appropriate) which seems to underlie the anti-Lawrence view. The former is generous, accords to subject-matter and intelligence the importance they

[1] Collected and Edited with an Introduction and Notes by Vivian de Sola Pinto and F. Warren Roberts.

ought to have, and has the courage of its convictions. The latter
is narrow-minded, excogitated (lit. crit. in the head) and stern
in a comically knuckle-rapping way. The anti-Lawrence party
seem to have at the back or perhaps front of their minds the ideal
figure of a perfect genteel poet, *sans reproche* and without fear
of critics. What matters is not that such a poet never existed, but
that this ideal figure, as far as one can make out his features,
resembles nothing so much as a deep-refrigerated macaroni
pudding. The determined worship of so false a god hints at a
strong element of narcissism in the devotees. 'How nice it is to
be superior!' Especially to Lawrence.

'Lawrence . . . was so uninterested in the poem as artifact that
he can't properly be regarded as a poet at all,' wrote A. D. S.
Fowler in *Essays in Criticism* several years back, while adding in
parenthesis, 'Not that his poems are not of great interest and
importance.' Well, let that go: it may be that the word 'artifact'
doesn't mean so much after all. 'As for Lawrence's wit, a not
unfair specimen is this, from one of his Prefaces: "These poems
are called PANSIES because they are rather PENSEES than anything
else".' As for this critic's understanding and good will, we must
hope that the foregoing is an unfair specimen. 'He felt no devotion
to language,' wrote Mr Gifford, echoing Mr Reeves:

> He was not a good poet in the technical sense. . . . He might
> have been a good poet had he been less himself. Impatience with
> poetic technique was, however, a part of him. He had not the
> craftsman's sense of words as living things, as an end in themselves;
> words were too much a means to an end.

It is interesting to have this definition of a craftsman as one
who has a sense of words as an end in themselves. And since Mr
Reeves goes on to say that 'Lawrence was an exciting and original
poet' and 'a poet of today—especially a young poet—can learn
more from the imperfections of Lawrence than from the technical
perfection of many better poets', one can only suppose that

'technical perfection' is a somewhat minor attraction. Certainly one is not left under the impression that by using words as a means to an end Lawrence was committing any mortal sin. The choice might seem to be between those who admire him and say so and those who admire him and make out they don't.

To be fair to Mr Fowler, he has made a good point. 'Revaluation has to be judicious. It would be necessary to distinguish clearly the poems on which the claim is based.' It must be granted that this *Complete Poems* (nearly 900 pages, not counting variants and early drafts)—however grateful many of us will be to have it—makes for oppressive, confusing and blunted reading. There is still room for a critical selection; none of those I have seen conveys a true sense of the fantastic variety and scope of Lawrence's verse. For all its *longueurs*, the *Complete Poems* does make one wonder whether it is not Lawrence's technique or lack of it that is resented so much as his range of subject-matter, the naturalness of his writing ('as the leaves to a tree') and its 'effortlessness'. Today, in an age of labels and syllabuses, we think of poets as possessing their 'special subjects', and we don't hold with 'effortlessness', we believe in paying our way.

Perhaps the best thing the reviewer can do, then, is to anthologize a little. One of Lawrence's avatars is the domestic poet, a gentle writer, concerned about everyday affairs, not with wonders sexual or metaphysical, a homely poet—a type unlikely to find favour with contemporary poetry-fanciers, who hold so elevated a notion of poetry and its purposes. 'Baby running Barefoot' may seem sentimental to those who wear their sentimentality with a difference. 'Corot' indicates how alive Lawrence was to art—ah, but that was the trouble, he failed to distinguish firmly enough between art and life!—to art outside himself; it is scarcely what one would expect from a *naïf*, from one who 'tries to beget children upon himself'. It also seems to have what might seem to be technique. 'The subtle steady rush . . . of advancing Time'

Is heard in the windless whisper of leaves,
In the silent labours of men in the field,
In the downward-dropping of flimsy sheaves
Of cloud the rain-skies yield.

In the tapping haste of a fallen leaf,
In the flapping of red-roof smoke, and the small
Footstepping tap of men beneath
Dim trees so huge and tall . . .

The dialect sequence 'Whether or Not' may be unacceptable
solely because it is in dialect: to me it seems a good, legitimate
poem, with its distinct and convincing voices, and a fine ending,
the outcome incidentally of Edward Garnett's objection to the
original ending and so not quite a case of monstrous partho-
genesis.

Another quality which Lawrence displays, trifling though it
be, is good practical sense, of a kind not always conspicuous in
those who by our loose journalistic categories are allowed
kinship with him. Thus, of teaching young people,

I must not win their souls, no never, I only must win
The brief material control of the hour, leave them free of me . . .

And 'Thought', from *More Pansies,* has a wide and, it appears,
perennial relevance:

Thought, I love thought.
But not the jaggling and twisting of already existent ideas
I despise that self-important game. . . .
Thought is not a trick, or an exercise, or a set of dodges
Thought is a man in his wholeness wholly attending.

'It's bad taste to be wise all the time, like being a perpetual
funeral.' And Lawrence's touch could be very light: his humour
played lightly over others, and he was able to laugh at himself.
'What ails thee?—' is a nice self-parody (or Connie getting even
with that hateful dialect), and in 'Peach', a notably neat little

poem, he recognizes how and why people sometimes felt like
throwing something at him, and offers a peach stone.

Within a few pages of 'Rhyming Poems' there is such diversity
as between 'She lies at last, the darling, in the shape of her dream'
and 'Am I doomed in a long coition of words to mate you?'
or between 'What a lovely haste for wisdom is in men!' and

> Sleep-suave limbs of a youth with long, smooth thighs
> Hutched up for warmth. . .

These last lines come from 'Embankment at Night, Before the
War', a piece of observation live and undoctrinaire, unsentimental
without being either callous or protectively clever. No doubt
the poem might have been more compact, concentrated, but no
one in his senses could regret that it was written and published.
'The Ship of Death' needs no commendation, it is the great
exception which Lawrence's non-admirers commonly admit.
But we might remark that it is not a solitary achievement:
several of the 'Uncollected Poems', written *c.* 1915, are comparable in the quiet solemnity of the run-on but unscurrying lines:

> And say, what matters any more, what matters,
> Save the cold ghosts that homeless flock about
> Our serried hearts, drifting without a place?

The much anthologized *Bird, Beasts and Flowers* have perhaps
been over-rated; but they do have fine things in them, evidence
of Lawrence's marvellous gift of empathy even with modes of
life for which he felt little sympathy, like the bat,

> Dark air-life looping
> Yet missing the pure loop.

Better still are the goat poems—

> Yet she has such adorable spurty kids, like spurts of black ink.
> And in a month again is as if she had never had them.
> And when the billy goat mounts her
> She is brittle as brimstone.
> While his slitted eyes squint back to the roots of his ears.

Has any other writer gone so far along this road? The insight is uncanny, a sort of magic, like Adam among the animals:

> I named them as they passed, and understood
> Their nature, with such knowledge God endued
> My sudden apprehension. . . .

But 'words are not Adamic', says Mr Gifford, and poetry (as we have been told) is made of words. (What are words made of?)

The weaknesses in Lawrence's poetry are so obvious that it seems unnecessary to dwell on them. In brief, at times he was downright bad in the very matters in which at other times he was superbly good. He could be uniquely sensitive and refreshing: he could also bumble on like a congress of cabbalists. He was gifted with a light touch: he was also cursed with a heavy hand. Thus in much of *Pansies* there is a pathetic straining after rhyme which defeats its own purpose, an ensuing serio-comic effect which fails to be either comic or serious:

> And it's funny, my dear young men, that you in your twenties
>   should love the sewer scent
> of obscenity, and lift your noses where the vent is
>   and run towards it, bent
> on smelling it all, before your bit of vitality spent is.

For Lawrence, as Aldington put it, 'writing was just a part of living. Take it or leave it.' Even Lawrence, though he lived more continuously, more intensely, with fewer rest-periods, than is the case with the mass of us, did not live always on the peaks. And he kept his trivialities for poetry in the way most writers of both reserve them for prose. Some of the poems here have their correspondences, more finely worked out, in the novels: compare 'Children Singing in School' with the famous Tevershall passage in *Lady Chatterley's Lover*. It isn't that the novel gave him more elbow room, for in the poems one often has the impression that he has treated himself to more space than he can occupy. One obvious advantage of the novel, Lawrence being the man he was, is that the argumentation and preaching are attached to characters who do other things besides argue and preach. The effect of some of the verse is of a pulpit and a microphone and a booming voice, but no human being in view.

And then you have the declamatory assertions of *Look! We Have Come Through!*, or the deadening reiteration, the rasping sterility of this, from *More Pansies*:

> Oh I have loved my fellow-men—
> and lived to learn they are neither fellow nor men
> but machine-robots. . . .

It is as if Lawrence sometimes woke up in the morning with a strong and perhaps not groundless distaste for the human race and thereupon wrote out of his irritation not one poem against it but four or five. He didn't inevitably, as he hoped to, exclude a 'repellent, slightly bullying' effect by putting his thoughts into verse: by the end of the outburst the reader finds his sympathy has gone where it wasn't meant to go. The pity of it is that, thus antagonized, the reader risks missing something good, perhaps 'Retort to Whitman', a few pages further on:

> And whoever walks a mile full of false sympathy
> walks to the funeral of the whole human race

—an utterance in one of Lawrence's characteristic modes, the Blakeian. There is much of Blake, too, which we would prefer Blake not to have written—except for a strong suspicion that in that case we wouldn't have any Blake at all. 'What fascinates me about the poems of Lawrence's which I like,' Auden has said, 'is that I must admit he could never have written them had he held the kind of views about poetry of which I approve. . . . Parnassus has many mansions.' Occasional boredom and exasperation is a small price to pay for a sizeable body of major poetry. If enthusiasm for Lawrence the poet is wrong, then it is a generous misdemeanour, a sensible error.

There was a Time: Herbert Read's Autobiographies

The Contrary Experience is Sir Herbert's *Prelude*, 'the story of the growth of a poet's mind'. While that mind has grown with the years, it has not changed much from its first shape and direction. Art captured him at an early age; 'Art is the redemption of Life', he wrote in 1916; and towards the end of this book, in a section not previously published, he tells us that 'my profoundest experience has been, not religious, nor moral, but aesthetic'. The love of art has been the prime constant among other constants; and just as Read has never lost his original strengths, so he has never quite overcome his original weaknesses. He has always exalted spontaneity over all else, yet his writing is often marked by predetermination: the sentiments are warm, at times (some might contend) overheated, yet there is a certain abstractness, a coldness, in their expression. The ultimate coldness of the aesthete, perhaps?

This is not the whole story, for Sir Herbert's story is a long and varied one, but it is true, I think, when he is expounding his ideas about art or politics or life. 'As soon as he reflects, he is a child.' Not the sort of child Goethe meant in speaking of Byron—indeed, when he is *not* reflecting, Read is like the child, 'open to the whole world without,' as he says in *The Tenth Muse*, 'but with an inward reserve which the child does not yet possess' —but rather a solemn precocious child. The signs of the autodidact are plain to see—they are honourable signs, and we can sympathize with his suspicion of formal education—but among them is an over-respectful attitude towards heavy thinkers and big words which conflicts with his fundamental beliefs.

When he philosophizes, we long for particularities, for illustrations in action, for concrete human instances: he has grown so much more abstract than his own account of himself would have. We are rarely quite sure of what he means by 'objective', 'subjective', 'idealism', 'realism'. Anarchism, he tells us, 'does not believe in plans, which are rational constructions that always leave out the imponderable and elusive factors of human feeling and human instinct'. Surely an anarchist, an enemy of prescribed forms, should avoid such prescribed terminology?—jargon which denies those imponderable and elusive factors that are of the essence of Read's business, which merely begs the questions that he seems so pre-eminently qualified to suggest the answers to.

'I love people with theories', he wrote in an early letter. And he has always loved theories too—more, one is tempted to say, than he has loved people.

> Anarchism asserts . . . that life must be so ordered that the individual can live a natural life . . . in a thousand ways the principle of anarchism will determine our practical policies, leading the human race gradually away from the state and its instruments of oppression towards an epoch of wisdom and joy.

Perhaps 'anarchism' asserts this, but such bare assertions are meaningless, and we expect more from Read, we want to hear something about some of those thousand ways. In 'The Artist's Dilemma' a striking contrast with the author's generalizing is afforded by the short dramatic extracts from Ford Madox Ford's letters and the welcome access of life which they bring to the page. Read's own writing offers an equally striking contrast within this book, in 'The Raid' and 'In Retreat' with their actualities and immediacies. 'Our chloride of lime is missing and cannot be found. Machine-guns very active.' Perhaps there is some reason—though still insufficient—why in the final volume of the *Pelican Guide to English Literature* Sir Herbert features only in the section on the literature of the First World War.

Sir Herbert being what he is, the book is plainly an event of some moment. I have perhaps made too much of this dissatisfaction, this central contradiction in his work, as it seems to me. Possibly because I am so often in sympathy with his basic tenets, artistic, political and 'philosophical', as to feel a special resentment when they are allowed to suffer by default, their significance undefined and untested. Other sections of *The Contrary Experience* do not give rise to this difficulty. Stimulating perceptions are scattered throughout, on formal education and 'negative capability', on form in poetry, on particular writers, on the physical context of our spiritual lives. The chapters dealing with war experience, lucid in scene and perfect in tone, rank with the classic memoirs of Blunden, Graves and Sassoon. The wartime letters which form 'Extracts from a Diary' are high-minded in theme and yet nicely informal, an agreeable blend of the author's abstract discursiveness and his lively depiction of persons and places. 'The Innocent Eye' needs no commendation: its dense detailed accounts of the author's childhood, testimony to an extraordinary memory, remind us of some Dutch paintings: 'the postman and the pedlar, and the scarlet huntsman . . . the snowman. . . . On Mondays the washed clothes flapped in the wind . . . hens, ducks, geese, guinea fowls, and turkeys. . . .' This is the green tree of life: it was to 'grey theory' that Sir Herbert lost his innocence. The only thing one might conceivably miss here is humour: the author's attitude is a little suffocatingly reverential.

Elsewhere one misses humour more badly. As when he tells us, apropos of his own unbelief, that 'many of my best friends . . . are devout Christians'. Always earnest, always rigidly honest, he is sometimes a little naïve—but there are worse things to be, in autobiography as in life.

Sir Herbert's last words, in the Preface, are sad ones. In the foreword to his *Annals of Innocence and Experience* he declared his persisting faith in man's natural goodness. That faith, he now

says, 'is certainly no longer tenable. The death wish that was once
an intellectual fiction has now become a hideous reality and
mankind drifts indifferently to self-destruction.' Here the anarchist
has turned tyrannical and is prescribing mankind's fate. Reason
no doubt is on his side, but Sir Herbert was never one to relinquish
himself entirely to reason. In one of the wartime letters he wrote,
'My pessimism does not deny all effort or defeat all hope—there
never was such a hopeful and ambitious soul as this . . .'.

Easy Lies the Head: C. P. Snow and the Corridors of Power

THE style is sometimes the man and, despite what the theoreticians say, the fictional hero is sometimes closely related to the creator. It is hard to tell whether the creator of the 'Strangers and Brothers' sequence is a very modest man or a somewhat self-satisfied one. Self-satisfied, because of the pervasive smugness, the transparent if subfusc gratification which the author derives from his acquaintance with men who matter and his intimacy with the ins and outs of the corridors which they walk. 'A kind of pleasure, the pleasure, secretive but shining, that they got from being at the centre of things': but hardly secretive in this case. Modest, because of the emotional moderation, the spiritual abstemiousness, which the author enjoins upon his creations. Because it is not a lord he loves, but merely a Parliamentary or even a Permanent Secretary. And because usually his corridors of power lead, if not to the grave, then to nothing especially grand or shining. The stock explanation is that, neither modest nor self-satisfied, Sir Charles Snow is simply the detached historian of the British Establishment, detached and accurate. So. This Establishment had hitherto inspired me with considerably more respect, or more fear, or more *something*, than does Snow's epic portrayal of it.

'When she wrote'—this is a minor character engaged on a biography of her late husband—'she didn't fuss, she just wrote.' The same can be said of Snow, and perhaps—which is not to ask that his personages should talk like Durrellian diplomats— he ought to try to fuss just a little. He employs clichés as such; not, for better or worse, wittily or questioningly; no, he has the

courage of his clichés. His style has been praised on the grounds
that it doesn't exist (like the only good German, etc.), and his
use of commonplaces has been defended as sound naturalistic
practice. That it to say, people talk in clichés—politicians, Civil
Servants, scientists especially?—and life consists largely of banal
situations, and Snow's themes are of such public moment that the
artist's fine Italian hand may not be allowed to distort the account.
There is a decent scruple at work here, which novelists of a
documentary sort can honestly feel; and it is best conciliated
by the reminder that a novel is only a novel, after all; or, better,
that a novel *is* a novel.

In one way and another I found *Corridors of Power* a lowering
experience. The fearful rumpus in *The Masters* was less dispiriting,
because we know that dons (still at that date an under-employed
race) tend to triviality the moment they cease to be profound.
'He longed for all the trappings, titles, ornaments and show of
power. . . . He wanted the grandeur of the Lodge, he wanted
to be styled among the heads of houses.' Whatever we may think
of such ambitions and of the benign respect which the author
accords them, it must be granted that a college was a suitable
setting for the subfusc intriguing which so fascinates Sir Charles.
The intrigues of this new novel concern a government and a
reasonably important public issue, the attempt of a Conservative
Minister to scrap Britain's independent Bomb. Yet the people
involved are as long-winded as the dons and considerably less
entertaining. Naturalism here reaches its climax, in what seems
little more than a waxworks show. Hansard, presumably a
naturalistic document, is distinctly more animated and (since no
one is so simple, or so aesthetic, as to take people's words, spoken
or written, as necessarily a true and complete representation of
their thoughts and feelings) hardly more deceptive than Snow's
stolid, cautious narrative. When there is so much craft in human
nature, surely we might as well permit our art to indulge in a
little art.

Naturalism, then, requires the chronicling of resounding commonplaces and even what might look like plain bad writing. Thus,

> It was often *naïf* to be too suspicious, much more *naïf* than to believe too easily. It often led to crasser action. But there were occasions—and this was one—where you needed to trust.

And,

> In fact, a nose for danger was the most useful single gift in the political in-fighting: unless it stopped one acting altogether, in which case it was the least.

Snow's didactic urge is endearing, and would be more so if by implication it didn't represent our masters as (more or less) honest (more or less) simpletons. His prose sometimes reminds one of orthodox Soviet writing: solemn, shrewdly simple, bucolically genial, heavily tolerant of minor sins, so ponderous in its humour as to be humourless—and apt to excite acute suspicion and alarm in the not-utterly-credulous.

But no, this is sheer sensationalism!—a mono-cultured reaction to Sir Charles's unrelenting temperateness, his judicial calm. I don't mean to suggest that we should elect hysterics or manic-depressives to rule us—or poets or novelists. But it seems a mere caricature of British sang-froid, of well-bred 'liberalism', when we are told that what Lewis Eliot and his wife—nice, Leftish people—chiefly feel over the Suez aggression is *humiliation*. They happen to be 'in a crowded drawing-room at the American Ambassador's house, deafened by the party's surge and swell', when the hurtful news is broken to them. Their American friends 'went on trying to cheer us up': a solicitude unhappily denied to those dead peasants around the Canal. However, humiliation is perhaps a strong emotion judged by the barometers that hang in the corridors of power. 'We mingled among the party'—a different party, this—'most of them rich and leisured.' With the worst will in the world I cannot believe that the rich and leisured are as consistently tedious and nerveless as most of Snow's guests and hosts show themselves. As ever, the author was seeking to be scrupulously honest, exact and un-romantic when he remarked, in *The New Men*,

> Put your ear to those meetings and you heard the intricate labyrinthine and unassuageable rapacity, even in the best of men, of the love of power. If you have heard it once—say, in electing the chairman of a tiny dramatic society, it does not matter where— you have heard it in colleges, in bishoprics, in ministries, in cabinets: men do not alter because the issues they decide are bigger scale.

But in this present book, where the issues are decidedly bigger-scale, he shows himself dreadfully unfair to those tiny dramatic societies.

There is little to be seen here of the inner life. Eliot is happy with Margaret, and *vice versa*: indeed the uxoriousness con-tributes generously to the suffocating smugness of the whole. Perhaps it is because Snow deems it advisable to inject a dash of mere humanity into all this high dignity that the Minister is given a mistress, otherwise supererogatory, since his sexual life features minimally if at all in his downfall. Hence, perhaps, such concomitant excitements as 'She was speaking without constraint, self-effacingness stripped off, codes of behaviour fallen away. Her face had gone naked and wild.' Or, 'He was speaking, as usual, the naked truth', when we didn't for a moment imagine the man was fibbing, and the truth in question (a Tory M.P. is indicating his reluctance to leave the Commons for the Lords) is hardly so momentous as to call for the epithet 'naked'. Nakedness has served before now to pep up dull parties. It is at a party in Lancaster House—'the occasion was the visit of some western Foreign Minister'—that Eliot muses thus:

> In this drawing-room the men and women were vigorous and hearty. 'Peach-fed' I had heard them called, though not by them-selves. There were some love-affairs floating around. But most of

them didn't chafe against the limits of the sexual existence. Often they got more out of it than those who did. But they didn't live, or talk, or excite themselves, as though there were, there must be, a sexual heaven round the corner.

That's Sir Charles's Establishment all right. They aren't going to get excited about nothing. They're a canny lot. They don't believe in *any* heaven round *any* corner, they haven't sufficient imagination to conceive of pie in the sky; peach in the drawing-room is good enough for them. 'I passed as a realistic man,' said Eliot in *The New Men*. 'In some ways it was true. But down at the springs of my life I hoped too easily and too much.' That must have been a long, long time ago.

To me *Corridors of Power* seems distinctly more wooden than the majority of its predecessors. It is only fair to record that *Time* magazine found the book 'the capstone of the sequence so far', 'on balance a very good novel', and 'a compelling novel of high politics'. Writing about Snow in *Meanjin* some five years ago Derek Stanford quoted Bonamy Dobrée as saying, 'Well, I suppose he's important because he writes about those things which really matter'. Taking the remark in perhaps not quite the same way, I would be inclined to agree with it. But is *Corridors of Power* the work of a sober patriot, soberly chronicling, or the machination of a cunning subversive, another Gunpowder Plot? Is Britain run by zombies, with a choice of zombies Right or zombies Left? An admirer of Snow has spoken of his 'immense, almost Johnsonian, weight of experience of society and knowledge of men'. Certainly some sort of weight is there. So perhaps this book *is* the 'great political novel' that the blurb claims. It is frightening that *Corridors of Power* should almost succeed in arousing nostalgia—almost—for the sort of politics which is accompanied by arrests, disappearances, riots, torture. There, someone seems to care at least.

Alexandrian Nights' Entertainments:
Lawrence Durrell's 'Quartet'

ALEXANDRIA *is* a rather melodramatic city, and not only by British-provincial standards. Its extremes of wealth and poverty are staggering. (Or were—my own experience of Alexandria was in the good old days of King Farouk; Durrell's 'Quartet' is set chiefly in the apparently even better old days of King Fuad.) Its beggars are the most horrifying in the world. Its population ranges from a simple fellahin through a cartoonist's cotton-pashas to the ultra-sophisticated society of Baudrot, *L'Atelier* and the big houses. Its sea is bluer than the most unlikely Mediterranean postcard. In the khamseen (which Durrell describes spendidly in *Justine*) the city honestly looks like the end of the world. Why, then, did Durrell feel obliged to paint the lily and throw an extra stench on the putrescence?

His characters can't have a drink in Place Zagloul without 'in the room above a poor wretch screaming with meningitis'. When we first meet her, Clea is reading *A Rebours*. Nessim's 'great house' is patrolled by 'black slaves': call them 'servants' and how the glory dims! The sustained set-piece of the masked ball in *Balthazar* belongs not to the Alexandrian 1930's but to the Renaissance Borgias, and (for we have the hang of it by then) it is only to be expected that the epicene Toto de Brunel should be found stabbed with a hatpin, that he should have been wearing Justine's ring at the time, and that (to bring us vaguely back into this century) he should transpire to have been a trusted agent of the *Deuxième Bureau*. 'Fateful words which I have so often recalled since,' we read later, 'for within a few months Fosca was to be a problem no more.' Dot-dot-dot, indeed.

'The Alexandria Quartet' seems to be built on the idea that one person can be different things to different observers, that a sequence of events can be interpreted in various ways and no way is any truer than another. The idea is neither novel nor true; or, if true, then true within such narrow limits that no tetralogy or 'quartet' or 'word-continuum' can safely be based on it. That Durrell manages to make it seem true for a while is a credit to his poetic talent: his 'views of Alexandria' are so sharply focused as almost to persuade us that *anything* he tells us is true even if it contradicts something else. It is also a discredit to his 'characters', who lack precisely character. Does Justine love Darley? Is she merely using him to conceal her love for Pursewarden? (And would this manœuvre be as likely as Durrell assumes?) Or is it the Palestine conspiracy which claims her real love? Was she or wasn't she raped as a child? Has she a 'wicked fashionable face'? Or a 'black stern' one? Did her child die in a brothel? Did she have no child? Durrell doesn't want to know. When everything is true, nothing is true. Off come the glamorous veils one by one—they are still coming off when the series 'ends'. Life isn't like this: more to the point, there seems no reason why art should be. Perhaps it is in a desperate attempt to endow his creations with character that Durrell deprives them of limbs. Capodistria wears a black patch over his eye, Scobie has a glass eye, and Hamid, Abdul and (in the end) Nessim are all one-eyed. Liz is completely blind, so is her daughter. Panayotis has had his tongue cut out. Balthazar loses his teeth and almost his hands. Clea loses a hand, Nessim a finger along with the eye, and Leila her beauty. Semira, on the contrary, gains a nose. Casualties among the minor non-characters are equally high: heads are chopped off, bits of ears removed, faces mashed by a hippo-hide whip, foreskins tumble in a continuous shower and eunuchs abound. Moreover, practically every horror happens at least twice—for instance, the camel being chopped up alive—or is told twice. But all the violence at Durrell's command cannot create *character*. And alas the two promisingly solid human creations of the quartet are undone by Durrell's lack of trust in them.

Scobie, the old seaman who has found a niche in the Egyptian Police, is far more of a presence than the heavily documented Justine. His honesty helps in that: 'If you have Tendencies you got to have Scope. That's why I'm in the Middle East if you want to know. . . .' He doesn't attach any spiritual distinction or arcane significance to his Tendencies; content to be a simple-minded old reprobate with a simple joy in living, he becomes rather more: a sun-cured Falstaff in a technicolour Dream of Dark Nymphomaniacs. But he too falls victim to his author's inability to leave well alone. No quiet death-bed, babbling of green fields, for him: the old chap is beaten to death while dressed in women's clothes. Then, by a *volte-face* more characteristic of the novelette than of paradoxical Alexandria, Scobie reappears as a local saint with an annual feast on St George's Day and a reputation for curing sterility. Yet perhaps Durrell was right there. Scobie was a natural eccentric, not (like most of the Alexandrians) a cultivated one; and, as the janitor of his tomb claims, he was 'a student of harmlessness'.

Justine of course is a *femme fatale* of ancient lineage:

> It would be silly to spread so much harm as I have done and not to realize that it is my role. Only in this way, by knowing what I am doing, can I ever outgrow myself. It isn't easy to be me.

That would seem mere claptrap—*Peg's Paper* bound in calf—and, a shadow herself, Justine can hardly do much harm to the shadows among whom she moves. The Palestine conspiracy is sketchy in the extreme: we cannot believe that a banker would put his money into it. Then there is the harm Justine does to Melissa, the cabaret dancer. . . .Melissa has her attractions. She works for her living: she doesn't dance with incredible grace (she doesn't even dance well); she doesn't 'seem an eagle', like

Justine, or 'gaze about her like a half-trained panther'. And she sleeps with Capodistria to pay Darley's debts, which (compared with the reasons or lack of reasons which the other females have for their amorous activity) seems reasonable. Yet we are told in *Justine* and again in *Mountolive* that when Pursewarden asks her, '*Comment vous défendez-vous contre la solitude?*' she replies softly, '*Monsieur je suis devenue la solitude même*'. A woman of such *esprit* could presumably (for she obviously doesn't enjoy sleeping with the cabaret customers) find more suitable employment in some local French cultural agency. But Melissa is doomed from the start: a pretty pathetic puppet of the Mimi variety, tagged with the legend 'the soft bloom of phthisis'.

The other solid creation, solid until his creator undermines him, is Pursewarden the novelist, the figure into which Durrell puts the unromantic, combative and sceptical side of his own nature, the side which shows itself in his best poetry. Despite the unpromising title of his trilogy, 'GOD IS A HUMORIST', he does have the air of a professional writer. His remarks on being a successful novelist are not irrelevant to Durrell's tetralogy: 'The answer, old man, is sex and plenty of it. . . . Lashings of sex . . . but remember . . . *stay buttoned up*. . . . Try and look as if you had a stricture, a book society choice. . . .' The situation is enriched by the fact that, while clearly involved in Pursewarden, Durrell identifies himself more explicitly with Darley, the unsuccessful novelist (so far unsuccessful, but *he* survives) whom Pursewarden is fond of teasing. It is Pursewarden alone who resists Justine's ambiguous spell. To Darley she is 'my tyrant'; to Pursewarden 'a tiresome old sexual turnstile'. He tells her, 'You have the impudence to foist yourself on us as a problem—perhaps because you have nothing else to offer?' And, even worse sacrilege, he actually *makes her laugh*. It is Pursewarden who refers to the 'cafeteria mysticism' of 'our friends' and remarks that 'Justine and her city are alike in that they both have a strong flavour without having any real character'. We all know people who put on a 'flavour' along with their scent or black tie before going to a party. Justine and company are inveterate actors; they act, they do not *do*. They demand so much and give so little. (Darley comments on Justine's 'almost deafening lack of interest in other people', and for her the Palestine conspiracy seems more a deliberate aphrodisiac than anything else, a high-class equivalent of poor Melissa's Spanish fly.) They make use of others who could otherwise be useful; a rude (and entirely non-political) word for them is 'parasites'. And one tires of them before long, well before the end of a tetralogy: their natural length is *Justine*, which remains for me the *raison d'être* of the quartet.

Durrell-Pursewarden's judgment on Justine and her city is devastating: yet Durrell-Darley ignores it and Lawrence Durrell writes a further three volumes. Of course Pursewarden, dangerous fellow, has to be put down. He commits suicide, an act for which (since for Durrell the novelist simplicity is unholy) two distinct motives are advanced. The first—his mistaken assumption that Nessim is innocent of arms smuggling—seems inadequate. 'Nobody kills himself for an official reason!' cries Mountolive, and few readers can have taken Pursewarden seriously as a member (albeit on contract) of the Foreign Service. The second reason is even more theatrical (this trouble-maker is to be thoroughly demolished!): it seems that Pursewarden loves his blind sister, that they had a blind child who has died, and that he kills himself lest his mere existence should endanger Liz's new love for H. E. Sir David Mountolive. 'I felt stupefied by the sad weight of all this calamitous information,' Darley mumbles somewhat inadequately, but then, for these Alexandrians a mere incest is nothing to write home about. Thus, by giving Pursewarden the most melodramatic finis of all, Justine and the quartet are 'vindicated' of his deflatory comments. In a review in *The Spectator* John Coleman countered Durrell's claim to have attempted 'an investigation of modern love' by adducing and applying the postcard message which Pursewarden is credited with having sent to D. H. Lawrence: 'I am simply trying not to copy your habit of building a Taj Mahal around anything as simple as a good f--k'. A further remark, of Darley's, can be adduced: 'Nobody in Alexandria can ever be shocked deeply; among us tragedy exists only to flavour conversation'. Yet, despite this plain warning, Durrell has attempted to build a sort of *Atrides* around a group of over-bred neurotics and sexual dilettantes.

The theatricality of the incidents is reflected in the self-conscious, melodramatic 'profundity' of the *aperçus* with which the composition is embellished. Thus, on the first page of the first volume:

> What is resumed in the word Alexandria? In a flash my mind's eye shows me a thousand dust-tormented streets. Flies and beggars own it today—and those who enjoy an intermediate existence between either.

Is that true? Is it well said? Is it even comprehensible? 'I have become one of these poor clerks of the conscience, a citizen of Alexandria'—what does that fine-sounding sentence *mean*? 'Women are very stupid as well as very profound' would be merely and obviously puerile in another writer. The observation that 'A woman's best love letters are always written to the man she is betraying' may be typical of Justine, but it is also typical of the novelette; while 'Life is more complicated than one thinks, yet far simpler than anyone dares to imagine' is a bad case of *fausse naïveté*. And those catalogues of Alexandrian names—a Colonel Neguib features in two of them—what do they contribute but a smack of snobbery? Even in my day there was usually a Romanoff or two in Baudrot, but the coffee didn't taste any different for it.

It is not pleasant to write thus of the prose of a poet whom one admires. I hasten to say that at its best Durrell's prose is extremely fine. The grim pictures in *Justine* of the dock area, Alexandria Main Station and the Attarine quarter are, in the way that art is, *authentic.* The festivals and especially the prostitutes' booths (one hears of 'radiantly beautiful' prostitutes) strike me as glamorized. But the 'clang of the trams shuddering in their metal veins as they pierce the iodine-coloured *meidan* of Mazarita' is overpoweringly evocative. The account of the duck-shoot on Lake Mareotis is so splendid that it seems blasphemous to intrude the supposed killing of Capodistria. The Coptic wake in *Mountolive* is equally exciting. And of course the work scores innumerable local successes: Melissa dancing with 'the air of a gazelle harnessed to a water-wheel'; Pombal on cocktail parties ('bottom-sniffings raised to the rank of formal ceremonies'); 'a prostitute singing . . . to the gulp and spank of a finger-drum'; Mountolive's encounter with the child prostitutes; the description of the harbour in *Balthazar* ('Dinghies . . . scuttling in and out among the ships like mice among the great boots of primitive cottagers') with its misplaced parenthetical comment, 'Fine writing!'; and Alexandria as Nessim enters it at dawn:

> The shrill telephones whose voices filled the great stone buildings in which the financiers really lived, sounded to him like the voices of great fruitful mechanical birds. They glittered with a pharaonic youthfulness. The trees in the park had been rinsed down by an unaccustomed dawn rain. They were covered in brilliants and looked like great contented cats at their toilet.

Alexandria, as one sees it at such moments, deserves better than the Alexandrians with whom Durrell peoples it.

The mistake was to try to make four books out of such tenuous *human* material, I think. Whatever its intention, *Balthazar* repeats those aspects of *Justine* which cannot really bear repetition, and the fact that the angle of vision has changed doesn't improve matters: shadows are seen, all the more surely, as shadows. It is not surprising that several critics have picked *Mountolive* as their favourite: 'I think this volume', V. S. Pritchett wrote optimistically, 'is the making of the quartet.' On the face of it,

Mountolive seemed the right answer to Durrell's problem at that stage: it was to show us a man doing a job of work, and it held out the prospect of 'a political and religious conspiracy' (the dust-cover had already whetted our appetites with an allusion to 'the sinister side of Egyptian life'). By this time the best-disposed of Durrell's readers, I should have thought, would welcome any sort of intrigue *not* amorous. Moreover it would appear that Mountolive is to be presented as a man at war with himself: the gifted individualist who must conform to the demands of his profession, in this case the very demanding profession of ambassador—a theme which could possibly be tragic and easily be interesting. True, there are sketchy but portentous references to his early years in the service: 'the love-affair with Grishkin which almost entangled him in a premature marriage; his un-happy passion for an Ambassador's mistress which exposed him to a duel, and perhaps disgrace'. Yet, two pages later, we hear how he was saved from marrying his little Grishkin, an altogether unsuitable ballerina:

> Fortunately she once or twice risked a public familiarity which froze me; once when the whole ballet was invited to a reception I got myself seated next to her believing that she would behave with discretion since none of my colleagues knew of our liaison. Imagine their amusement and my horror when all of a sudden while we were seated at supper she passed her hand up the back of my head to ruffle my hair in a gesture of coarse endearment! It served me right. But I realized the truth in time, and even her wretched pregnancy when it came seemed altogether too transparent a ruse. I was cured!

'Coarse endearment'! Poor Grishkin was apparently a mere Czech, certainly no Alexandrian. Mountolive was a young man at that time, and Grishkin's parting taunt—'You are only a diplomat. You have no politics and no religion!'—settles his hash and makes the rest of his history redundant. His reflection 230 pages further on that 'he had now joined the ranks of those who compromise gracefully with life' comes as a comic anti-climax. We have every reason to believe that he was born into those ranks, his Third Secretary-ish involvement with an Egyptian lady (the permissible 'bed dictionary'?) notwithstanding, his unwitting visit to a children's brothel notwithstanding, his name notwithstanding. In fact he is the stock figure of the 'brilliant diplomat,' making witty and charming speeches in fluent Arabic and French, blessed with greying temples, beloved of all his female staff—a caricature even of a breed which runs to caricature. Though Durrell is not deceived on the point, he makes curiously heavy weather of placing Mountolive. And the reader feels disappointed: he had expected sterner stuff than this. Mountolive may be more honest than his Alexandrian acquaintances but he is equally flaccid; at the best, we sympathize with his 'difficult position'.

And so in *Clea* 'naturalism' gives way to a reasserted and intensified romanticism. Capodistria turns out not to be dead. Balthazar attempts to cut off his hands. Clea (erstwhile lesbian) makes love with Darley during an air-raid. The pregnant Fosca is accidentally killed by a warning shot from a Vichy battleship in the harbour. The Pursewarden incest is revealed. Clea is harpooned underwater and Darley has to hack her hand off (happily she finds she can paint better with an artificial one). And the whole desperate brew is spiced with fortune-telling and magic: there is a long letter from Capodistria (based on a footnote in a *Life of Paracelsus,* the author tells us) describing the manufacture and use of homunculi. Some good posthumous Scobie and Pursewarden and the fine incidentals (Darley's entry into war-time Alexandria, for instance) cannot do much in the face of all this. The quartet runs out in a sort of hectic boredom, like Justine herself: 'under every sofa the same corpse, in every cupboard the same skeleton? What can one do but laugh?' Then, at the very end, we hear that Justine and Nessim have 'broken through' in some undefined way: 'It is something much bigger this time, international. . . . I can't tell you any details.' A rocket plot? A cabbalistic Summit? Moral Rearmament? And to think that in *Justine* Darley had said of himself and his mistress that 'We were human beings not Brontë cartoons'!

The reasons for the quartet's resounding success, on various levels, are not hard to find. It creates through the senses a place, a city, even if in the long run it dulls those same senses. It offers some genuine tough farce of the kind of *Volpone*. It contains fine writing as well as 'fine writing'. It approximates to the English idea of a French novel; and, I suspect, translates well into French. It is worlds apart from the Welfare State (wouldn't you just love to keep a black slave?). Its politics are happily archaic. There is a good deal of talk about art (not too much?). It provides us with some choice time-honoured Grand Guignol. X- as well as H-Certificate tastes are catered for, but safely this side obscenity. It raises moral questions—which is always good—and then disposes of them among amoral characters—which is better. In brief—another recipe for success as a novelist?—when Durrell is good he is very good, and when he is bad he is horrid.

Public Faeces: the Correspondence of Lawrence Durrell and Henry Miller

Lawrence Durrell and Henry Miller. A Private Correspondence, edited by George Wickes: or the transactions, over 400 pages and twenty-five years, of a small but active mutual admiration society. It must be granted that this is not a case of you-scratch-my-back-I'll-scratch-yours. For the partners are quite disinterested; they are utterly sincere, alas. It can only be supposed that the ungrateful publisher has some enormous grudge against the two of them, since the making public of this 'private correspondence' will hardly enhance the reputations which they have so painstakingly built up with the collaboration of an unnerved and gullible international public. Even gullibility, even international gullibility, has its limits.

The correspondence opens in August 1935 with a fan letter from Durrell. *Tropic of Cancer,* recently published, 'strikes me as being the only really man-size piece of work which this century can really boast of. . . . It's the final copy of all those feeble, smudgy rough drafts—*Chatterley, Ulysses, Tarr,* etc.' The outburst has the captivating enthusiasm of youth: Durrell was only twenty-three. Miller's reply is short and to the point. 'I particularly prize your letter because it's the kind of letter I would have written myself had I not been the author of the book.' Miller was only forty-three. Durrell then confesses to being a writer himself, and Miller asks, 'Why don't you send me something of yours so that I can return some of the audacious compliments you pay me?' Which shows a nice nature. A little later Durrell takes off 'a Britisher of the old flag-waving type . . . quite nice but thick in the attic', who has borrowed *Tropic of*

Cancer and doesn't object to 'the fellah consorting with buggahs, and all that' but draws the line at his pinching things from whores. Interesting, that. It had always struck me that for the uncensorious reader this episode might well be the only one which would stick in the mind—or the gullet.

Miller claims to feel like a Chinaman. 'I'm nuts about China.' And this is the prelude to a good deal of wishful-orientalism on both sides, until Durrell lashes out at Zennery in 1958. Similarly an early portentousness on Durrell's side—'I AM SLOWLY BUT VERY CAREFULLY AND WITHOUT CONSCIOUS THOUGHT DESTROYING TIME'—looks forward to *The Alexandria Quartet*. A little later and Miller is writing a huge book on *Hamlet* but can't bring himself to read Shakespeare's version and asks Durrell to 'give me the low-down on it'. He writes to T. S. Eliot (a minor but engaging character in this correspondence) to tell him about Durrell, but complains that Eliot 'seems to treat me very gingerly and cavalierly'. Throughout their relationship each does his utmost to help the other along: in these early years Miller goes to enormous trouble to launch his young friend: so much is unequivocally impressive.

Durrell sends Miller a prose poem and enables him to return an audacious compliment. 'This puts you in a class with Léon-Paul Fargue. It's far superior to Breton or to Dylan Thomas. . . . You're a stinking genius!' Durrell's grateful reply, in which he mentions that he is working on *The Black Book*, 'a chronicle of the English Death', is rather nicely signed, 'Derivatively yours'. This is not unduly modest, since in the next letter he seems to be rating Miller higher than Shakespeare. This document Miller describes as 'the finest letter I ever received in my life'.

In March 1937 Miller receives the manuscript of *The Black Book* and is immediately transported.

> You are *the* master of the English language. . . . This is way beyond Lawrence and the whole tribe. . . . It's like the Black Death, by Jesus. I'm stunned. My only adverse reaction is that it's too colossally colossal.

We do not feel, here or elsewhere, the slightest doubt as to the genuineness of Miller's admiration: it makes for more palatable reading than Durrell's own admiration for *The Black Book*: 'I like it, frankly . . . I think it's a book Huxley could have written if he were a mixture of Lawrence and Shakespeare', though the critic in him admits that 'the affectations and literary flapdoodle stick a bit'. When (despite or because of Eliot's personal admiration for it) Fabers want *The Black Book* expurgated, Durrell is thinking of capitulating, but *Vade retro, Satanas*! Miller warns him sternly in one of his best letters. *The Black Book* is published in Paris the following year. Miller continues to rhapsodize over *The Black Book*. Apparently it isn't too arty for his tastes; what he seems to admire most in it is such phrase-making as 'we can send out to the clitoris for an ice' (cf. *Tropic of Cancer*, 'I will bite into your clitoris and spit out two franc pieces').

References in Durrell's letters of 1944 look forward to *The Alexandria Quartet*. 'The Alexandrian way of death is very Proustian and slow . . . one has never had anything lovelier and emptier than an Alexandrian girl. Their very emptiness is a caress. Imagine making love to a vacuum. '(Yet he imagined it through four long volumes.) He meets a woman who provides him with a lot of material about 'the inside of Egypt' which is to come in very useful; rather ungallantly he describes her as '*Tropic of Capricorn* walking'. Alexandria, he informs Miller, is rich in 'sexual provender of quality'. 'It's funny the way you get woman after woman; and exactly what it adds up to I don't know. . . .' In this case it added up to that world-beater *The Alexandria Quartet*, which Durrell announces a little later: 'I have a wonderful idea for a novel on Alexandria, a nexus for all news of Greece, side by side with a sort of spiritual butcher's shop with girls on slabs'. The Alexandrian 'Book of the Dead' is to be more exotic than our English dead.

In 1946 Miller reports a meeting with Frieda Lawrence. 'We get on famously. She said to me once, "If only Lawrence had known you when alive. You would have been the very friend he was looking for."' He adds in parenthesis, 'I wonder'. Three years later Miller remarks of an essay on him which Durrell has written for *Horizon*, 'Merlin, you say somewhere. Mais, c'est vous! If any one can seduce, drug, exalt the English, it is you.' Prophetic, indeed, though not quite in the way intended. But Durrell is unable to return the compliment when *Sexus* comes out: the mysticism is fine but it is lost 'in this shower of lavatory filth which no longer seems tonic and bracing, but just excrementitious and sad'. It is Durrell who has changed, not Miller or Miller's work. Yet however strongly one agrees with Durrell's onslaught, one has to admit that Miller's reply is (and especially in view of the history of their relationship) magnificently dignified, and by far the most moving document in this collection. Even the hostile reader is glad to see Durrell recanting immediately, in a cable which crosses with Miller's letter. Unhappily the running commentary supplied by the editor, vulgar throughout, gets particularly excited at this juncture and rather mars the effect in advance: 'But Miller's magnanimity is equal to Durrell's candour. What might have been a crisis proves a climax. . . .'

As the commentary informs us, Miller is 'full of wonder and admiration and amazement' when *Justine* appears in early 1957. Durrell confirms that the novel 'has had a tremendous press in England—rather a worried plaintive note from the dovecots where our literary men drowse but enthusiastic withal'. The second volume reminds Miller of Valéry, 'those aesthetico-religious-metaphysical speculations especially. I'll say this, there is nothing like this *Justine* in all English literature—what I know of it, at any rate.' The two cannot agree over Kerouac, however. 'Good, very good, surpassingly good,' says Miller, but Durrell is clear-headed and firm about Kerouac's attitudinizing. The editor interrupts again, to tell us that 'the entire correspondence describes a perfect arc, beginning with Durrell's fan letters and ending with Miller's. Now it is Miller's turn to acclaim Durrell

as the Master . . .' and the correspondence comes to a halt with
a long, lively, chatty and amiable letter from Big Sur dated
31 October 1959.

The increasing dissimilarities between the two correspondents
emerge fairly clearly as the book unfolds. Durrell is changing,
sobering up, while Miller remains exactly the same, self-intoxi-
cated. In general, the one is strong where the other is weak.
Miller has had a hard time, he has the right to complain, much
more cause than has Durrell, who in fact complains more. Miller
is a man of principle: he will not compromise with publishers
or laws. Likeable if exasperating, he is a naïve and generous being.
Durrell shows more willingness to compromise—the need is less
on his side—and does not strike us as in the least naïve. Unlike
his friend, he is critical, he has doubts and he voices them: we
gather that he had doubts about publishing his own contributions
to this correspondence. There is more to Durrell, we feel, than
appears here. He soon begins to hold part of himself back:
Miller gives the whole of himself, ten times over.

Durrell is gifted for depicting people's physical mannerisms
and for the description of places. Miller is good at human ex-
ternalities but can describe little beyond shabby hotel bedrooms.
Durrell has a sense of humour (it must sometimes embarrass
him). Miller is innocent of such a trait, an innocence which he
shares with the hack pornographer; the latter, though, is content
with reducing the sexual act to meaninglessness, whereas Miller
believes that the meaninglessness he thus procures *means* something, means highly and means holily. Something to the same
effect might be said of the sexual complications of *The Alexandria
Quartet*, but where Miller is the conscious anti-artist, the messiah,
Durrell is the conscious artist, the aesthete: Chanel ('Scent like a
river-pilot led me there') in place of disinfectant, sophistications
in place of rant.

My résumé may have been slightly tendentious. There are,
it should be said, passages in this book which do not induce

incredulity, alarm or despondency: passages sufficient to make a small book, just as *The Alexandria Quartet*, less its aesthetico-religious-metaphysical confectionery, would make one novel, and as Miller's *œuvre*, less the excrement and much of the mysticism, would make one book. The editor thinks otherwise. His first words are, 'The complete Durrell-Miller correspondence in half a dozen scholarly annotated volumes will not be ready for publication until the next century . . .'. What is going to kill reading in our time is writing.

Contrary Wise: the Writings of Mary McCarthy

REVIEWING for *Encounter* Mary McCarthy's book of essays, *On the Contrary*, Angus Wilson finds the author slightly guilty of arrogance and highmindedness. Her remarks on contemporary artistic celebrities and the taste which makes them celebrities remind him of Dr Leavis. With the exception that 'Dr Leavis has been wise enough to confine himself to criticism', whereas Miss McCarthy 'has laid herself too open to counter-attack. She has written novels and they are not very good.' It seems a rather mean line to take, that a person's critical views can be dismissed, in any effective way, by a sort of 'Ya! What did *you* do in the War, Miss?' We don't demolish Arnold's criticism by adducing his poetry, which is not *very* good. Miss McCarthy's novels are not *very* good, by her own standards as an admirer of Dickens, Eliot, Tolstoy and Dostoevsky. But Mr Wilson means that they are *poor*. They seem to me, by current standards, distinctly superior—and even, by standards less circumscribed, to possess a degree of distinction.

I wish to propose that Miss McCarthy's healthy sense of humour saves her from arrogance and that she is not *disastrously* high-minded. She would like people to be better than they often are, but she doesn't offer to pull out their finger-nails because they aren't. Perhaps the difficulty here is that, like Angus Wilson, she is a wit: but her wit is blunted by charity (or, others might feel, made meaningful by it). '*Difficile est satiram non scribere*' in our times. So, difficult to write anything other than satire, or of course that most rewarding form of it, pornography. Poison in jest, we murmur excitedly, as (lightly disguised in Dr Leavis's hood and gown, it seems) Miss McCarthy creeps up on some unfortunate American intellectual, a glittering instrument in her upraised hand. But no, she doesn't stab him, she probes: she doesn't want to kill him, she only wants to know how he lives. There *is* a difference. Admittedly, Miss McCarthy looks so much like a satirist that it must be a disappointment to find that she is merely a moralist. No self-respecting wit likes to see the tools of his trade misused: a stiletto employed as a scalpel, for instance.

In a particularly lively essay Miss McCarthy hunts down the symbol-hunters. 'Like everything in America, this search for meanings has become a socially competitive enterprise; the best reader is the one who detects the most symbols in a given stretch of prose.' It is indeed a chastening thought, that the mental and sense activities of a barely literate peasant engaged in reading a piece of prose or verse are likely to be complex perhaps beyond the point of describability, whereas the same activities in a university student reading the same passage under the supervision of a teacher would appear to be skin-thin and simple to the point of idiocy. A *really means* Z, 'iron gates of life' *really means* hymen, or *vice versa*, etc., etc. Miss McCarthy has suggested the reason: the peasant is not participating in a competition.

Writers too can win valuable prizes in this competition:

> Literary symbolism, as taught in the schools and practised by certain fashionable writers . . . is centrifugal and flees from the object, the event, into the incorporeal distance, where concepts are taken for substance and floating ideas and archetypes assume a hieratic authority.

Objects and events are boring, shabby, mean. This sort of writer procures through the manipulation of 'symbols' an unfocusing of the object or event, an invitation to the self-indulgent or lazy imagination to indulge itself further. (Somehow most symbols turn out to be sexual ones: symbolic organs can play on for ever, I suppose it is, whereas real ones run short of breath.) The proficiency and the excitement are all in the chase: the fox when caught is a bedraggled little wretch, shabbier and meaner than any real object or event could be. Miss McCarthy's recommendations to the student of writing are characteristic in their intelligence, clarity and firmness. Start with a pattern of symbols, if you will, but if the pattern hasn't been shattered by the end, then the writing isn't worth much.

The writer must be, first of all, a listener and observer, who can pay attention to reality, like an obedient pupil, and who is willing, always, to be surprised by the messages reality is sending through to him. And if he gets the messages correctly he will not have to go back and put in the symbols; he will find that the symbols are there, staring at him significantly from the commonplace.

Miss McCarthy has just cited Hegel, that the tree of life is greener than the tree of thought. The saying is also quoted by Taub, the somewhat brutish 'leader of the realist party' in her short novel, *The Oasis*. 'Realism': Miss McCarthy remarks in an essay, 'If someone tells you he is going to make "a realistic decision", you immediately understand that he has resolved to do something bad.' One notices, by the way, many links between this author's various works, fictional and otherwise. But my point concerns the conscientiousness with which she goes about her task of exploring conscience and scrutinizing motives. 'Bad' characters like Taub are given good things to say, and even to do. 'The tree of life . . .' is an especially good thing to say, I suspect, in that Miss McCarthy may think fit to warn herself that through their constant self-analysis her characters come near to reducing her novels to groves of thought—groves of academe, indeed, since they are all artists, intellectuals or holders of political opinions.

To say that Miss McCarthy is conscientious in her examination of conscience is not, obviously, to imply that she is zealously seeking out that little bit of Heaven which lingers on in the worst of us. If her 'bad' characters are given their due, then her 'good' ones are continually brought under suspicion. Her microscope reveals sinister similarities where notable differences might be expected. Mulcahy of *The Groves of Academe* may be, as Miss McCarthy describes him in an essay, 'unsavoury'. But he needs to keep his job at Jocelyn College in order to keep his family (snotty-nosed though *they* are), whereas Domna, his sweet young colleague, a Turgenev heroine, is fighting to preserve her moral virginity, that quaint honour, rather than anything else.

Miss McCarthy does tend to nag. Motives are unearthed under motives unearthed under other motives. What a loss to the F.B.I.! It is a point of honour with her to attract our attention whenever anyone resorts to the scales of conscience in order to gauge just how much moral relaxation they may permit themselves in view of an earlier moral severity over and above the call of duty. Scrupulousness becomes obsessive. And in reading through the McCarthy canon one soon finds oneself predicting with fair accuracy the next start of some or other thoroughbred conscience. She wants justice to be done, and to be seen to be done: and it is a little fatiguing to watch justice being done at such length. Perhaps Mr Wilson is right in finding her prissy at times. This might account for the strident accents which she occasionally displays in speaking of sexual activity. The quasi-rape in *A Charmed Life*, for example: 'He heard Martha laugh faintly as she pushed his head away from her tit . . .'—not pornographic, but forced.

But let us too strive to be honest with ourselves. It could be that what we resent in her characters is their mental calibre. When we would be toying with an ashtray, they are leafing through Apollinaire: they play-read *Bérénice* in French for an evening's relaxation; the more backward among them merely quote Kierkegaard. We come to feel we are reading above our means.

In fact Miss McCarthy pokes fun at the very tendencies we are tempted to ascribe to her as the vices of her virtues. Taub, the snake in Utopia, calls for an emergency meeting of the colony's council to discuss the behaviour of an unnamed person. '"Bad conscience," he explained stonily, regarding his confederates with a look almost of warning. "That's how we get these moralists. Make each one think it's *him*."' More devastating is the story of Keogh in *The Groves of Academe*, the visiting 'poet of the masses', who inadvertently gives the impression that Mulcahy had formerly been a Party comrade. Summoned to the office of the college President, he is happy to state the truth: Mulcahy never joined the Party. But things are not that simple at Jocelyn, or with Miss McCarthy. As a liberal, the President is obliged to renew the contract of a supposed Communist, but he is quite free to dispense with the services of an unco-operative temporary instructor. Realizing that the pro-Mulcahy movement is fuelled by the belief that Mulcahy is a modern martyr, and that unwittingly he has played the stool-pigeon after all, Keogh tells Mulcahy what he has just told the anti-Mulcahy party. Then he asks himself whether he oughtn't to go back to the first party and tell them of how he has told Mulcahy of how he told them that Mulcahy was never a Communist:

> But as the ridiculous question, like a repeating decimal, propounded itself to him, he struck his open left hand a blow with his right fist. *No*, he inwardly shouted to himself; *Keogh, keep out of this, or they will get you.* . . . Possibly they were all very nice, high-minded, scrupulous people with only an occupational tendency towards back-biting and a nervous habit of self-correction, always emending, pencilling, erasing; but he didn't care to catch the bug, which seemed to be an endemic in these ivied haunts.

Essentially, what saves Miss McCarthy from being a sort of campus Compton-Burnett, however, and her fiction from degenerating into a game of moral Snakes and Ladders, is simply her novelist's gift for evoking physical presence, her respect for objects and events. Together with the rights and wrongs of 'the Mulcahy case' we note the man's granulated eyelashes, the scraps of toilet paper stuck on his shaving cuts and the ash-plant he carries in imitation of Stephen Dedalus. Just as we heed not only the words of Bentkoop, the follower of Niebuhr and Barth, but also the way 'his deep young voice creaked, like a pair of high shoes ascending a dark stairway with precaution'.

When introducing *The Oasis* as the *Horizon* prize winner in February 1949, the Editor alluded a mite nervously to 'what seems a certain coldness and inhumanity in the writer'. Her wit and intellectuality have long been established, as also her 'masculine mind' (but see the feminine face on the wrapper of *Sights and Spectacles*, 1959), and more recently she has been described as 'the steeliest lady in American letters' and a 'quill-wielding porcupine'. There is more to her than that. In one of her essays she attacks passionately those sexual reformers who fancy they are redeeming human relations when they replace poetical words like 'passion' and 'healing' by steely intellectual terms like 'functioning' and 'adjustment'.[1] And she tells us that what turned her against Communism was—no tortured self-inquisition, no labours of intellect or conscience—but simply the odd way her Com-

[1] The sad thing, it seems to me, about her latest novel, *The Group*, is that whatever the author's intentions, the ethos of 'functioning' and 'adjustment' has taken over. An epic of contraception, baby-feeding, toilet-training, and divorce and burial techniques, it smells overpoweringly of the surgery and the pharmacy. An unkind critic might point up the novel's weakness—issuing as tediousness—by adducing Miss McCarthy's extemporizations on 'Shakespeare's Women' in *Vogue* for July 1964. Of Rosalind, Beatrice, Rosaline, Miranda, Celia, she says, 'I've always felt they were rather like Vassar girls, or like the ideal Vassar girl of my time, or at least what the faculty *wanted* us to be'. The Vassar girls of *The Group* are certainly literary rather than living characters—demonstrators of the latest domestic appliances—and the novel itself shapes as more an endorsement than (however understandingly) a questioning. On Cleopatra's death Miss McCarthy comments, 'the asp at her breast is like a male member'. Oh dear, whose sex life is *she* seeking to reform? Couldn't she have found a poetical word or two—even if not 'passion' or 'healing'—to use here?

munist acquaintances behaved when it was suggested that some person called Trotsky might perhaps be given a hearing.[1] Miss McCarthy, too, is truly 'a listener and observer, who can pay attention to reality, like an obedient pupil', and more often than not she gets correctly the messages which are meant for her.

---

[1] A character in *The Group* remarks, '. . . that was the big thing they taught you at Vassar: keep your mind open and always ask for the evidence, even from your own side.'

The Inadequate American:
John Updike's Fiction

O F late a combination of circumstances—insomnia, the duties of a reviewer, tropical lethargy—have led me to a rather massive reading of current fiction, and thence to the conclusion that the real threat to the human species is not the Bomb but current fiction. 'Not with a bang but a whimper': Eliot's words acquire an extra significance. Perhaps our Western world will end that way, with the gloating whimper of the writer, his hand on the reader's neck, and the suffocated whimper of the reader, his head pressed down into a pile of other people's laundry. 'We are intimate with people we have never seen and, unhappily, they are intimate with us,' wrote Wallace Stevens. 'Democritus plucked his eye out because he could not look at a woman without thinking of her as a woman. If he had read a few of our novels, he would have torn himself to pieces.' We are considerably more sophisticated than Democritus. Why tear ourselves to pieces when we can put our feet up and crumble in comfort?

If one were compiling a dirty-laundry list, the name of John Updike would come nowhere near the top. One might not include it at all, though (having read *Rabbit, Run* twice with a year between readings) I personally wouldn't feel inclined to leave it off. The intimacies Mr Updike presses upon his readers are not exclusively sexual, but they still have a suffocating effect which reminds me of how an old Egyptian queen killed herself— by diving into a specially constructed tower filled with fine ash. I am aware that great literature is honest and painful and unpleasant and terrifying, and that for major novels the next best thing to no ending is an unhappy one. The new platitudes—

134

new?—are as easy to mouth as the old ones, and they seem to have an extra sticking-power about them. Thus *The Waste Land*, whether properly understood or not, left more of a mark on the post-war Japanese consciousness than the rest of the Occupation put together. Hopeful theologians might take this phenomenon as an indication that, though we lay claim to disbelief, the modern world is acutely conscious of its original sinfulness. What monuments of sentimentality, of simple-minded humanism, are those old barn-stormers *Macbeth* and *King Lear*!

John Updike is a remarkably skilled writer, but to me he seems hardly an author at all. He is less a maker than a dismantler, though the magic of his style has won the admiration of a number of critics (including Mary McCarthy) with whom I tremble to disagree. I feel like that oafish Mario letting off his home-made pistol at the suave Magician in Thomas Mann's story. And perhaps it is pedantic to ask that so entrancing an anatomist should have something more to show at the end of it than a stripped skeleton and a bucket of waste flesh and blood. Yet I note that several of Mr Updike's admirers have described him as a 'poetic' writer, and expect when used by practising poets the epithet, however approvingly intended, commonly carries an admission that something equivocal is going on which would take more of the critic's time to investigate than he feels able to afford.

Of the Farm is Mr Updike's fourth novel. The previous one, *The Centaur*, was a fairly obvious case of mythology dragged in by the ears to bolster up a thinnish story-line. The obviousness is in a way endearing: people who don't try to disguise the fact that they are cheating can scarcely be called cheats. But they might still qualify for the adjective 'bare-faced'. And bare-faced is what Mr Updike's opening is:

> Caldwell turned and as he turned his ankle received an arrow. The class burst into laughter. The pain scaled the slender core of his shin, whirled in the complexities of his knee, and, swollen broader, more thunderous, mounted into his bowels.

Caldwell, a teacher of general science at Olinger High School, clatters away on his 'three remaining hooves'—he is also Chiron—to Hummel's Garage, where Hummel—who is also Hephaestus—will cut through the arrowhead with an acetylene torch. The story and the myth exist uneasily side by side, merging chiefly in minor points and diverging in major respects, so that human life is no more mythologized than the myth is demythologized. Hummel's garage hands are Cyclops simply because they are smiths and wear goggles and one of them is actually one-eyed. A luncheonette is run by a Mr Minor Kretz (Minos) and a post office is managed by a Mrs Passify (Pasiphae): the two establishments share a building: that's all.

Caldwell's pupils give him a bad time, but they love him really. Caldwell loves them, and teaching, really, but is oppressed by a feeling of inadequacy. For one thing, he can't keep discipline, as is pointed out by Zimmerman, principal of the school and the mildly lecherous Zeus of the Olympian shadow cabinet. Caldwell is a man with elephantiasis of the conscience, a fearful ditherer, a dyed-in-the-wool humanist, a good, exasperating man—and he is in no way helped by having a centaur wished on him.

According to the myth as quoted by Mr Updike at the outset, the immortal Chiron, suffering from an incurable hurt, offered himself as a sacrifice in place of Prometheus. Zeus acceded to his prayer and allowed him to die. In Mr Updike's book Prometheus is Caldwell's fifteen-year-old son, Peter, who suffers not from an eagle pecking at his liver but from psoriasis, a lesser embarrassment but at least etymologically Greek. The novel seems to end—for it is left extremely vague—with Caldwell committing suicide. Mr Updike's ending is in Greek, which a little research traces to Apollodorus, who is telling us that Prometheus accepted Chiron's immortality so that the centaur could find relief in death. But on the realistic plane there is no question of Peter doing his father a favour or gaining from his father's suicide: it will hardly bring relief to his skin ailment. But then, no real attempt is made to link Peter with Prometheus, apart from the initial letter. And apart from giving him a girl-friend called Penny (why not Dora?), who has a little box (guess where?) in which perhaps hope resides—or Peter's hopes reside. That's the trouble with this sort of hermaphrodite production: if you insist on faithfulness to the myth you are being pedantic, if you insist on a realistic reading you are being facetious or even indecent.

The pity of it is, all this mythological paraphernalia was unnecessary, and *The Centaur* would otherwise be Mr Updike's best novel. Perhaps it still is, unless that place is held by his first novel, *The Poorhouse Fair*, a perfect little cameo of old age, perhaps too perfectly posed (in retrospect one wonders whether it isn't a group-photograph of the defeated Titans languishing in Tartarus) and of sharply limited interest. Caldwell is a good character (in both senses of the phrase), richer than any of the thumb-nail portraits of *The Poorhouse Fair*, while the school scenes of *The Centaur* are lively, and some at least of the human problems are real enough. Far from gaining a dimension from the Olympian parallels, this story of men and women is actually trivialized thereby. Perhaps Mr Updike, who is a very consciously sophisticated writer, suspected that he was on the brink of sentimentality—humanist, all too humanist!—and mustered up these ancient divinities lest he should have nothing better to offer us than a modern American who was positively and clearly likeable.

The publishers tell us that *The Centaur* was 'originally conceived as a contrasting companion' to the preceding novel, *Rabbit, Run,* a book whose eponymous anti-hero (*pace* Miss McCarthy) was notably unlikeable. Rabbit Angstrom is on the run throughout, he runs away from his wife, his mistress, his parents, his jobs. Caldwell runs away from his pain—not the pain of that old arrow (X-rays show he doesn't have cancer), but the pain of the inadequacy he feels in the face of his beloved young hooligans, and perhaps life in general.

If an author has set out to create a feeble character there is little point in the reader complaining that the character is feeble. But we can legitimately complain that Rabbit soon grows boring. He runs away from his wife not once but twice, he runs away from his mistress (an incongruously grand name for the poor girl) not once but twice. Where Caldwell's feeling of inadequacy is inexplicable—no teacher expects to work miracles— Rabbit's inadequacy is all too explicable. 'That was the thing about him', muses his mistress, 'he just lived in his skin and didn't give a thought to the consequences of anything'. With Wallace Stevens's remark about unwelcome intimacies in mind, we feel that the trouble here is, we know more about Rabbit than there really is to know. If, as it seems, these two novels are companion studies in the Inadequate American, then Mr Updike's popularity speaks volumes for the national masochism. But *Rabbit, Run* has something which *The Centaur*, happily, hasn't—a whole smothering of dirty laundry, those 'fashionably audacious erotic passages' which, as Norman Podhoretz has said, merely 'expose the adolescent level of Updike's sexual attitudes'. Rabbit has been really good at something, he was a high-school basketball champ, and this is what makes him, in his own eyes and perhaps in Mr Updike's too, a bit of a tragic figure. 'After you're first-rate at something, no matter what, it kind of takes the kick out of being second-rate,' he says, in excusing himself for walking out on his 'second-rate' relationship with his wife. But even so he is still pretty good at something, he's quite a champ in bed. So maybe this 'inadequacy' isn't all that hard to accept.

If Joey, who narrates Mr Updike's new novel, *Of the Farm*, is also inadequate, then his inadequacy is comparatively mild and apparently commonplace. He and his new (and second) wife and her eleven-year-old son visit Joey's mother down on her farm. The mother has a thing about this farm, though 'What's the point of a farm nobody farms?' asks young Richard, in what seems a vaguely symbolic utterance. Mother and wife quarrel, conventionally, bitterly yet not irretrievably, over Joey and over

Richard. Joey finds himself defending his wife against his mother and his mother against his wife—fortunately Richard, 'the most adult member of the party, can look after himself—and if their mutual hostility pains him, then their moments of amity upset him equally, for he feels 'excluded'. 'My wife', 'my mother', 'the farm' (since he is jealous of his mother's preoccupation with her acres)—it is all very neat and contrived, as if some sophisticate is amusedly performing for a psychiatrist of low intelligence. Joey tells us that it was his mother who made him dislike his first wife. 'I am always a little behind my mother, always arriving at the point from which she has departed.' His new wife tells him, 'You never should have left your mother's womb,' to which he wittily (and assentingly) replies, 'It was wonderful in there. Perfect room temperature.' There is a little byplay with Tampax (not included in 'the rather embarrassing variety of hygienic items' unpacked by his wife), which the kindly critic might defend as 'symbolic' in that when Joey brought his first wife to the farm his mother could provide this needful commodity but now she doesn't stock it any more. Though what it could usefully be symbolic *of* is hard to see. Mr Updike doesn't like endings, but his non-ending in this case is almost happy: the mother has a queer turn, hostilities are suspended, and the rest of them return to the peace and quiet of New York.

Symbolism in *Of the Farm* is no more than a gentle velleity. You can take it or leave it—and since you cannot get your fingers round it, it seems better to leave it. Here Mr Updike makes no real effort to camouflage the thinness of his material, whether with generous sexual detail or by means of mythological shadow plays. *Of the Farm* is more or less honestly naked, thin and point-blank. Whereas the technique of *The Centaur* seems a rather naïve form of sophistication, the technique of this new novel is a sophisticated exercise in naïveté. The writing is as usual: never a cliché, never a crudity (except when planned), nothing borrowed, everything new; it is nearly always alive, and yet its life seems autonomous, having nothing to do with any larger life, with the life (as one would have said) of the novel. The splendid incidentals cannot be properly so called because there is nothing much for them to be incidental to. What's the point, one wants to ask, of a novel that has no point?

Mr Updike's writing shows at least one characteristic of major authors like Joyce and Thomas Mann: a mass of interrelations run between his various works. For instance, the Pennsylvanian location, and the Episcopalian/Lutheran and town/country complexes. Caldwell is briefly prefigured in the story 'Home' ('though for thirty years a public-school teacher, he still believed in education'), Joey's father was a teacher, like old Hook of *The Poorhouse Fair* (whose 'flaw had been over-conscientiousness'); and Mr Prosser in 'Tomorrow and Tomorrow and So Forth' is another sorely tried but unembittered member of the profession, while Caldwell's rather fulsome amiability appears in the sick father of 'A Traded Car'. Minor Kretz's luncheonette pops up momentarily in 'Sunday Teasing' and Peter's skin disease in *The Poorhouse Fair* and in 'The Happiest I've Been', while Rabbit's mother, like Joey's, is 'somehow too powerful, at least with me'. But these interrelations, rather than enriching the whole, only make one feel that Mr Updike's work is cannibalistic, that it feeds on itself. Despite their air of being something special, many of the short stories are like Fred Platt's puns in 'Who Made Yellow Roses Yellow?'—'impeccable but fruitless'. And *Of the Farm* is an impeccably dressed short story, with nowhere much to go, which takes a little too long getting there.

Mr Updike, it seems to me, has the talents of a good nature poet, not of the Wordsworthian class, but one of those who 'rest in Nature, not the God of Nature'. His cornfields and his cars (he is the laureate of the second-hand automobile) have much more presence than his people. Though long ago he found a way of writing, as yet he doesn't seem to have found something to write about. But he still has time.

Down Cemetery Road: the Poetry of Philip Larkin

'LONG and eagerly awaited,' to quote the sober and accurate blurb, *The Whitsun Weddings* (as, with his characteristic sense of where to put the stress, he has entitled this new collection), 'will not disappoint Mr Larkin's innumerable admirers.' For not only does Mr Larkin write like an angel, as many a poor devil does once in a long while, he *always* writes like an angel. Well, apart perhaps from four or five lines which read pettishly or clottishly (an angel doing his damnedest to swear—cock! balls! get stewed!) or just don't read very well. Practically nothing here disappoints, and practically everything here reminds us how distinct Mr Larkin's poetry is—in the way Edward Thomas's is—from all the verse which might be thought to be like it. How distinct and superior.

No, a rational admirer of Edward Thomas would hardly be overcome with a sudden disappointment that Thomas didn't write like Yeats or Brecht. Disappointment is certainly not the word. Simply, this angel is so often a sad angel, wryly reflecting on how vainly he would have beaten his luminous wings in this void world, had he determined to beat them. And perhaps it is not ridiculously out of order to feel a degree of impatience at the sight of so marvellous a skill in conveying the feel of living joined with such a valetudinarian attitude towards life.

That was a mouthful—and Mr Larkin is averse to mouthfuls:

> Words as plain as hen-birds' wings
> Do not lie,
> Do not over-broider things—
> Are too shy.

Not, however, that he could be called a debunker. If now and then he patronizes his characters (such as poor Arnold, who 'married a woman to stop her getting away/Now she's there all day'), he never sneers at them. If anyone takes a beating in this book, it's the author himself. And if Mr Larkin's cheek doesn't sport a ready tear, none the less compassion for others is never too far away; and there are even rare intimations of a sort of muted glory. He writes of failure, or insufficiency rather, or rather of velleities and second thoughts, of dubious buses not too bitterly missed, of doubts about doubts, and there is a gentleness, even a dry sweetness, to his tone of voice.

'Love Songs in Age', if you paraphrase it, reduces to an observation, more an observation than a complaint, that love doesn't inevitably, or perhaps just doesn't, 'solve, and satisfy, and set unchangeably in order'. And yet what has gone before, what leads up to this fairly trite or more truly meaningless deduction (what is this thing called order, anyway?), holds a tenderness so charmingly conveyed as more to rebut than to support it. At least love seems to have done *something*. A pity, then, that the deduction should be there, merely words on the page. There is occasionally an element of the arbitrary about Mr Larkin: as if he doesn't altogether trust poetry, not even his own.

'Toads Revisited' (see *The Less Deceived*) is more determinedly and successfully glum. Work is to be preferred to leisure on the grounds that it kills time (the days where, as another poem says, we live) more effectively. It is a proposition which, without asking for a footnoted thesis on the subject, one might consider a bit bleak and blank, seeing that leisure doesn't get much definition ('The lake, the sunshine,/The grass to lie on') and work —an in-tray and a loaf-haired secretary—gets even less. But then, that loaf-haired secretary sounds rather agreeable, a pleasing instance of synecdoche, and it is difficult to feel angry with a poem which ends,

DOWN CEMETERY ROAD

Give me your arm, old toad;
Help me down Cemetery Road.

It is less difficult to do so in the case of 'Self's the Man', a
thinnish gloss on the niggardly proposition that marriage has so
many pains that perhaps celibacy has fewer—perhaps. 'Talking in
bed ought to be easiest', but gets less and less easy as the years
pass. True, that old toad takes it out of you, but think of the poor
bachelor—he talks to himself! No doubt the problem is a pretty
central one. Goethe himself faced it—

I will confess to you, friends;
I find it most disagreeable to lie alone at nights.
But it's quite abhorrent to go in fear of serpents
On the paths of love, of poison under the roses of pleasure . . .

—but then he found Faustina and all was well. For Mr Larkin,
there are serpents everywhere; he disposes sadly but nimbly of
the alternatives and never makes a choice. Poor married Arnold
doesn't get a chance to read the evening paper; poor single Mr
Bleaney shivers on his single bed in his single room.

In another poem an apple core missing the wastepaper basket
is briefly and elegantly interpreted as an omen of doom, a sign
of original failure. But who really wants to be one of those chaps
who hit the bull'e eye every time, wastepaper basket or spittoon
or what-have-you? Mr Larkin will have nothing to do with the
age-old homespun wisdom which tells us, 'If at first you don't
succeed . . .'. Elsewhere and fairly clearly he seems to be reminding us that East West, Home's Best—'These are my customs
and establishments'—while on another page, 'Home is so sad,'

Look at the pictures and the cutlery.
The music in the piano stool. That vase.

No one but Mr Larkin could have written the line, 'Those are
my customs and establishments'. The quality of reverence in his
work has been noticed before: 'Churchgoing' remains the most

143

obvious example of this. An unsolemnly reverential attitude and a sense of mystery lightly worn, these (if nothing else has) have diverted him securely from the sentimental toughness, the parochial modishness and the shrill smart-aleckry to which in our day 'a gift for words' seems naturally to tend. It is part of his sadness—or maybe I am being obtusely solemn—that for him customs are less a way of life than a way of dying:

> separate ways
> Of building, benediction,
> Measuring love and money
> Ways of slow dying.
> The day spent hunting pig
> Or holding a garden-party,
>
> Hours giving evidence
> Or birth, advance
> On death equally slowly.
> And saying so to some
> Means nothing; others it leaves
> Nothing to be said.

But it is 'Dockery and Son', a companion-piece and sequel to the earlier classic 'I Remember, I Remember', which promulgates Mr Larkin's homespun melancholia at its most explicit and least appealing. The question is, to be or not to be a father? To have or not to have a son? And again the alternatives seem equally unpreferable:

> Life is first boredom, then fear.
> Whether or not we use it, it goes,
> And leaves what something hidden from us chose,
> And age, and then the only end of age.

With all due respect to *timor mortis*, you don't have to be Superman to find this a wee bit unadventurous.

In other poems—for his habit of using only as many words as he needs doesn't make him a simple character—Mr Larkin has

other things to say about love and life. The title-piece is a nice
Short View of England from British Railways, but despite the
splendid actuality ('the reek of buttoned carriage-cloth'), I'm
not sure about its somewhat grand climax. The conclusion seems
willed—wishful thinking though indeed a good wish: rather than
being changed by their change, the brides are lost under

> the perms,
> The nylon gloves and jewellery-substitutes,
> The lemons, mauves, and olive-ochres. . . .

But in this field 'An Arundel Tomb' is wholly and finely successful, committing itself to its findings, and finding

> Our almost-instinct almost true:
> What will survive of us is love.

This poem and 'Ambulances' ('a wild white face that overtops/
Red stretcher-blankets' as a *memento mori*, a poor soul lying
alone on a bed 'inside a room/The traffic parts to let go by') and
'Mr Bleaney' (the classic of the poetry of the bed-sitter, not a
gloomy piece but a shiveringly grim one) seem to me the prizes
of this collection.

So glum's not always the word. And even when it is, even
when one is unable not to dissent from this sick-bed view of
the human condition, one has to admit that what Mr Larkin does
he does so well as to come near to making cowards of us all.
His wit is insidious, and elegant ('Death-suited, visitant, I nod'),
and by no means provincial. Among his admirers is at least one
Chinese-educated Chinese poetess—an admiration which I adduce
in that a classical Chinese education is less than celebrated for
fostering a catholicity of interest or a taste for the frail or frivolous
or far-flung.

In verbal fastidiousness and a severe beauty of rhythm, Larkin
is reminiscent of Edward Thomas, whose melancholy seems to
me, however, a mite less complacent, a considerable mite richer.

At times he has the appearance of a mid-century Emily Dickinson;
at others—

> To compare his life and mine
> Makes me feel a swine:
> Oh, no one can deny
> That Arnold is less selfish than I.
>
> But wait, not so fast:
> Is there such a contrast?
> He was out for his own ends
> Not just pleasing his friends

—of Stevie Smith turned peevish. But more often—a characteristic and endearing persona—the reader thinks of the clever sad-
faced clown, raising ambiguous smiles:

> On shallow straw, in shadeless glass,
> Huddled by empty bowls, they sleep:
> No dark, no dam, no earth, no grass—
> *Mam, get us one of them to keep.*
>
> Living toys are something novel,
> But it soon wears off somehow.
> Fetch the shoebox, fetch the shovel—
> *Mam, we're playing funerals now.*

Does this book constitute an advance on *The Less Deceived*?
Perhaps not markedly—Mr Larkin seems to have arrived all at
once at where he was going—though this judgment is of course
cheerfully open to invalidation. At any rate *The Whitsun Weddings*
certainly doesn't constitute a retreat; and not to retreat is something of a rarity among our poets. The collection not only
deserves to be greatly successful, it will be—and, it seems likely,
successful beyond and above and below the small dutiful mob
who have already made Mr Larkin their poetry choice.

III

The Marquis and the Madame

Justine: *Pamela* rewritten as pornography. *Juliette*: a female *Tom Jones* reconstructed in the same spirit. *Miss Henriette Stralson*: *Clarissa* minus Clarissa. *Augustine de Villeblanche*: refined smut yielding to gross sentimentalism, very much of and for its period. *Les 120 Journées de Sodome*: just what it says. But if there seems little reason for literary people to concern themselves with Sade, he has found a new lease of life among philosophers and anthropologists. Bored and uneasy with our little lives we resort to the greater amplitude of symbols. Bardot, Byron, Hitler, Hemingway, Monroe, Sade: we do not require our heroes to be subtle, just to be big. Then we can depend on someone to make them subtle.

In her essay, 'Must we burn Sade?', Mme de Beauvoir devotes some seventy pages of subtle explication to the plain Marquis. Scandalized by the neglect into which he has fallen, yet repudiating the obvious topsy-turvy whereby he has been deified, she asks that he be regarded as a man and a writer. Even so it is not exactly as author nor as sexual pervert that he interests her, but by his efforts to justify his perversions, to 'erect his tastes into principles'. We are all great moralizers, especially where our 'tastes' are concerned. 'He dreamed of an ideal society from which his special tastes would not exclude him.' Don't we all? And Sade's dream is clearly defined in *Les 120 Journées de Sodome*, with its small society of libertines, protected from the mean prejudices of the outside world, wealthy enough to procure any diversion they can think up and unlimited supplies of every variety of human flesh. Or in Minski's castle, in *Juliette*, in which the furniture consists of naked girls artistically arranged and the owner lives *'selon l'état de mes couilles,'* which are kept in prime condition by large helpings of gammon of boy accompanied by sixty bottles of Burgundy at a sitting.

Minski's castle, it would seem forgiveable to suppose, is the dream world of the impotent and Minski himself bears the hero's expected characteristics: '. . . *de dix-huit pouces de long, sur seize de circonférence, surmonté d'un champignon vermeil et large comme le cul d'un chapeau.*' The obvious thing about Sade's fiction—it was outside Mme de Beauvoir's purpose to remark the obvious—is that it is *par excellence* obscenity of the most basic sort, as it were a pattern for pornographers. It runs, quite insultingly, to the form which it lays down for itself. Incidentally, Minski's ejaculatory ability reappears, though with a nice touch of humour, in a pot-boiler by his admirer Apollinaire.

In *The Marquis de Sade,* a selection recently published in English by John Calder, the following passage is left in French. I will risk translating it:

> One of my friends is living with the daughter he has had by his own mother; only a week ago he deflowered a boy of thirteen years, fruit of his commerce with that daughter; in a few years this same boy will marry his mother

—and, continues the narrator, the friend is still young and intends 'to enjoy still more fruits that shall be born of this wedding'. These genealogical acrobatics correspond to (and are followed by) the physical acrobatics beloved of the hack pornographer. But *honi soit* . . . and Mme de Beauvoir thinks better than I do. 'Juliette was saved and Justine lost from the beginning of time.' A less cosmogonical interpretation of the two might have it that Juliette is the bad girl who will do anything and Justine is the good girl to whom everything is done, the two stock figures of the pornographic scene.

As for Sade's philosophical disquisitions, they might serve to justify his tastes as revealed in the fiction, except that the philosophy is ludicrous—a *Modest Proposal* unironically intended—and the tastes are (I should have thought) self-evidently unamenable to justification. The philosophy is basically this: if you enjoy wickedness, it shows that Nature intended you to be wicked, and it would be wicked not to be. There seems nothing very original here. 'Thou, Nature, art my goddess': Edmund is a somewhat richer character than any of Sade's creations. The rest follows predictably from this first principle. 'There is nothing more refined than the carnal liaison of families': or, in language less gallant, incest is more Natural than non-incestuous connection. Similarly, for the pornographer any hint of tenderness is to be shunned like the plague: genuine perversion is an onanistic activity to which a second party is necessary as a tool, whereas tenderness implies the recognition of the other party as a person in his or her own right. The case against love is put neatly by Belmor in *Juliette*: it is useless in that it doesn't increase sexual enjoyment and positively pernicious in that it 'causes us to neglect our own interests for those of the thing loved' and adds this thing's pains and troubles to the sum of our own.

Notwithstanding, Mme de Beauvoir tells us that 'eroticism appears in Sade as a mode of communication, the only valid one' between persons. Since she then admits that 'every time we side with a child whose throat has been slit by a sex-maniac, we take a stand against him', it is possible that she is using the word 'communication' in some highly special sense, paradoxical to the rest of us, reserved to philosophically-trained intellectuals. For the rest of us, Sade's message on this point might seem to come to, F – – – you, Jack (or Jill), I'm all right.

Some of the ideas advanced in *Français, encore un effort* are respectable enough—his republicanism, anti-clericalism and opposition to the death penalty—but they are neither novel nor respectably argued. Elsewhere his recommendations are simple: murder, rape, torture, sodomy, cannibalism, arson, coprophagy, necrophilism, bestiality ('*le dindon est délicieux*'), etc. For Mme de Beauvoir, Sade's value, his contemporary importance, lies in the fact that 'he chose cruelty rather than indifference'. His sincerity—indifference, I suppose, cannot be sincere—encourages her to hail him as 'a great moralist'. The aptest comment on this description is M. de Bressac's casual remark to his servant, which I quote from memory: 'Now, Joseph, you b– – – – Justine, and then we shall feed her to the dogs.' Mme de Beauvoir shares one of her protégé's characteristics: humourlessness.

The Calder selection contains nothing from *Justine* but, considering the obvious difficulties, it conveys (with the help of short passages left in their native French) a just hint of its author's preposterousness. 'Must we burn Sade?' asks Mme de Beauvoir. Now that you mention it, why not? The world is littered with literature. And Sade teaches us little about human nature which we couldn't gather from a few minutes of honest introspection. But maybe we can learn something more useful from Mme de Beauvoir's solemn excogitations, something about our scornful reluctance to face the realities of our selves and of the selves of others, and our preferred contemplation of modish dummies, those highbrow status symbols, ourselves as heroic monsters or grand victims, our inflation or reduction of ourselves and of others to ingeniously explicated strip-cartoons, as unreal as the wicked Juliette and as empty of life as the virtuous Justine.

The Passion of Indifference :
Henry de Montherlant

'AS FOR ME, my daily bread is disgust,' says Don Alvaro in
The Master of Santiago. 'God has given to me in profusion the
virtue of loathing.' By this criterion Henry de Montherlant is
a man of profuse virtue, for he can dislike even those characters
whom he has created to do his loathing for him. Typical of him
—despite his dissociation of himself from anything 'typical'—is
his treatment of Mlle de Bauret in the comparatively early novel,
The Bachelors. A minor character, whose actions indicate kindly
if careless impulses and nothing which could be called vicious,
Mlle de Bauret is abruptly subjected to several pages of intemper-
ate abuse. 'Her bosom, *miserabile dictu,* was on the whole conspicuous by its absence.' That perhaps qualifies as fair comment,
though the young lady's bust dimensions bear little relevance to
her part in the book. 'In politics, needless to say, Mlle de Bauret
had progressive ideas.' Well, at least this tells us what Montherlant
thinks of progressive ideas. But when the author says, 'Although
heterosexual, she had not married, because she had nothing; and
she had even preserved her virginity—though it was hardly
worth preserving', the disgust and contempt in his voice can
hardly be justified by acknowledging that since Montherlant
created her he is free to deal with her as he will.

He did not create France, which incurs a similar contempt in
the same novel. 'The whole thing was imitation American, which
is to say that it was typical of present-day France; since for some
time now the national genius has largely consisted in copying.'
The 'whole thing', incidentally, is M. Octave's habit of typing his
letters, which one would hardly have thought a mortal offence,

even in 1934. The trouble with these comments is that they come from outside, they are gratuitous, they are (if the description isn't inappropriate in view of their violence) mere asides. The author's temperature shoots up without warning and without apparent cause. He is himself aware of this dubious behaviour. 'We must apologize for having spoken of Mlle de Bauret with a sort of shudder which is quite out of place in this narrative. But we were unable to suppress it.' A marvellously arrogant anti-apology!

There are a number of fine things, too, in *The Bachelors*, which makes this insistent cantankerousness all the more regrettable. Similarly, the account of the relationship between Costals and Solange Dandillot in *The Demon of Good* and *The Lepers*, though markedly lowering in its effect on the reader, is undeniably fascinating. Solange is slowly done to death, the death of a thousand cuts, and Costals acts as her executioner. As they embrace, 'she felt a need to go to the closet, and while she is away Costals remembers that Arab mare he once had, so proud and delicate that she would never stale or dung when he was on her back'. But the surgeon—someone has spoken of Montherlant's 'clinical detachment', a horrifying judgment on clinics!—the surgeon continues cutting long after poor Solange is dead. The unintended sympathy which the reader begins to feel for her grows sharply when he finds, at the end of this fantastically argumentative novel, that a scholarly appendix has been granted Costals for his further and quite redundant reflections on the 'moral inferiority of woman'. For example, 'Cows tread each other, though they get no pleasure; through a stupid imitation of the male.' We note that Montherlant is ready to discredit the human by adducing both its similarities to and its dissimilarities from the animal. The dissection of Solange is magnificently telling, up to a point—and then the feeling grows that all this is like a highly skilled matador expending his techniques on a hobbled cow. Cruelty to dumb characters.

The note to *The Lepers* (the Routledge translation of 1940) gives Montherlant's reactions to the public's habit of identifying him with his heroes. 'If the public confounds me with Costals, it is mistaken in so doing: but I am indifferent to the fact, it is no business of mine.' Had he wished to attack the institution of marriage, he says, he would not have chosen someone as unsympathetic as this character to be his mouthpiece. Yet it seems to me that he does not really answer his interlocutor's question: '. . . you have made it so obvious that something of yourself has gone into Costals. Why be astonished, therefore, if the public tries to identify you in him, and not M. Maurice Leblanc in Arsène Lupin?' Montherlant is literally correct, though, in that, while using Costals to destroy Solange, he also makes clear how unlikeable he considers Costals:

> 'I love great cities,' Costals said passionately, dreaming of all the human material in them for him to corrupt. And, like an alternating current, he felt the three phases of his relation to the world pass through him: (1) how to enjoy it; (2) how to guard against it; (3) how to jeer at it.

But then, does Montherlant set much store by likeableness? Certainly, compared with the virulence he shows towards Solange, his attitude to Costals is one of indulgence. Possibly Henri Peyre was going a little too far when he spoke of 'the author's hatred of himself': Montherlant hates other people, people of a different kind, more. What does he *not* hate, what does he admire? Pride, virility (of a sort which characterizes itself by despising women), isolation or independence, courage and style (his literary style is not to be judged by translations, readable as are Terence Kilmartin's)—the virtues of the bullring.

'There have been three passions in my life,' Montherlant has said, 'independence, indifference and physical delight.' In the hero of his new novel, *Chaos and Night*, independence has degenerated into a pathetic unassailable bigotry, indifference is all too potent and physical delight makes next to no appearance. Don Celestino, a Spanish republican aged sixty-seven (the author's own age at the time of publication, Peter Quennell remarks in the introduction) has passed twenty years of exile in Paris. Every morning he searches through the newspaper. 'If there was no mention of Spain he was mortified. If Spain was criticized, he was mortified. If Spain was praised, he was mortified, because it meant praise for the Franco régime.' As a study in depth of a political doctrinaire, one for whom the war still continues, for whom the world never changes, for whom principles mean everything and people nothing, the book has a good deal of point. 'You're a caricature of a man of the Left,' his friend tells Celestino, 'just as Don Quixote was a caricature of a knight-errant.' The novel has that sort of point, that's to say, until the point is blunted by too much hammering. Again Montherlant is not content to let his story tell the tale, he must intervene in person, and his person is crushing. Celestino, the anarchist, has realized in 1936 that 'the State acquires some meaning when it allows you to kill legally those of your compatriots who do not think as you do. So, long live the Republic!'—this passage occurs on the twenty-seventh page of the narrative: Celestino is quickly put in his place. And a little later, 'the reader must already have discovered that it was Celestino's speciality never to see reality for what it is'. Celestino's 'humour'—incidentally the book has little of the humour and none of the generosity which the reference to Don Quixote might lead us to expect—is perhaps the subject for an essay or a short story rather than a novel: the reader feels a growing claustrophobic discomfort as the walls steadily close in round the author's chosen subject. Slawomir Mrozek made a rather similar point in a very short story, 'Birthday', with its tame progressive kept in a playpen as a domestic pet.

Chaos and Night is typically Montherlant (*pace* M. Montherlant again) in its generalizations, mostly of an unkind tendency, though the unkindness is not always immediately obvious. 'The brief-cases of Parisians are stuffed with sausages and loaves of bread, since it is the men who do the shopping instead of their wives.' That is, the men are not real men—and more's the pity because, as *The Lepers* has it, 'there's less stupidity in a man's codpiece than in his brain and heart'. V. S. Pritchett remarked several years ago that Montherlant's epigrams do not wear so well. And alas they incline to be so loud. We notice too the device which leads the sentimental reader to suppose that the author is about to say something nice about somebody for once. Thus, 'in the whole crowded room' of the Café de Bondy 'the only person of any distinction was a Negro. Distinguished and melancholy.' But then one reads a little further. 'Distinguished because only he was lunching alone: melancholy because he knew that, whatever apocalyptic changes the future might bring, he would always be black.' And we are aware of the pleasure, barely concealed, which Montherlant derives from the collapse of a relationship. 'All's well that ends well,' as he says here, and several times in *The Lepers*, in the sense that all's well that ends. Celestino deliberately quarrels with his few friends and then breaks with his daughter. He is left only with his principles, concerning whose unreality we have already been fully informed, and the enjoyment he gets from watching bull-fighting.

France and the French come off badly in the earlier part of the book; but Celestino is a Spaniard, and the fact that he has found refuge in France is no reason for liking the place, whether or not his creator does. Then he is called to Madrid on family business. 'He had braved the bull, for the first time literally, at the age of fifteen'—like Montherlant himself, according to the biographical note attached to *The Master of Santiago*. 'This time he was braving the bull by going into a Spain that was fraught with danger without being forced to go.' His panic when he crosses the frontier is the point at which we feel most deeply for this cantankerous, perverse and (it must be confessed) rather boring old man. But what sort of Spain does he encounter? Madrid is a busy bourgeois city, full of 'empty faces or happy faces, in other words what one sees in every town'.

The novel has its triumphs. The account of Celestino in Paris stepping into the street to 'fight' the oncoming cars as if they were bulls, and his memories of past *corridas*, 'those enchanting ballets sometimes performed by man and beast in the heart of the clamorous arena'—passages which are comparable, or almost comparable, to the splendid description of the migrating wild geese towards the end of *The Bachelors*. The chance to attend a *corrida* once again is perhaps more powerful than the family business in drawing Celestino back to Spain. Yet the *corrida* which he goes to outside Madrid—and perhaps Montherlant is being cruel to himself now, perhaps he does hate himself—is vulgar, artificial, farcical, and (powerfully recounted) culminates in a horribly botched *mise à mort*. 'All was disillusionment: the revolution, the war, his youth, the people, the bulls,' Celestino muses on his way back to Madrid, his body throbbing with fever. 'At least France did not mean disillusionment, because France had never meant anything to him.' Rather pathetically Montherlant seeks in a prefatory note to dissociate himself from Celestino's disillusionment: despite 'the uninhibited tone in which my characters and I speak of the Spaniards here', he wishes to confirm 'the profound blood-friendship which has bound me to the Spanish people ever since my adolescence, and of which I have given countless proofs'.

Alone in his hotel room Celestino suffers a series of sharp pains in his back. This is the moment of truth, and the truth which is revealed to him is that

> there was chaos, which was life, and night, which was whatever exists before life and after life. . . . There was non-sense, which was life, and non-being, which was what exists before life and after it. Or rather, wasn't there only non-being and an appearance of being? *'Nothing exists, since everything ceases to exist when I cease to exist.* That's what I ought to have understood sooner: *nothing exists.'*

Hence the greatest power in the world, more powerful than hatred even, is indifference. The fourth stroke kills him. But the end is not yet. Three men come to arrest Celestino, 'for politics'—his pride is posthumously assuaged—and find him apparently murdered, with four wounds between his neck and his shoulder-blades, 'four thin, clean holes which might have been made by a knife or a sword'. The fairy-tale ending—the stigmata presumably convey that Celestino was not the bullfighter but the bull—is of course utterly out of tune with the insistent harshness, the unrelenting unforgivingness, the grudging realism which have gone before. Perhaps for that very reason, however his reason may boggle, the reader is not inclined to dismiss it with a pitying or contemptuous smile: at least it is something *different*. Alas, there is a final irony—it comes at the very end and one assumes it is irony: the words inscribed on Don Celestino's tomb are *Laus Deo*. It seems that once again, superb fighter as he is, with dash, finesse, fearlessness, strength and learning, Montherlant has been fighting a bull unworthy of his steel.

Too Many Caesars: the Poems of
C. P. Cavafy

OURS is a noisy, virile, goody-goody and flaccid world. In new countries run by new statesmen all sorts of brand old ideas are retreating to the fore. Such as banning juke-boxes, not for aesthetic reasons but because they interfere with the proper serving of the State: and banning films with love in them because love is a disturbing element; and banning other films which tend to corrupt in other ways, like *Superman*, not because they are ideologically tendentious but because they instil in people inefficient notions or irrelevant ambitions. After seeing *Superman*, a young boy in one of these new countries attempted to fly out of an upper window. He broke his leg, and maybe will never be able to serve the State as serviceably as he (or the State) would wish.

Ah, you may say, but things are different elsewhere: nearer home the old Adam is really on the rampage. Well, there seems to be plenty of mechanized vice, certainly—the old Adam in his senility—and of course there is juvenile delinquency, an activity which takes such standardized forms that one suspects it to be one more manifestation of conformity. At all events, all this is in the hands of the reformers.

> However, the handicap and the hardship
> are that these Reformers make
> a big story out of everything . . .
>   For everything,
> for the least thing, they inquire and investigate,
> and immediately they think of radical reforms,
> with the request that they be executed without delay.
> They also have a bent for sacrifices. . . .

How health-giving, in this degenerate context, is the presence
of a 'decadent' poet! A decadent poet with a strong sense of
irony, a firm compassion for the unheroic living who in every
age feed the politicians if not the guns, and a keen worm's eye
view of History. In his poetry Cavafy is no saint; a bit of a cynic,
at least where the big important things are concerned; in short,
and taking the one adjective with the other, a civilized human
being. He is willing to settle, not triumphantly, for the second
best, although he knows what the first best would be. How
agreeably dissimilar from some of our modern intellectuals who
are ready to settle for the third best while pretending it is the
first—and from those others, the reformers, with a bent for
sacrifice, for sacrificing the common man's common pleasures to
their uncommonly high opinion of their own taste and authority.

Cavafy is very honest. If one doesn't altogether admire his
homosexual love poems, it is not because he prettifies or pro-
pagandizes, but because there is a little too much self-pity, in
much the same way as some writers of unhappy heterosexual love
poems pity themselves—and his love is more likely than theirs
to be unhappy, since it has so few lines of defence. He wrote
his poems out of 'the foul rag-and-bone shop of the heart': he
did not pass his heart off for a spick and span mid-twentieth-
century supermarket. Not that his heart is all *that* foul. He abhorred
melodramatics; he was something of an aristocrat, a connoisseur,
an imperfect gentleman.

It is not that Cavafy reminds us we are merely human. He
reminds us that we *are* human. His persons may not be conscientious citizens, but neither are they beatniks or anarchists or
'other sounding matters of the sort'. They are imperfect—'Imperfect? Does anything human escape that sentence?'—they are
individuals needing in some degree to be, trying to be, not
altogether managing to be, members of a society. They usually
lack power, and perhaps it is a losing battle which they fight, a
succession of small Thermopylaes—

and they merit greater honour
when they foresee (and many do foresee)
that Ephialtes will finally appear,
and in the end the Medes will go through

—but it is better (this old-fashioned decadent would say) to fight a good, losing battle than to brandish arms noisily in a victorious, bad war.

The first English translation of Cavafy at length, by John Mavrogordato, came out in 1951: a poetic event of unusual importance. A second translation has appeared, ten years later, from America, costing twice as much, but still cheap at the price. In addition to the complete edition published in Alexandria in 1935, and translated by Mavrogordato, Miss Rae Dalven gives thirty-three 'early poems'. W. H. Auden remarks that translations of Cavafy, no matter who the translator, are always recognizable as translations of Cavafy; but, with four exceptions, these early poems could have been written by anybody. It seems a pity that the claims of posterity, *et cetera*, should have prevailed over Cavafy's wish that none of them be collected.

Mavrogordato's volume has the advantage there. In respect of a biographical note on the poet Miss Dalven has the advantage. The notes to the poems are much of a muchness. And between the two introductions—Rex Warner's to the first, Auden's to the second—there is little to choose. Both are interesting, and Warner's is slightly more to the point. Auden is rather prissy about Cavafy's erotic poems. 'Cavafy does not, perhaps, fully appreciate his exceptional good fortune in being someone who can transmute into valuable poetry experiences which, for those who lack this power, may be trivial or even harmful.'

They rose from the mattress,
and they dress hurriedly without speaking . . .
But how the life of the artist has gained.
Tomorrow, the next day, years later, the vigorous verses
will be composed that had their beginning here.

'But what', Auden wonders, 'will be the future of the artist's companion?' Cavafy has touched on that question several times: 'then he lost his position, and then his reputation', or even

> quickly, by heavy labour,
> and by common debauchery, so wretched, he was destroyed.

As Auden says, Cavafy does not glamorize, whether History or homosexual love. There is not the slightest tendency to corrupt in the man's work. His erotic poetry won't *make* any homosexuals, any more (I would have thought) than Yeats's erotic poetry will make heterosexuals. And it is too late to seek to reform Cavafy the man.

Auden raises a second interesting point, perhaps not strictly relevant, concerning what he calls Cavafy's 'patriotic poems'. Cavafy's persons are often drawn from the world of the Hellenistic states under Rome, and their love of country is surely too aesthetic, too resigned, too wry, to be termed 'patriotism'. As Auden remarks, their love and loyalty reside chiefly in the Greek language, which has survived political defeat and impotence: against that language and love of it is set military conquest, political intrigue, big talk and the rest of what is generally implied by 'patriotism'. From the tone of his remarks we may suspect that Auden is envisaging the downfall of Anglo-American civilization and the survival none the less of the English language. Agreed, Cavafy is 'topical': but topical not so much in treating of falling nations and lost power as in his concern with fallen man, and with men who are unwilling to be absorbed into the State as the price of official regeneration and perhaps comfortable survival. If you like, it is their country which such men love, but we shall have to find another word than 'patriotic' for them.

I doubt whether the new translations bring us anything especially new. In general Miss Dalven's use of English is more correctly English, and more 'contemporary'. Yet I confess, with a faint blush, to preferring the charm of Mavrogordato's mild eccentricities. 'The Senators making no laws what are they sitting there for?'—this fits better into the helter-skelter of long questions followed by short answers, in 'Waiting for the Barbarians', than Miss Dalven's bleak 'Why do the Senators sit and pass no laws?' Miss Dalven is more economical with words, often to advantage, though at times her economy approaches that of a bill of lading. In 'The Trojans', her 'downdrag of destiny' is more forceful than Mavrogordato's 'animosity of fate', and in 'Philhellene' (in Auden's sense, a 'patriotic poem'), her 'So we are not un-Greek, I reckon' scores over 'So we are not quite greekless, I believe'.

But Miss Dalven has gained in clarity at the cost of forfeiting something of that tenderness which accompanies Cavafy's irony. Mavrogordato has

> Poor though you find it, Ithaka has not cheated you.
> Wise as you have become, with all your experience,
> You will have understood the meaning of an Ithaka.

Miss Dalven ends this particularly fine poem, 'Ithaca', with the line, 'You must surely have understood by then what Ithacas mean', which makes her sound rather impatient with this dim traveller. She ends 'Caesarion' thus:

> still hoping that they would pity you,
> the wicked—who murmured 'Too many Caesars'.

But it is Mavrogordato's lines which I shall continue to remember:

> Still hoping that they would have mercy on you,
> The baser sort—chattering their 'Too many Caesars'.

It must be Miss Dalven's briskness, rather than a desire for a greater Greekishness, which betrays her into 'pseudo-supports himself', where Mavrogordato simply has 'pretends to keep himself'. Her use of the common forms of Greek names ('Phoebus') is more sensible than Mavrogordato's dogged transliteration ('Phoibos'). It should be remarked that Mavrogordato often rhymes, whereas Miss Dalven writes conscientiously free verse: and the effects secured by rhyme—sometimes of emphasis, sometimes of softening of tone—outweigh the occasional inversion and obscurity which Mavrogordato incurs. Incidentally, Miss Dalven invariably uses the horrid word 'deviate' to render Cavafy's description of the nature of his eroticism, where Mavrogordato makes do with 'lawless'. If 'lawless intoxication' is a bit grand, then 'deviate erotic drunkenness' sounds too much like a rather grave police charge.

For my own part, I remain faithful to Mavrogordato's Cavafy, by and large. But this is not to regret Miss Dalven's Cavafy. He is a major poet, and a very pertinent writer in his dealings with history, not with the Supermen who soar into fame, but with the men who fall and break their legs. He deserves more than one translator, and surely this new version will find new readers for him.

As will perhaps the welcome reissue of *Pharos and Pharillon*, E. M. Forster's collection of scattered anecdotes from Alexandrian history: a characteristic mixture (much the same in Faroukian times, perhaps not utterly different in the age of Nasser) of theology, politics, gossip, sensitive understandings and farcical misunderstandings, all lenified in Forster's alembic.

The author shows himself here a sort of genteel Cavafy, a sweeter-natured observer of the scene, sweeter because not deeply involved, a Cavafy applying himself to a *The Times* third leader. There is nothing here of what Rex Warner calls, in introducing Cavafy, the 'vigorous assertion of emotion . . . together with and underneath the controlled attitude, the steady point of view'. A quiet amusement replaces the quiet irony or quiet desperation of the Alexandrian poet. One of the pleasantest and probably (despite a slight cosiness of tone) the most valuable of these essays concerns Cavafy himself; and we are reminded that Forster was perhaps the first Englishman to recognize him and to make available samples of his poetry in translation.

He had tried to lead Greece, then he had tried to lead mankind. He had succeeded in both. But was the universe also friendly, was it also in trouble, was it calling on him, on him, for his help and his love?

That, of Alexander, is one of Forster's gentle confidence tricks. This—

> The Bedouin, guiding it (the plough), will sing tunes to the camel that he can only sing to the camel, because in his mind the tune and the camel are the same thing

—this is Forster at his strongest, making other people come sharply alive for us—small thanks though he is likely to get from them for it!

Since History deceives, perhaps it might as well deceive us pleasantly. Even opium dens, even hashish dens, vanish like a mirage when Mr Forster appears on the threshold. 'There is really nothing to say when one comes to the point.' Still, Forster says it very well—even if at times one doesn't altogether believe him.

Svevo's Progress: or, The Apotheosis of the Poor Fish

Each of Italo Svevo's three novels is a 'Life'. But the difference in liveliness between the first and the last is striking. *A Life* (1893) is a simple and sad story, predictable and yet—while obviously a superior work by the standards of current fiction—not altogether cogent. It is difficult to present convincingly the sort of character who is utterly lacking in convictions: the weak character tends to emerge as a weak characterization. And unhappily Svevo makes his character commit suicide for reasons which are almost—the official formula is not so ironic in its effect as Svevo may have intended—'quite unknown'.

The simplicity of approach is intimated on the first page, in Alfonso's letter to his mother. The country boy has come to work in a Trieste bank: 'I feel such a need to breathe some of our good pure air coming straight from its Maker. Here the air is thick and smoky.' Poor Alfonso, he is doomed from the start, though (one would have said) doomed to tuberculosis or malnutrition rather than death by his own hand. And 'country boy' is a misleadingly robust description of him, for he is handicapped by an education and a degree of culture. 'Generally he read serious works of criticism and philosophy, which he found less tiring than poetry or art.'

For Alfonso his 'culture' is an escape from life, an unsuccessful attempt to escape: it returns him to life even less qualified to cope than he was before. 'A well-written book gave him megalomaniac dreams, not due to the quality of his brain but to circumstances; finding himself at one extreme, he dreamt of another.' Unhappily he strikes up an acquaintance with the boss's daughter, a young lady whose interest in culture derives from something worse than enervation of character or unfriendliness of circumstance—from vanity and snobbishness. When there is no more spring in their emotions than in a snail, plainly a mutual taste for novels or for talking about novels is not likely to bridge the social and economic gap between them, not in Trieste at the end of the nineteenth century.

Macario warns Alfonso about Annetta's true nature at the very beginning of their tepid relationship, indeed before their relationship begins. None the less, for some unexplored reason, Alfonso pays half-hearted court to her. They even collaborate on a novel, Annetta's role being to write it, Alfonso's to admire what Annetta has written. Alfonso despises Annetta, Annetta despises Alfonso, and they continue to court each other quarter-heartedly.

Other well-meaning persons warn Alfonso, plainly enough. Annetta, one of them says, is 'a vain little thing who wanted to see someone die of love for her, but had not succeeded so far'. But an irresistible lack of force drives him on, and eventually they make love, or some shadow of it. Admittedly this happens only once, but the vague talk about Annetta's sensuality doesn't explain how she came to 'give herself'—the expression is peculiarly incongruous—to someone of inferior class, and one moreover whose physical presence, hero though he is, remains so indistinct. He is described at the outset as 'tall and strong', but later, in the company of Macario (himself 'tall and strong'), we hear that in size Alfonso was 'so small and insignificant that Macario felt fine beside him'.

The act of sexual collaboration proves too much for them, and mutual indifference sets in forthwith. 'His love for Annetta and his repugnance for her both seemed colourless.' Alfonso returns to the village, but only to be present at his mother's sickbed. Her doctor now begins to show more interest in her, and Svevo comments sadly that perhaps this was a benefit Signora Carolina derived from her son's arrival, 'for a person's life seems precious mainly because of the value others put on it'.

Returning to the city after his mother's death, Alfonso finds

Annetta engaged to Macario and himself in indefinably bad odour with his employer. After a curiously obscure brush with Annetta's brother and an ensuing challenge to a duel—presumably a social transgression cannot be dealt with except obscurely—Alfonso gasses himself; the country boy chooses a metropolitan way of death. 'He knew neither how to love nor to enjoy; he had suffered in the best of circumstances more than did others in the most painful ones.' Suicide might be thought to be Alfonso's one successful act in life, except that by this time we are so used to him failing that we cannot accept the author's ruling. The case is altogether different with Guido Speier in *Confessions of Zeno*, since Guido is not the chief character and, though he too may lack sufficient reason for suicide, he was in truth hoping to win sympathy and respite from the burden of financial failure. By a mischance the stomach pump which Guido was counting on failed to arrive in time.

Though this account of *A Life* indicates the novel's self-imposed limitations, it fails to do justice to the quiet clarity and decency of the writing, and above all Svevo's gift for making plain the mediocrity of a character without the least trace of a sneer. Svevo is always at his best in the vicinity of a death-bed, and the mother's last days are movingly related. He is almost as good in the vicinity of finance, and the atmosphere of the bank is evoked with the minimum of documentation, by a scattering of light hints and natural touches.

Svevo's second novel, *As a Man Grows Older* (1898), though its hero is similarly a poor fish, is a marked step forward. It has a good deal of quiet charm, often what seems a deliberately faded charm, and it is innocent of straining after effect or significance. Emilio, a bachelor of Trieste who has once published a novel, falls vaguely in love with Angiolina, not definitely enough to marry her, but just enough to feel hurt and indignant when she deceives him, as (it is clear to the reader) she is practically bound to do in the circumstances. There are foretastes of Zeno. For instance, Emilio has banished religion from his own home, but is gratified and reassured to find that his intended mistress is a believer: 'What a blessed thing religion was!' Zeno tells us repeatedly that, if *he* were religious himself, he would spend all day in church, nothing else in the world would matter. But, worldlier than Emilio, Zeno would never have attributed rapid progress with a new lady friend solely to the fact that 'she had found him so reasonable that she felt she could trust him completely'. Before long Emilio and Angiolina come to despise each other hardly less than do Alfonso and Annetta, and Emilio's reflection that 'he had possessed the woman he hated, not the woman he loved' could well come from Alfonso at the corresponding stage in his courtship.

Yet in the central relationship of *As a Man Grows Older* there is a strong and credible element of sensuality, of natural appetite. Moreover the novel contains a powerful character, Emilio's sister Amalia, colourless in her life but powerful in her decline and death, a process which is described at length and in lucid and dramatic detail. There is nothing elsewhere in Svevo's work to compare with this, not even the death of Zeno's father, for he exists chiefly as an adjunct to Zeno, or to Zeno's 'disease'. Certainly Amalia's death-bed throws the rest of the book (as I suppose the moral requires) into the shade. Svevo's sense of irony is developing; and Emilio, having lost both his mistress and his sister, settles down to 'a love of quiet and of security' and 'the necessity of looking after himself'. As the years pass, Angiolina merges in memory with Amalia, the physical beauty of the one with the spiritual qualities of the other, to become a 'lofty, splendid symbol'. Emilio's taste for literature has, after all, proved to have its uses. He survives.

The hero of Svevo's last novel, *Confessions of Zeno* (1923), not only survives, he triumphs. Third in this sequence of poor fishes, Zeno is the one who gets away. He gets away with quite a lot. It is as if Svevo has revolted against his earlier attitudes, or against their one-sidedness, their excessive simpleness. Perhaps, under his cod's clothing, the poor fish may be something of a dolphin, even at times a bit of a shark? And here it is Guido, robust and successful, the proficient violinist who understands Bach better than Bach understood himself, the Tuscan-speaking dandy, the charmer who wins the beautiful and virtuous Ada—it is Guido who kills himself, while Zeno, invalid and dilettante, goes on to recover the family fortunes and build a family and a fortune of his own.

The sickliness of Svevo's heroes, their physical enervation, is gloriously caricatured in Zeno. Continuously beset by mysterious aches and pains, he lives on avidly while strong characters die off all around him. His nerves, it seems,

> were so sensitive that they already gave warning of a disease from which possibly I was going to die only twenty years later. They might in fact be called perfect nerves, their only disadvantage being that there were very few days when they left me in peace.

The *Confessions* were written at the suggestion of Zeno's analyst (who supplies a nicely pompous and uncomprehending preface), or rather his ex-analyst. Towards the end Zeno cries,

> How can I any longer endure to be in the company of that ridiculous man, with his would-be penetrating eye, and the intolerable conceit that allows him to group all the phenomena in the world round his grand new theory?

For Zeno's trouble has been diagnosed as that of Oedipus: which enchants him (what an impressive pedigree the disease has!) but doesn't, even in 1915, deceive him. The association with Sophocles may titillate his vanity, but neither his common sense nor his sense of humour nor his status in the Triestine bourgeoisie nor indeed his vanity will permit for long this assimilation to a barbarous, dead mythology. Zeno is alive, civilized and very real. He remarks of his analyst, 'He must be the only person in the world who, hearing that I wanted to go to bed with two lovely women, must rack his brains to try and find a reason for it!' It is really the analyst who is sick, who is abnormal.

The truth is, Zeno is an extraordinarily normal and healthy man. He is one of the toughest characters in fiction: he needs to be, if he is to think about himself so minutely, so intensively, so protractedly, without turning into an absolute monster or dissolving into thin air. Rich enough not to have to do any real work, he has plenty of time to suppose that there must be something wrong with him. He is the most cheerful type of *malade imaginaire*, since his maladies never prevent him from doing or not doing whatever he would have done or not done otherwise. The 'search for health' is equally imaginary, a device for occupying the intervals between adventures and for justifying (Zeno enjoys big words and large conceptions even though he doesn't exactly trust them) his immense and unremitting interest in himself. 'Health cannot analyse itself even if it looks at itself in the glass. It is only we invalids who can know anything about ourselves.' It must be his 'illness' (or it might be his 'search for health') which leads him to take a mistress, seeing that he genuinely loves and admires his wife. It must be this too which causes him to give up his mistress—or causes him to cause her to give him up—seeing that she is a wellnigh perfect mistress. *He* is ready to tell us as much, but he declines to hear the same explanation from his analyst: common sense is all against it, and in any case one expects better things from a doctor.

When the *Confessions of Zeno* first appeared in English translation, in 1930, Frank Swinnerton spoke aptly of its 'amusing and mischievous illustrations of the adjustments of conscience by which sinners are able to continue respecting themselves'. When Zeno is about to take a mistress, he falls ill with conscience, and his wife assumes that his suffering is caused by the imminent marriage of Ada, her sister and Zeno's first love, to Guido. Zeno's indignation is such that it at once dispels the pangs of conscience. 'I honestly felt that she was wronging me; I was not guilty of such a crime as that.' A similar touch occurs in *As a Man Grows*

Older, when Emilio taxes his mistress with infidelity: she has been seen with another man, in a café, drinking chocolate. Angiolina flares up in righteous indignation: 'Chocolate! I who simply can't endure it! The idea of my drinking chocolate!'

Much of the humour of the *Confessions* derives from the fact that Zeno *sometimes* deceives himself or errs in interpretation. During his honeymoon, 'I was prone to assume the dignified pose of an equestrian statue,' he tells us, amusedly, complacently. The honeymoon was spent in Italy, visiting the galleries, and Zeno misses the point of Augusta's remark, reported directly after: 'It is lucky one only has to visit museums on one's honeymoon, and then never again!' Any interpretation of that remark other than the obvious, superficial one, wouldn't fit in with his settled conception of his wife as 'the personification of health'—that is, a splendid woman, but not too bright.

But if Zeno always, or mostly, deceived himself—or was tediously striving to deceive us—his company would prove intolerable over four hundred pages. A genuine *malade imaginaire* is deceiving himself: Zeno is an imaginary *malade imaginaire*. The *Confessions* move nimbly to and fro, from self-deception to engaging attempts at deceiving the doctor (and the reader) to truth-telling. (An instance of the latter is when he, the great self-analyser, the foremost expert on Zenology, points out that 'to explain to somebody how he is made is only another way of authorizing him to do as he likes'.) And what emerges from this agile to-and-fro is, not a very sublime character admittedly, but the truth about Zeno.

Like his predecessors, then, Zeno is a self-examiner, but on a vaster and minuter scale, and what he sees, far from depressing and disabling him, keeps him vastly stimulated. He is not the narrow, exclusive kind of egoist, for the egos of others amaze him almost equally. As a tragic figure a poor fish cannot amount to much, however humane his creator: but his comic potentialities are enormous. Zeno has been described as a Triestine

Charlie Chaplin, but he is much further removed from the tragic, or pathetic, than this would suggest. In some respects he resembles Falstaff—witty in himself and a notable cause that wit is in other men—except that he is thoroughly Triestine and bourgeois and in little danger of having his heart killed by anybody. For a hypocrite, he is a relatively honest man. Thus, during the period of his rivalry with Guido he consoles himself by playing the Kreutzer Sonata. And pretty well, too: the battle for Ada is not hopelessly lost. 'One's own violin,' he adds, 'resounds so close to one's ear that it reaches the heart very quickly.' The truth is sometimes too harsh to be faced squarely: Zeno will then squint sideways at it. In this way he is enabled to carry on with the battle of existence—but before long he will himself demolish the consolations and vindications which he has fabricated. There is much of the rascal about him, but nothing of the prig.

Tottering on the brink of death, as he likes to imagine, Zeno maintains a zest for living, is endlessly fascinated by all the sad and lovely contradictions of human life. Ada, the perfect woman, makes the mistake—as Zeno sees it, though not the reader—of preferring Guido: in fact, as things turn out, it *is* a mistake. A succession of mistakes and misapprehensions leads to Zeno affiancing himself against his conscious will to Augusta, Ada's plain though kindlier sister: as things turn out, this is no mistake, for Ada loses even her good looks, while Augusta gains them. Zeno has more luck than he deserves: he makes up for poor Emilio and poorer Alfonso. Yet the luck is not wantonly bestowed by a doting author, for Zeno's disposition is such as to attract good fortune. Towards the end of the novel he informs Guido, now patently the under-dog, that 'Life is neither good nor bad; it is original'. Alfonso and Emilio might well have produced a set of melancholy and flaccidly 'cultured' variations on the first part of that epigram, but neither could have delivered himself of the second part.

Having already switched from law to chemistry, the young

Zeno asked his father's permission to change back to law. The
father remarked good-naturedly that Zeno must be mad. The
grateful son, wishing to amuse his parent, underwent a thorough
examination in order to obtain a certificate of sanity, which he
then carried in triumph to his father. The latter, 'in an agonized
voice and actually with tears in his eyes', exclaimed, 'Ah, then
you really are mad!' But *Confessions of Zeno* is not only much
funnier than Svevo's other novels, it is richer in very nearly every
way, a splendid complex of wit, irony, shrewdness, tenderness
and dry compassion. If the earlier books derived from Flaubertian
realism and from the confusion of literature and life called
bovarysme, the *Confessions* are nearer to the nobler and larger
tradition of the *Bildungsroman,* and at the point where this genre
overlaps with the picaresque. There are similarities with Thomas
Mann's *Confessions of Felix Krull* and even with *The Magic
Mountain.* And just as the equivocal hero of *Wilhelm Meister's
Apprenticeship* is finally likened to 'Saul the son of Kish, who
went out to seek his father's asses, and found a kingdom', so
Zeno, incredulous paterfamilias, goes out to seek roses for his
daughter, inadvertently crosses a military frontier, is prevented
by the confused outbreak of war from rejoining his family, and
later—with the help of the war—finds himself become a successful
speculator in his own right. 'I really am well, absolutely well. . . .
Of course I have pains from time to time, but what do they matter
when my health is perfect?' It was business, his business, that has
cured him, and, he says, he would like his late analyst to know it.

James Joyce, who encouraged Svevo to persevere in the face
of public neglect, remarked in a letter to his widow, 'The important thing is that Svevo be read and written about.' Had Joyce
managed to overcome his reluctance to set up as a literary gent
and written about Svevo himself, perhaps the English might
have overcome their ingrained suspicion of the European novel
and actually read the *Confessions,* at least, this masterpiece of a
period rich in master-novels.

Common Bird or Petal: the Poetry of
Hugo von Hofmannsthal

O F the trio, Rilke, George and Hofmannsthal, it is the latter
who has attracted the least attention outside Germany. The
Poems and Verse Plays—a bilingual selection of poems and six
verse plays, edited and introduced by Michael Hamburger—is an
admirable undertaking, but it is not likely to start any critical
landslide in Hofmannsthal's favour. He emerges from it as the
most attractive personality of the three, but the least forceful
artist.

Hofmannsthal was an aesthete, conscious of the sterility of
aestheticism, and seeking to escape from his own aestheticism.
A great deal has been made by the critics of his 'solution of the
antinomy between art and life, introspection and activity,
individualism and community'—to quote a phrase from Mr
Hamburger's introduction. Obviously this 'crisis' (as presented
in the Chandos Letter and indeed pervasively) offers a fine oppor-
tunity to the philosophically-minded sort of critic; and it is
interesting to note how English critics turn philosophic—and
turn Germanic—when they are engaged with German writing.
They trust the artist: far from trusting the tale, they hardly seem
to notice it. Mr Hamburger's introduction is painstaking and
thorough, yet it doesn't give the reader much idea of what
Hofmannsthal's poetry is *like*. It makes explicit, though complicated, what is already perhaps too explicit (though more
graceful) in the work. The translations are more truly enlightening: they (and notably Mr Hamburger's own) are of a very
superior kind, and remind us that we seem to be entering a new
era in the translation of German poetry.

Hofmannsthal's problem was not a new one. Art is beauty: art must have to do with life it if is not to starve: yet life is often not beautiful. Rather than conveying a sense of what life is, Hofmannsthal is most adept at conveying the aesthete's recognition of the emptiness of his own sort of existence. The theme is already summed up in an early poem, 'The Youth in the Landscape'. Coming to see 'that the world's destinies were his by kinship', the youth decries 'the riches he had found in his own soul', for now 'only the need of serving made him glad'. To use Hofmannsthal's terms, he is preparing to penetrate out of 'pre-existence' into 'existence'—but we do not witness the outcome of the penetration.

The smith in *Idyll* stands for participation in 'real life', presumably, and the centaur (the 'lover of journeys') for the dream or for art. When the smith's wife runs off with the centaur and the smith kills her with a spear, the reader is left feeling that the villain of the piece (in so far as there is a villain) is the smith rather than the centaur. In the morality-style verse play, *Death and the Fool*, Claudio, 'the utterly unloving and unloved', is an enervated, more cultivated and narrower version of Goethe's Faust. 'What do I know about human life? . . . at the most, I studied it.' When he complains that he is not ripe for death, Death reminds him:

> What all men have, you, too, were given:
> An earthly life, to be lived in earthly fashion.

The apparitions enter of three persons whom, through his non-commitment, Claudio has betrayed. He then falls dead, after announcing that Death can compress into one hour more life 'than once the whole of life had space to hold', a sentiment which seems to imply a curious conception of life's possibilities and an odd celebration of them.

'How strong is all that's common, life is filled with it,' we are told in *The Marriage of Zobeide*, and again,

> O fool,
> whoever scorns what's common, seeing that life
> consists of what is common, through and through.

Yet one finds little that *is* common in these plays, which partake of the aristocratic and ritualistic nature of Yeats's theatre. In *The Emperor and the Witch*, the Emperor (of Byzantium) can only end his seven years' enthralment to the beautiful witch by not touching her for seven days. 'I want human, human kind!' He succeeds, the witch turns into an old woman, and he can now give himself freely to his wife and children, to 'real life'. Yet here too the reader may feel that his sympathies have been enlisted for the witch. Trying to convince himself, Hofmannsthal hardly manages to convince the reader that a meaningful choice has really been made.

There is, that's to say, a strong impression of *voulu* about this writing. We see what Mr Hamburger means in speaking of the unity within the diversity of Hofmannsthal's productions; but the reference to Goethe only brings out how much greater Goethe's diversity is and how his unity is less forced, less conscious, than that of Hofmannsthal's 'repertory'.

Hofmannsthal's verse has a consistent measured grace (admirably reproduced in the translations), on the cold side, but still distinct from the lofty, sacerdotal and more-refined-than-thou poetry of Stefan George. Yet George's cold arrogant aestheticism is at any rate in focus, it has an incisiveness and force which compel admiration: it has the courage of its (as they seem to me) largely distasteful convictions. George's ivory tower was armour-plated. Hofmannsthal impresses us as 'a better man', more scrupulous, concerned for the outer world and its denizens, less godlike in his assurance. Yet—suffering perhaps from the vices of its virtues—his verse often seems slightly out of focus, deficient in incisiveness and cogency. He is puzzling out, whereas George knows—and is stating. 'Every complete poem', Hofmannsthal wrote, 'is at the same time premonition and presence, longing and fulfilment'—yes, but is this too much to ask, or perhaps too much to be conscious of?

What another poet might theorize about in his journal, might deduce from the poetry he has already written, Hofmannsthal talks about in his verse. Perhaps it was as a way of escape from his obsessive preoccupation with one or other aspect of the antinomy that he turned to translations and adaptations. It seems that it was thus—and notably in his collaboration with Richard Strauss—that as an artist he found himself best able to penetrate out of 'pre-existence' into 'existence', to take his place in a society of men.

Beyond Irony : Erich Heller on
Thomas Mann

A STUDY of Thomas Mann by Professor Erich Heller—that
was indeed something to look forward to, if with a certain
trepidation. For in his previous book, *The Disinherited Mind*,
flights of smooth profundity alternated with rude air-pockets.
From being cogently present, the author would abruptly 'go
through the wall as though it were thin air', to use the words of
one reviewer.

This phenomenon still happens in *The Ironic German*, but
rarely. When it happens, we admire and are disappointed, but
at least we are not discouraged from reading Thomas Mann. For
here Heller is less impelled to preach, is indeed less apocalyptic,
fairer to his subject, and fairer to his reader. Discussing the
irreconcilability of art and life as propounded by so many
modern artists, from Tonio Kröger ('it is all up with the artist
as soon as he becomes a man and begins to feel') to T. S. Eliot
('the progress of an artist is a continual self-sacrifice, a continual
extinction of personality'), Heller says:

> Amid all this aesthetic pother the suspicion grows that there must
> have been a time when the artist shared the reality of his fellow-men,
> and was distinguished from them not so much by a unique vision
> and agony as simply by the power to give surpassing form and
> shape to the common intimations of meaning. . . . The aesthetic
> transcendence is then, perhaps, nothing but an optical delusion
> enforced upon the eye by the dark prospect of a historical period,
> and caused by a pathological narrowing of the common vision—
> by an insidious deficiency in the concept of what is real.

To measure the difference of tone we need but adduce his quotation in the earlier book of Kierkegaard's statement, 'the individual cannot help his age; he can only express that it is doomed', and his large addendum to it: 'And this is the only way in which he can bring help to it'.

The Disinherited Mind was hardly 'about' literature, or life. What was its subject? Unreligion? The mass disgrace of humanity? The present book is, largely, about literature and so about life. Heller shows himself more Goethean than Kierkegaardian; he once refers to Kierkegaard as a 'great moral hypochondriac'. Though he tells us that he has long been fascinated by Thomas Mann, there were few signs of that author's influence in *The Disinherited Mind*. It was at the very end of Mann's long career, after his minute and relentless exploration of human powers and impotences, following the burnt-out and broken figure of Adrian Leverkühn with the surging of the queenly bosom of Dona Maria Pia, and forgetting neither in the experience of the other, that he could write (in the essay on Chekhov, published in 1954):

> But still one goes on working, tells stories, gives form to truth and thereby regales a needy world, hoping darkly, sometimes almost confidently, that truth and gracious form will avail to set free the human spirit and prepare mankind for a better, lovelier, worthier life.

It was beside the point to describe Heller's cast of mind as now more Goethean. Rather, he has laid himself open to Thomas Mann.

His discussion of Schopenhauer and Nietzsche begins by being interesting and pertinent. Most notably, the passage relating the clash between 'Will' and 'Idea' to *Buddenbrooks* is truly illuminating, because Heller throughout has old Buddenbrook, Consul Buddenbrook and Thomas Buddenbrook, that declining (or ascending?) series, firmly between his fingers. The philosophical discussion later becomes only interesting,

Heller defends his procedure, of quoting, glossing, developing Schopenhauer, Nietzsche and Mann in the same long breath, with his usual skill:

> the peculiar understanding of life which is embodied in a work of literature—and it is this *understanding* which determines also the *formal* aspects of the work: its organization and its style—may have crystallized in the contact between the writer and a philosopher, between an imagination and a thought. In such a case the philosophy will be as relevant to the nature and quality of the writing as is its vocabulary, rhythm, or syntax. Indeed, every major literary work has a *syntax of ideas* upon which it may ultimately depend for its rank and status.

And defends it so modestly (considering the extent to which he makes use of it) that still to have doubts seems ungracious. One would be more confident in one's defence of the procedure, as he says—or in one's rejection of it—'if we were, in fact, surer of the precise difference, in every respect, between literary and philosophical comprehension'. That difference seems to me, at any rate, suspiciously large. Is it simply a question of individuality? That some of us are predominantly philosophical, others predominantly literary, in our mode of comprehension, and that to count on a true co-operation of literary and philosophical perception would be, as Leavis said in a similar context, 'to count on the attainment of an arduous ideal'? 'It is possible for an idea to move a man passionately, and possible for a man to fall in love with an idea.' Yes, the idea may be philosophy, but literature is about the love affair, *is* the love affair, and usually no merely platonic one at that. Surely he would be a remarkably specialized being who, in reading Mann's fiction, would say, 'But this is Schopenhauer, this is Nietzsche' more often than he would say, 'But this is life, this is me'. In an un-English way, Heller is in love with ideas, and successfully so. But large tracts of this book made me feel that *Buddenbrooks*, *The Magic Mountain*, *Doctor Faustus*, help towards an understanding of Schopenhauer and

Nietzsche far more than these philosophers help towards an understanding of those novels. 'Every man, philosopher included, ends in his own fingertips,' said Lawrence. Even an *avant-garde* woman artist from Munich, one may add, remembering Heller's account of what she said to Mann after reading *Buddenbrooks*: 'I was not bored by your novel, and with every page I read I was astonished that I was not bored'. Mann would not be a great novelist did he not provide amply for his readers' fingertips. He never quite goes through the wall. At times Heller's mixture of philosophical discussion and particular adduction from the fiction is exactly right: what we read is all-assuring, and we cannot tell which is the gloss, which the glossed. At other times Heller goes through the wall, seems to be addressing a different audience in a different lecture-room on a different topic.

He pokes lively fun at the technique of 'close reading'; as he says, it is frequently 'a strenuously elaborate manner of special pleading', in fact a smug substitute for real reading. Even so, if 'literary analysis, however close, can neither assess, nor explain or prove, the *quality* of a literary work', neither can those ends be properly achieved without literary analysis. There are two altogether different sorts of 'literary analysis': one is performed by a curiously primitive form of mechanical computer, and it is this one that Heller demolishes. But when he says,

> it is good to realize that 'close reading' is merely the virtue of a vice: of that lettered illiteracy which is the ruinous price paid for universal education,

then one feels he ought to have given his own words, especially the word 'ruinous', a little 'close reading' of the other sort. A closer reading and use of Mann might have kept his philosophical digression in better order and under the orders of his subject matter. And in fact his section on *Death in Venice*, where he deliberately 'reads closely', impressed me as the most valuable part of the book, and not merely (though he takes this view) as an analysis of Mann's 'literary technique'.

Mann's *Meditations of a Non-Political Man* (1918) demonstrates how an artist of his range and perceptiveness will hardly be able to swallow those lumpish modes of thought and behaviour which we call politics. 'The Conservative Imagination', Heller's chapter on the *Meditations*, is itself somewhat indigestible. And in spite of Mann's statement that the *Meditations* 'shows the intellectual foundation of my literary work', we may doubt whether it is worth the sheer amount of attention which Heller gives it. Considering, that is, the existence of *The Magic Mountain* (1924). As Heller puts it, in the *Meditations* the brothers Mann— Thomas, the ironic conservative pessimist, and Heinrich, the windy republican optimist—face each other:

> the one, nobly enraged by the ignominy of the ruling powers, courageously proclaiming with catastrophic platitudes his belief in a better future; the other, indignant at the untruth of high-minded and highfalutin rhetoric, supporting with many a true insight into the human condition an insupportable cause. It is the exact picture that Thomas Mann himself was later to draw of the struggle, with Naphta and Settembrini fighting it out in *The Magic Mountain*. . . .

Yes, except that *The Magic Mountain* is more exact: that is, more meticulous, more exhaustive, more persuasive, more 'truly interesting'. And in approaching the novel by way of the *Meditations*, Heller occasionally distorts the greater work. The sentence of Heller's which I have quoted above ends thus:

> with Naphta and Settembrini fighting it out in *The Magic Mountain*, paradigmatic victims, perhaps, of one of the most disturbing perversions of an age in which all profundities tend to be sinister, and shallow all the friendlier thoughts about man.

Compare this with Castorp's reflections in the section titled 'Snow':

'Yes, yes, pedagogic Satana, with your *ragione* and your *ribellione*,' he thought. 'But I'm rather fond of you. You are a wind-bag and a hand-organ man, to be sure. But you mean well, you mean much better, and more to my mind, than that knife-edged little Jesuit and Terrorist, apologist of the Inquisition and the knout, with his round eye-glasses—though he is nearly always right when you and he come to grips over my paltry soul, like God and the Devil in the mediaeval legends.'

The two passages are near in meaning; yet there is still a considerable difference of meaning between them.

Then, in this matter of conservatism *versus* radicalism, there is Heller's statement—close to C. P. Snow's letter but far from Snow's spirit—that 'the poetic imagination is naturally more a glorifier of memories than a designer of utopias'. That is perhaps somewhat more than a half-truth. The modern artist, remembering Shakespeare, isn't likely to harbour any simple-minded faith in 'progress'. (Will he, though, forgo the use of a modern w.c.?) But surely it is not a question of 'progress'—it must be a long time since any reasonably intelligent person expected to gain on all the swings and all the roundabouts too—rather, of contending against evils which are forever springing up. These evils exist in utter disregard of our glorification of memories; and in that their manifestations are always in some sense 'new', so new weapons against them have always to be found. The 'conservative imagination', as Heller describes it, has all the urbanity, wit, irony and profundity of the statesman who is perpetually in opposition. No doubt we need him. But what if he were alone, left indeed in solitary state, with nothing to oppose except the problems of the present and the future? My own philosophizing seems all the more ingenuous, beside Heller's; I should have been content to propose that Mann, the totality of his work considered, is a good deal more 'ironical' towards the claims of conservatism, too, than Heller makes him out to be. This touches on one difficulty of the book: naturally Heller has every right to express his own opinions (how could he help but do so?), but the reader cannot always tell from his mode of exposition and style of writing (often resembling Mann's) whether it is his own opinion he is expounding or his subject's.

As concerns the *Meditations* we must agree that Mann was no more a fellow-traveller of Fascism at that time than he was of Communism when 'waving and bowing to the Press cameras of the "People's Democracy"'. His political meditations might be said to have been non-political in that no conservative politician adorning his age would truly comprehend, let alone be guided by, them. Political comprehension being what it is, we may be forgiven for still feeling that this was the one point where Heinrich Mann rose superior to his brother. What party congress would devote time to this sort of motion?—

> Could it be that what I am . . . does not correspond exactly to what I think and believe, and that I am destined to further precisely that which on these pages I have called 'Progress' through the very act of conservatively opposing it—opposing it by means of 'literature'?

That Heller quotes this (from the *Meditations*) is a measure of his concern for scrupulousness. Careful and subtle as he is, yet Mann (as in this passage) is more subtle and generally (I would say) easier to grasp. I feel that the commentator does push his subject, however gently, along a discernibly political path—the way of conservatism. He blames the radical artist for having an opinion ('the responsible artist is a political sceptic'), and yet he appears to be praising the conservative artist *for* his opinion, as though 'conservative', as Heller conceives the word, can be equated with 'non-political'. Perhaps at the time when Mann wrote the *Meditations*, this seemed the case—yet even then he hardly made that equation with much confidence. In his fiction he is too acute a moralist to want to make it: his fictional people come from a deeper part of his being than that which 'meditated': personal enough in all conscience, yet less subject to the personal and historical stresses which bear upon the *Meditations*.

This seems an example of Heller's often scarcely perceptible intervention; he is speaking of Mann's essay on Chekhov:

> He quotes with cautious sympathy even one of the sillier remarks of the not often silly Chekhov, a remark directed at the old Tolstoy's 'reactionary morality': 'Sober reflection and a sense of justice tell me that there is more love for mankind in steam and electricity than in chastity and fasting.'

Firstly, who—Mann (whose sympathy is 'cautious') or Heller—considers the remark 'silly'? Secondly, in what way is it silly? Would it be less silly to say that sober reflection etc. tell us there is more love for mankind in chastity and fasting than in steam and electricity? Or is the remark silly because meaningless, because it all depends and there is no mention of what it depends on? If the latter, one can still suggest that the implied choice often and urgently confronts us in one form or another. What is missing from Heller's discussion of the remark, as from the remark itself, is the context of the thinking—its application to events and people—and *that* we find in Mann the novelist. It is of course one aspect of his greatness, and it is that which again and again defies the commentator to find anything more useful to say than, 'Go and read Mann!'

Consequently, if I say that Heller doesn't sufficiently bring out the fact that Castorp's preference for the liberal humanist Settembrini is one reflection among others in the novel of Mann's preference, and that Mann, for all his ironic scepticism, would rather be simple and right than profound and wrong—then, in so saying, I am over-simplifying, exaggerating in the other direction. Perhaps I had better conclude with the suggestion that Heller doesn't give enough weight to such explicit statements as this:

> Schopenhauer has not a good word for 'progress', and even less for the political activity of the people, the revolution. His behaviour

in the '48 was grimly, comically petty—one cannot put other words to it. His heart was not at all with those who fanatically enough hoped at that time to give a direction to German public life which might have meant a happier turn to the whole of European history down to our day, and which was to the interest of every intellectual man—the democratic direction.

It is interesting to find this in the essay on Schopenhauer, which was written in 1938, and cannot be taken as one of Mann's nods and becks towards the German Democratic Republic. (Of course, another external explanation can be found for it . . . and we are driven back to the fiction, and to literary criticism. . . .)

To sum up. The present reader received from *The Ironic German* a little of that feeling which Heller ascribes to the reading of Lukacs: 'the unsettling sensation of a wisely conducted tour over firm ground with sudden detours, taken at the beckoning of the *idée fixe*, over large patches of thin ice. The result is a vague distrust of the wisdom even of what is undeniably wise.' By no means at all times. The individual successes are too many to recount. I would mention, though, the characterization of 'the daring literary device of Thomas Mann's later works: the calculated and artistically mastered incongruity between the meaning of the story told and the manner of telling it'. Towards this—of which one aspect is that apparent incongruity of stance whereby cool humorous appraisal is combined with loving warmth or (in *Doctor Faustus*) inconceivably endured personal agony, and which is of the very essence of this author—Mann must have been helped by Goethe. Among the literary ancestors of Felix Krull, Heller might have included Wilhelm Meister, dubious hero of a book hardly less 'licentious' though stiffer-faced and not nearly so nimble in its handling of this sort of irony.

Then there are the excellent insights and asides (which, in 'Conversation on the Magic Mountain', are given to Q as well as to A); the insistence that 'almost every successive work not only adds to the illumination of his previous writings, but reveals them as actually bigger than they seemed when they first appeared,' and that all this is achieved without monotony; the enlightening treatment of *Tonio Kröger* and *Joseph and his Brothers*; the brief but pithy consideration of *Doctor Faustus* (and if Heller has said too little about the tremulous hope, the 'light in the night', we grant that it is difficult to say anything on this score, 'utterable only in the lowest whisper', without saying too much); and the few comments on *Felix Krull*. The latter are all too few. Heller refrains from longer discussion on the grounds that the comic 'puts an end to the debate', for it is 'the human spirit's one and only self-inflicted defeat that is almost indistinguishable from victory'. There he goes through the wall again. Is there so little to be said about our one victory, officially unrecognized though it may be?

Erika Mann ends her homely touching account, *The Last Year*, with these words:

> Dear, beloved 'Magician', Grace walked with you to the end, and you went forth in tranquillity from this green earth about whose fate you have so long and lovingly distressed yourself.

'The ironic German'. Yes, Heller expounds the nature of that irony in brilliant fashion. But is it the best title, for so sincere a study of one whose voice, for all the subtlety of his mind, was rarely muffled by irony? 'There is still something left in me which is not mere irony, something which is straightforward, warm, and good', Thomas Mann wrote to his brother Heinrich in 1901. He could have said the same fifty-four years later. There is a case for calling him the straightforward German. As straightforward as a long and loving distress, never turned away from and never given in to, could allow.

Three New Germans

Günter Grass

    Günter Grass's first novel, *The Tin Drum*, is the *Tristram Shandy* of the age of Adenauer, cynical instead of sentimental, combining innuendo with a violent explicitness unimaginable to Sterne. And generous in digressions, many of which, farcical or fantastic or shocking, are superb set pieces in themselves.

    This species of novel needs space. But Grass took more space than was good for his novel. The physical density for which *The Tin Drum* has been justly admired is weakened by its author's prolixity, his spotlighting of details which fail to prove significant, and his habit of continually reminding the reader of things which the reader would not have forgotten or missed if he hadn't been distracted by reminders of other things which he wouldn't have forgotten or missed if . . .

    Critics have fastened on the work's 'amorality' as a possible source of dissatisfaction, especially outside Germany. It is true that Oskar, the three-foot dwarf who can shatter glass with his voice, is neither Nazism nor the agent whereby Nazism is to be exposed and condemned. But there is no categorical reason why he should be either, and plenty of reasons why he shouldn't be. The reader is perfectly able to judge what is happening around Oskar without Oskar having to nudge him into horror or pity or rage. Obviously Oskar is rather low on personal morals: his job is to survive, and for a dwarf in his brutal milieu this is a full-time job.

    No, what is wrong is not that Grass hasn't written an allegory, but that what he has written, the way he has written it, demands to be taken as allegory and then renegues on its own invitation.

Grass manipulates private obsessions, dwelling on them with the peculiar intensity which we rightly associate with allegory of however subtle or complex a kind; he repeats themes and images with a finger-pointing deliberateness which betokens a thesis. Something approaching Thomas Mann's meticulousness, his exhaustiveness, is deployed in the service of what turns out to be a dirty joke or a slapstick anecdote. With Mann in mind, one might suggest that Oskar has fallen, and fallen with notable vigour, between two stools, between Felix Krull, realistic villain, and Hans Castorp, allegorical hero.

The potted history of Danzig, the manic listing of regiments, the nuns, the preoccupation with bodily functions, apparently gratuitous yet never casual or merely 'commercial': all this must mean something. The author *is* committed—but to what? To something we can share in? Oskar maintains that the authentic political partisan 'who undermines what he has just set up, is closest to the artist because he consistently rejects what he has just created'. Perhaps this is what is happening in *The Tin Drum*.

In reviewing the novel Neal Ascherson remarked that 'the reader is adjured to be alert to these themes and correspondences, as if *The Tin Drum* could be unravelled by pulling certain master-threads'. Grass is a painter, and his symbols, Mr Ascherson suggested, are not organic, but recur in the way that mandolin shapes recur in the work of Picasso. Nevertheless *The Tin Drum* is eminently readable, even or perhaps especially if you permit yourself to skip, and a rich stew in a time of watery gruels. Many readers will be content to leave it at that.

Cat and Mouse is a different kettle of fish: a short work, so thin in texture that now those putative 'master-threads' can be followed through from beginning to end. To me they seem to end in precious little. The book is all threads and tricks. The mouse of the title is (among other things) the Adam's apple of the hero, Mahlke: a mouse which looms as large as an elephant, trampling its way through the story along with the other objects which decorate Mahlke's neck, screwdrivers, medallions, a stolen Knight's Cross and a legitimately acquired one. What the cat can be, besides a literal feline once attracted by the quivering of Mahlke's oversize thyroid cartilage, is up to the reader. Possibly the sunken minesweeper into which the hero finally disappears, possibly the author himself playing with his mousy readers. Its real presence is on the dust-jacket, designed by Grass.

The scene is Danzig again, but a pale shadow of the happy drumming ground of little Oskar (who makes a fleeting appearance in these pages). The surface of the novel is too frail to support the weight of documentation which Grass lays on it, the naval expertize for instance, let alone that portentous Adam's apple. There are moments of miraculous freshness and hallucinatory clarity, but often the action is repetitious, mystificatory or (in the case of the patriotic schoolmasters) satirical in a wearily slapdash way.

Cat and Mouse is crammed with style, or 'stylistics': the recurrent images, blankly catalogued ('Mahlke's throat and Mahlke's aunt, Mahlke's sugar water, the parting in the middle of his hair, his gramophone, snowy owl, screwdriver, woollen pompoms, luminous buttons . . .'); the calculated but senseless uncertainty ('Your house was in Westerzeile. . . . No, your house was on Osterzeile'); the narrator's habit of referring to Mahlke in both the second and the third person in the course of the same sentence; the coy refusal to name the Knight's Cross except by some circumlocution, 'that very special article, the abracadabra, the magnet, the exact opposite of an onion . . . the thingumajig, the Iwillnotutterit'. Mahlke himself remains a cluster of reiterated physical traits: 'as for his soul, it was never introduced to me. In the end, all I really had to go by was his neck and its numerous counterweights'—and perhaps his sexual member. Again, that curious mixture of obsessive fascination and blank absence of interest. The parts are manipulated with loving care: the whole crumbles before our eyes.

Less than a quarter the length of *The Tin Drum*, this second novel requires a far greater effort to get through. Much of the time it reads like a parody, perhaps by Mary McCarthy, of the extremer productions of a Creative Writing School. More like that—though I may be wrong, my observations are based solely on the translation, and I hope I am—than a basic document in the German literary renaissance.

Uwe Johnson

Was it the momentous intention behind *Speculations about Jakob* which gained it the Prix des Editeurs, or its achievement as a novel? We shall hope that it was the intention which was honoured, though some of us might suspect meanly that it was the achievement which impressed. For obscurity is again or still the hallmark of quality, and a profitable working motto for new novelists would be Make it Hard.

Jakob is a young but responsible railwayman in East Germany, in a city on the Elbe. His adopted sister Gesine is working for Nato in 'the other Germany'. His mother moves her residence from the East to the West. Jakob, Gesine and Jonas, an intellectual teaching philology in East Berlin, are all under surveillance by Herr Rohlfs, a conscientious agent of the East German state. Jakob visits his mother in the West. On his return to the East he is killed by a train while crossing the tracks as was his custom.

It is here that the book begins. Various people—it is usually difficult and sometimes impossible to tell who they are—speculate on Jakob's death, and necessarily on his life. It was a foggy night. It could have been an accident. Jakob was an experienced railwayman, able to sense a train miles away. It could have been suicide. It could have been elimination.

This is a mystery with little cloak about it and no dagger at all. For once the complaint might be indeed that the book is excessively unsensational. Herr Rohlfs is a not unsympathetic figure. He acts according to his lights, he believes in order and obligation and grows petulant at the spectacle of 'everybody leading his life as though he hadn't been told what to do'. This sentence is the 'crudest' of Johnson's explicit criticisms of Herr Rohlfs' State. No one is really unsympathetic. 'Is it tolerable that reality takes place,' says (or thinks) doubting Jonas, 'and we censure it according to its adherence to or infraction of theoretical rules?' This question is the nearest we come to an epitome of the book's thesis. On the last page Jonas stretches out his wrists for the handcuffs of Herr Rohlfs. This is the book's most dramatic moment.

What times we live in! The rueful exclamation comes equally from Herr Rohlfs and from the suspects he is watching. In other times Jakob and Herr Rohlfs could have been friends: as it is they are not precisely enemies. The taxi-driver who took Jakob and Gesine to the station tells Herr Rohlfs that the fare was seventy marks, but Gesine's account has it that he charged them eighty-five. It is not the times that are out of joint in this particular, but human nature—perhaps with the implication that no State, however efficient, and no political philosophy, however comprehensive, can quite contain the old Adam.

The reader will be grateful for the blurb's assurance that the fog in which he wanders is 'the very climate of life under Communism' and not the result of his own stupidity. Uwe Johnson, though, is less party-spirited and less precisely censorious than the blurb. We hear nothing positively good from him about West Germany or Western democracy. He is certainly not catering to hot or cold warriors. *Speculations about Jakob* is not political, except in being anti-political. Its villain is ideology, ideology carried to such extremes of theoreticalness and given such all-embracing terms of reference that it perverts at all levels the individual lives in its charge without managing to control them. Yet at times it would seem that Johnson is looking at the situation from the opposite viewpoint as well: grand ideals are perverted though not entirely overthrown by grubby realities. The taxi-driver is not a good socialist, he cheats and lies.

The author, says the blurb, 'is concerned not with a portrayal of confusion, but with confusion itself'. Exactly, and there the trouble lies. We cannot interest ourselves in confusion unless we can understand it: Johnson *should* have portrayed, he should have portrayed in the way that art does and must portray, understandingly. If none of the characters here is really unsympathetic, neither is any of them really sympathetic. They remain determinedly enigmatic. Now—to put it crudely, which Johnson never does—the theoretical implication of this may be that under a totalitarian régime people dare not reveal themselves to others, they must cultivate enigma. Or that in a situation where two political systems confront each other, and neither seems acceptable and there is no third alternative in view, then some people will consider it useless to—or more proper not to—reveal their thoughts and feelings, their misgivings and desires. But it is easy enough to justify Johnson's procedure in abstract terms like this: and as one does so, one finds oneself admiring one's own ingenuity and hence admiring the novel restrospectively, one's self-concocted idea of the novel. For alas the novel is a form of art. We cannot for long excite ourselves over the fate of enigmas. If they do not reveal themselves to the reader, how can the reader tell that they dare not reveal themselves? Can such figures be the *victims* of a total ideology? The reader, while he is reading, is likely to feel that they are made to measure for such an existence, they exactly deserve the politics they have got.

The style of the book is consistently rebarbative; it is clearly Johnson's style, not the responsibility of the translator, who seems to have gone to great pains to reproduce the painfulness of the original. Johnson cuts abruptly from one group of speakers to another, from the present to the past, and he serves up too many speculations to too few facts. He is wilfully obscure, wilfully abstract, for occasionally a character threatens rather splendidly to come alive, as when Gesine is describing Herr Rohlfs. 'The way he barks at the waiter. Like a sick Great Dane who hasn't had enough sleep.' Jakob, for all the speculation devoted to him, has no more than the makings of a likeable young man. The most vital presence in the book—reminding us of Günter Grass's dust-jacket—is a cat.

If we take 'theory' as the villain of *Speculations about Jakob* and 'life' as the hero, then the book turns out a very sad one. For the villain wins. But this is another way of saying that the theme of the work is truly serious and urgent and it would be a very considerable novel indeed if only it were readable.

Heinrich Böll

'What portion in the world can the artist have,' asked Yeats, 'but dissipation and despair?' Hans Schnier, the hero of Heinrich Böll's latest novel *The Clown*, doesn't take to dissipation—he is an innocent, a pure person, irretrievably monogamous, and cognac costs money—nor completely to despair. The book ends with him begging outside Bonn Railway Station, the first coin falling into his hat. Charity? But he is singing for his supper. And rather the charity of passing individuals than a retainer, a grant, a subsidy. For this way no group, no institution, no party is buying the clown and his services.

The novel begins with the 27-year-old clown arriving in Bonn, down on his luck, with a swollen knee and without his beloved Marie. The Catholics have seduced Marie away from him, persuaded her to marry one of Them and thus (in Schnier's view) to commit adultery, double adultery even, since (he tells himself) she will surely return to him one day. Alone in his room, between making telephone calls to various acquaintances who might help him, he recalls the past. Such is the form of the novel.

Lacking action in the usual sense of the word, yet *The Clown* moves with a remarkable purposiveness, its constituents working singlemindedly together. Possibly for this reason it may not prove altogether acceptable. The sensitive contemporary reader

prefers to be knocked flat by a velvet glove and there is perhaps
too much iron in evidence here. I think it is the case that the irony
is rather too insistent. So many of Schnier's acquaintances have
suffered a postwar sea-change into something not so strange
though certainly rich enough. His mother, once so zealous that
the 'Jewish Yankees' should be driven from 'our sacred German
soil', is now president of the Executive Committee of the Societies
for the Reconciliation of Racial Differences and 'lectures to
American women's clubs about the remorse of German youth'.
Brühl, a schoolmaster of Blood-and-Soil tendencies, is now a
professor at a Teachers' Training College, a man known for his
'courageous political past': he never actually joined the Nazi
Party. Schnitzler, instrumental in forcing the young Schnier into
the Hitler Youth, wrote a bad novel about a fair-haired French
lieutenant and a dark-haired German girl which incurred the
displeasure of the National Socialist Writers' Association (a careless use of the palette) and caused him to be suspended from
writing for some ten months: the Americans welcomed him as
a resistance fighter, 'gave him a job in their cultural information service, and today he is running all over Bonn telling all
and sundry that he was banned under the Nazis'. These are
people with whom (it is made plain, plainer than necessary)
you cannot communicate. You ask them a personal question and
you get a party answer. They are not interested in helping lone
clowns.

Böll takes his epigraph from Romans xv. 'To whom he was
not spoken of, they shall see: and they that have not heard shall
understand.' Paul had been preaching the gospel where Christ's
name was unknown, where he could not build upon another
man's foundation. Schnier is a gifted mime, he could make an
excellent living in Leipzig with his 'Cardinal' or 'Board Meeting'
turn, and in Bonn with his 'Party Conference Elects its Presidium'
or 'Cultural Council Meets' act. But the trouble is, he wants to
do the latter numbers in Leipzig and the former in Bonn: he

apparently lacks 'audience-sense'. 'To poke fun at Boards of
Directors where Boards of Directors don't exist seems pretty
low': and the same with Elections of Presidiums where presidiums
are not elected. There is an obvious parallel here with Schrella's
story in Böll's previous novel, *Billiards at Half-past Nine*. A
refugee from the Nazis, Schrella was imprisoned in Holland for
threatening a Dutch politician who said that all Germans ought
to be killed. When the Germans came in they freed him, a
martyr for Germany, but then realized that he was on their list of
wanted persons, so he had to escape to England. In England he
was imprisoned for threatening an English politician who said
that all Germans should be killed and only their works of art
saved. The clown's job is not to confirm but to disturb, to preach
to the unconverted. Böll's further gloss on the text from Romans
would seem to have it that, in the world as it is, *real* Christian
feeling exists outside the Churches, *real* socialism outside the
socialist parties, *real* concern for racial harmony and *real* chances
of it outside the Executive Committee of the Societies for the
Reconciliation of Racial Differences. . . . And, perhaps, *real*
married love outside the marriage certificate.

Schnier then is an active non- or anti-party man, not merely
an elegant ironist on the side-line. How he behaves as an artist
consorts exactly with how he feels as a man. Art should be free—but
that doesn't mean that art exists for the sake of art. He abandons a
highly successful number called 'The General'—and perhaps this
makes him no artist at all?—because after the first performance he
is visited by the widow of a general killed in battle, 'a little old
woman'. There are generals who are good men, or there are
good widows of generals, or pathetic little old women. Similarly,
however bitterly Schnier feels the defection of Marie, he admits
that there are Catholics who are good men, indeed he admires
Pope John immensely. It is Catholic*ism* he is against, the party
line, the party men, the people who begin sentences with the
words, 'We Catholics . . .', just as he is against those who begin

their sentences, 'We Protestants . . .', 'We Atheists . . .', 'We Socialists . . .', We Germans . . .' and so forth. He will never make a 'great satirical artist', because he refuses to generalize, because 'strangely enough I like the kind to which I belong: people'. Life is indeed hard for a clown unless he is prepared to toe a Clown party line of one sort or another.

The rhetorician seeks to deceive his neighbour, Yeats said, the sentimentalist to deceive himself. Böll deals nimbly with his rhetoricians, but his clown is something of a sentimentalist, perhaps, a little too sorry for himself. In his lamentations for Marie he grows maudlin: a clown should be able to cut his losses, to shoulder a broken heart and march on. But the sorrows of unrequited monogamy are a rare phenomenon in current fiction, and it may be that our conditioning inevitably makes them seem embarrassing. Elsewhere I am more sure that Böll's tact has forsaken him. Our sympathies go astray when Schnier informs us that his mother (on whom we are already fully informed) was a ban-the-bomb campaigner for three days until a business friend told her this policy would lead to a slump in the stock market. At times Böll can be strident, as when Schnier thinks of the people who helped Marie and him in their hard times 'while at home they sat huddled over their stinking millions, had cast me out and gloated over their moral reasons'. Possibly explicitness of this order, this insistence, is intended as a guard against a self-indulgent or merely self-protective irony, against that habit of 'keeping your superiority feelings fresh in a refrigerator of irony', as a character in *Billiards at Half-past Nine* puts it. Böll doesn't want his novel read as a cosy, remote 'allegory', a mere parable about The Creative Artist in Relation to Church and State in an Age of Technology (to borrow a lecture-title from his earlier book, *Tomorrow and Yesterday*) or the Condition of Twentieth-Century Man (who is never you or me). Every now and then a clown must be allowed to be very simple and straightforward and unsophisticated.

Böll has something to say, and not of course merely something about the Germans. He says it several times. A common weakness of writers with something to say is their inability to understand that saying it four times is not necessarily four times as effective as saying it once. But to have something to say—how rare this is! Unlike Uwe Johnson in *Speculations about Jakob*, Böll doesn't erect reading-difficulty into a law; although retaining the flash-back technique of *Billiards at Half-past Nine*, this new novel is less gratuitously involuted, with a positive stylishness of clarity and competency, and free from fussiness. Unlike Günter Grass, Böll doesn't obscure his real meaning with a barrage of private emblems. Unlike certain British comtemporaries, he doesn't seek to obscure the absence of meaning with an aura of bogus 'symbolism', to disguise as high metaphysics a bedroom farce or an Arabian Nights' sexual dream. 'I would rather read Rilke, Hofmannsthal and Newman one by one than have someone mix me a kind of syrup out of all three,' remarks Schnier apropos of a sermon by an 'artistic' prelate. There are few novels coming out these days which aren't either a kind of syrup or a kind of emetic. *The Clown*, I have omitted to mention, besides being one of these few, is at times very funny, as well as sad, as well as salutary.

Dog Years: Günter Grass's Third Novel

IMPRISONED in Grass's new and corpulent book a thinner but very considerable novel is struggling to get out. The question, which I find difficult to answer with much confidence, is: does it manage to emerge? There is no end of excess fat for it to cut a way through: at the same time it is a muscular piece of flesh and blood, endowed with sharp teeth, at least thirty-two of them.

Dog Years, stretching from the early 1920's up to 1957, falls into three sections. The first, narrated by Herr Brauxel, owner of a very special sort of mine, deals with the childhood of the two main figures, Amsel and Matern, who become blood-brothers with the help of a penknife, though Amsel turns out (when such things start to matter) to be half-Jewish. At this time however, Matern, the tough, the sportsman, protects Amsel, the plump clever boy (artistic too, he creates prodigious scarecrows) from the other lads. This section could even be said to possess a good deal of simple charm.

The second book, a hefty slab of 230 pages, takes the form of letters addressed by Liebenau, a slightly younger man, to his cousin Tulla, the Tulla Pokriefke of Grass's previous novel, *Cat and Mouse*, and carries the narrative up to 1945. Liebenau is a rather drab, rather feeble person, Tulla is a fearsome wench, quite a creation in her own right, but having little to do with the essential story of Amsel and Matern. This second section is terribly hard going. Grass appears to have been influenced by the question-and-answer sequence of *Ulysses*; the epistolary form is irritatingly 'literary' and the reiterated fairy-tale formula—those hundreds of paragraphs beginning 'There was once . . .'—creates portentousness rather than power or pathos. Many a reader will fall by the way, which is a great pity, since it is here that the central event of the novel is recounted. Nine masked S.A. youths climb over Amsel's fence, knock out the fat sheeny's teeth, all thirty-two of them, and roll him in the snow. Eight of the assistants are named, the ninth (it is plain to the reader, though not to Matern) is Matern. When the snowman melts, out steps a thin young man, who heads for a dentist and thirty-two gold teeth, who survives, who in fact eventually becomes a mine-owner, the owner of a mine which (we are told with stultifying frequency) 'produces neither potash nor iron nor coal'. Grass's overwhelming taste for the allegorical, or perhaps we should rather say the quasi-allegorical, betrays him into doubling this transformation scene with the sea-change of Jenny, the fat little would-be ballet dancer, who is rolled into a snowball by nasty Tulla, and emerges as a thin ballet dancer when the snow melts. What is Jenny doing in the book? Just another figure, you may say, featuring legitimately on so large a canvas, with no need to 'do' anything in the book. But she loses her toes in an air-raid, and we last see her in her bar 'Chez Jenny', a faded spinster, serving her special lemonade to Goldmouth (or Brauxel, or Amsel of course), a well-to-do mine-owner with a chronic hoarseness which (though Matern attributes it to excessive smoking) he traces to a certain January snowfall. . . . The lemonade contains several drops of a magic essence, a Gipsy recipe—Jenny was a Gipsy orphan—and also a little mica—Jenny's adoptive father, the schoolteacher Dr Brunies, was a keen collector of mica stones. Once you have started an allegory, it is difficult to stop it.

The third section, related by anti-Fascist Matern, tells of Matern's search for vengeance in postwar Germany. The pace accelerates: there is no risk of the reader falling by the way now, he is swept splendidly along. The addresses of ex-Nazi wrong-doers—small-shots or at the most medium-shots—are revealed to Matern among the graffiti on the wall of the Gents lavatory in Cologne Central Station. He sleeps with the first culprit's wife and with the daughter of number two; since in the case of number three no wife or daughter is available, Matern kills his pet canary;

the fourth he punishes by throwing his stamp collection into the fire. . . . Matern acquires gonorrhoea and during the next six months distributes it freely over West Germany—'the milk of vengeance'—with special attention to the female relatives of former Nazi officials. Denazification he calls it. He attempts to wreak vengeance on Martin Heidegger too—what did all that talk of Being and Nothing do, except help people to convince themselves that there wasn't a bad smell, or if there was, then it didn't come from that pile of bones, or if it did, then the bones weren't human bones?—but only succeeds in wrenching off the philosopher's gate and throwing it into the philosopher's garden. The philosopher himself is as abstract, as evasive, as his philosophy.

But vengeance is growing thin—'Who wants to tear open old wounds if the opening of wounds gives pleasure?'—and, in the Germany of the economic miracle, Matern is growing fat and scant of breath. Grass is clearly wise in thus de-demonizing the avenger. For what form could vengeance appropriately take? And who is the man who could administer it? Not, at any rate, Matern, who has belonged to both sides. There is a nice reference in a young people's 'open and dynamic' radio discussion to 'Adolf Hitler, builder of the Reichsautobahn'. It is as if the Ghost of Banquo found himself offered the seat of honour, given a good wash and haircut, plied with beer and schnapps and complaisant female relatives, and taken out to night-clubs on expense accounts. . . .

This section is full of marvellous set-pieces, and on the whole the symbolic (the fairy-tale, the allegorical) and the realistic manage to co-exist fairly comfortably. Thus the fashionable new night-club, 'The Morgue', where the customers eat off genuine operating tables with genuine dissecting instruments, the waiters wear surgeon's robes and masks and rubber gloves, and the bill has the form of a death certificate. Prepared to wreck the joint, Matern is upset by the pudding, a dentition-shaped affair to be tackled with spatula-shaped instruments, and vomits his guts out in the toilet. 'A lot of people get that way the first time,' the attendant assures him. 'Take some strong coffee and a slug of schnapps and you'll be all right.'

Grass's last novel, *Cat and Mouse*, was something of a give-away, I thought, a piece of work so thin that its 'allegorical' skeleton obtruded, in a way it didn't in the dense composition of *The Tin Drum*—and alas its bones could be seen to lack articulation, its symbols were too often wantonly private. *Dog Years* is an altogether more powerful work, with a recovered density of detail and documentation, but it has no cohesive presence to match that of Oskar the dwarf drummer. Matern and Amsel are not dwarfs, but men. The dwarf (who makes a number of inoperative appearances in this new novel) was an outsider: Matern and Amsel are insiders, and therefore (given Grass's symbolizing stress) 'representative'. Disbelief is not so readily suspended here; fantasy demands, more imperatively than in *The Tin Drum*, to be reconciled with realism, the individual story with national history, the 'symbolic' with what it symbolizes. And the reconciliation cannot always be made—at least, cannot always be seen to be made.

Central to the book, it would seem, is the idea of the blood-brotherhood of German and Jew, with emphasis laid on the blood as well as the brotherhood. Each needs the other, the German the Jew, the brotherhood the blood. This is represented parable-wise in the faustball business. Amsel was the 'born play maker', the middleman, the arranger, the brains, while the 'unstoppable' Matern piled up the points. If the symbolism is acceptable here it is largely because of the expertize Grass displays, he *knows* about faustball. Perhaps the idea is acceptable too. Matern believes too easily, he is receptive to myth; Amsel is disbelieving, Matern's only expressed objection to him is that 'nothing was sacred to him'. Each is necessary to the other. The situation offers the possibility of mutual aid and correction—also of murder. But the associated idea, that the Jew *wants* to be beaten up—Amsel had always desired gold teeth instead of those drab natural things, and the forged passport obtained some weeks in advance of 'the miracle in the snow' mentions as a distinguishing mark his 'Artificial denture. Gold crowns'—this seems merely disgusting. Matern is forever grinding his teeth, he is known as the Grinder (the deep tortured Teutonic soul, Wagnerian percussion?), whereas Amsel throws his teeth away and is proud to be known as Goldmouth (the sophisticated, un-natural, gilt-edged Jew?). It seems merely a sick joke, a mere extension (if that) of an old racist theory.

One readily understands the difficulty Grass faces. He doesn't want just to write another 'anti-Nazi' book: *that* has long since become a heavy industry, a respectable profession, everybody is against atrocities. Indeed, 'satire' is universally fashionable. . . . At the same time Grass *is* appalled by what was done in the name of Nazism, and by all that has been forgotten in the name of reconstruction and economic recovery. Do we forget because we must—or because we will? One solution, especially congenial to Grass's gifts, is to glance sideways at the horrors, through the eyes of children. 'Bet you that's a human bone. . . .' Another expedient is to fall back on the ambiguities, the pedantic word-play, the experimental techniques of what was once called 'modernism'. In an essay in *Commentary* for May 1964, which I recommend by way of remedying the certain deficiencies and possible injustices of this present account, George Steiner has remarked on Grass's recourse to the late 1920's and the consequent 'outmoded flavour of his audacities'. The German economic miracle had no counterpart in literature: *there* the lost ground has taken longer to make up.

But too often Grass seeks to extricate himself from this central difficulty—the problem, to put it simply, of dealing freshly and feelingly with a numbed subject—by means of a calculated vacillation between the grim and the farcical, between the portentously 'significant' and the unrelated *tour de force*, between realism and fantasy. Symbolic-smelling red herrings lure the reader off on wild-goose chases, and allegorical hounds, let off their leashes, howl oracularly and then disappear into thin air.

Mystification lies thickly about the identity of Herr Brauxel (or Brauksel or Brauchsel), the opening narrator, and is simultaneously rendered senseless by the broad demystificatory hints which accompany the mystification. Matern poisons Harras, the fine German shepherd who sired Hitler's favourite dog. Why? Because Harras 'symbolizes' Nazism? Nonsense, Harras is just a dog. Throughout, a symbolic italicizing goes hand in hand with an apparently deliberate blurring of the print, so that one asks in bewilderment whether Grass is striving to sharpen his meaning or seeking to prevent it from emerging.

This obsessive play with motifs and emblems goes on even in the concluding pages, the *Walpurgisnacht* as Steiner calls it, when Brauxsel-Haseloff-Goldmouth-Amsel takes Matern on a tour of the mine which 'produces neither potash nor iron nor coal'. The cable of the pit cage is made of 'seven times thirty-two wire strands wound round a hemp-clad steel core', and the mine (which, Matern says, is 'hell, indeed') consists of thirty-two stalls (or circles): the magic number is the number of Amsel's lost, or found, teeth. Incidentally, what the mine produces, and very profitably since there is a world-wide market, is mechanical scarecrows, representing by sound and movement the cardinal human emotions and actions, weeping, laughing, hating, copulating, philosophizing, practising democracy, playing games, conducting business. . . . 'This meticulously organized inferno,' as its owner describes it, is an incredible *tour de force*. But what otherwise is it? Not a hell for people at all, not even for other people. It is, and that is the trouble, *incredible*, a gratuitous act of the imagination: incredible, where the apparition of the Devil to Leverkühn in Thomas Mann's *Doctor Faustus* is, incredibly, credible.

Reviewing the novel on its original appearance, a writer in the *Times Literary Supplement* contrasted Grass's deliberate 'demythologizing, de-heroizing and, as he puts it, de-demonizing' of Nazism with the 'demonizing' of it which Mann performed in *Doctor Faustus*. Mann thus 'paid a paradoxical tribute' to the 'perverse appeal' of Nazism, whereas Grass's task has been 'the more difficult and more effective task of exposing its vulgar shoddiness from the inside'. I am not altogether sure that de-demonizing is what Grass is invariably doing here. There is some ambiguous Wagnerianism in the novel; the Virgin Mary appears to Matern and exhorts him to poison the dog Harras; and Brauxel's mine may owe a little to the Devil's account of Hell (and the concentration camps) in *Doctor Faustus*: '. . . the thick-clotted diapason of trills and chirps lured from this everlasting dispensation of the unbelievable combined with the irresponsible . . .'.

Nor, which is more to the point, is it so certain that de-demonizing is 'more effective'—if by that is meant salutary—than Mann's so-called demonizing. The account of his pupils denouncing Dr Brunies for not hanging a flag out on the Führer's birthday, while again one can understand Grass not wishing to make a song and dance about it, is even cosy. Heinrich Böll's novels achieve a degree of de-mythologizing with much less ado and with more clarity, which I would have thought indispensable to de-mythologizing. And, in as far as such an exercise is right and proper, hasn't the de-demonizing of Nazism and the exposure of its 'vulgar shoddiness' been carried out more effectively than any novel could do it by Adolf Eichmann? 'I sat at my desk and got on with my job. . . .'

No, for all Grass's violence and for all Mann's heavy nine-teenth-century elegance, *Doctor Faustus* strikes one as having been written in blood and tears and *Dog Years* in ink and poster-paint. I think Grass is often at his best when scurrilous, when he is lashing out with a rough and angry tongue, but Mann can make him look actually genteel. All the same, *Dog Years* is a staggering performance. With such energy and inventiveness it can afford or very nearly afford some major failures of form and uncertainties of intention. I still feel, though, that like Amsel and Jenny, the book could profitably have spent a few hours inside a snowman, having some of its excess fat boiled out.

Aimez-vous Goethe?: an Enquiry into English Attitudes of Non-liking towards German Literature

'Naturellement, you think I have in mind your ferocious discipline, and que vous enchaînez votre art dans un système de règles inexorables et néo-classiques, forcing it to move in these iron bands—if not with grace, yet with boldness and esprit. But if it is that that I mean, I mean at the same time more than that when I speak of your qualité d'Allemand; I mean—how shall I put it?—a certain four-squareness, rhythmical heaviness, immobility, grossièreté, which are old-German—en effet, entre nous, one finds them in Bach too. Will you take offence at my criticism? Non, j'en suis sûr—you are too great. Your themes—they consist almost throughout of even note values, minims, crotchets, quavers; true enough, they are syncopated and tied but for all that they remain clumsy and unwieldy, often with a hammering, machine-like effect. C'est "boche" dans un degré fascinant. Don't think I am finding fault, it is simply énormément caractéristique, and in the series of concerts of international music which I am arranging, this note is quite indispensable. . . .'

(Fitelberg, the impresario, *Doctor Faustus*)

Introduction: Not all English non-likers of German literature non-like it for all of the reasons about to be cited, of course. Nor should it be assumed that these various reasons are all equally reasonable, or unreasonable. They are all real reasons in that they exist, at least.

(1) Since the essence of scholarship lies in its exhaustiveness, its refusal to leave anything unsaid, no matter how obvious it might seem to the layman, we must commence with the following proposal: Many English people do not like literature of any sort, not even English literature. Further, among those who like English literature—indeed, among those who must like English

literature a lot, since they make their living out of it—there are many who don't like foreign literature of any sort: on the grounds that it is foreign to them, they are innocents abroad, they might be horribly hoodwinked by a false rhythm or a corrupt metaphor.[1]

(2) Research indicates that the commonest or most commonly-voiced English objection to German literature has it that this literature is wordy, philosophical, humourless, highly abstract and crammed with details. In brief, heavy-handed. The objection comes equally from those who have read some German literature and from those who haven't read any because they know it is wordy, highly abstract, crammed with details, etc. Largely it derives from atavistic memories of Goethe and a nervous perusal of the opening pages of *Buddenbrooks*. If this is not altogether an idle prejudice, it is (especially as regards the two writers referred to) an unfortunate one. The German mind appears to be naturally more ruminative than the English—and more pedagogic. We like our novelists to arrive; the Germans are content to watch their novelists travelling hopefully, slowly and instructively. Thus all the landscape gardening in Goethe's *Die Wahlverwandt-schaften* (*Elective Affinities*)—though it must be granted that this particular item might carry the implication that human relationships cannot be as neatly planned as an estate. (A piece of symbolism too gross by far for our sensitive British stomachs.) Thus all the discursuses and excursuses of *Faust*, or of Thomas Mann's novels. (The greatest European novelist of the twentieth century? Thomas Mann, alas!) Thus *Wilhelm Meister*, that cultural hitch-hiker, of which work Goethe is reported to have said, 'I should think a rich manifold life, brought close to our eyes, would be enough without any express tendency, which, after all, is only for the intellect'. (But then, Goethe was an old fox by anybody's standards, and often contrived to eat his cake and moralize over it.)

[1] For the opposite or 'libertarian' point of view see Professor Enright, 'Reflections on Foreign Literature', *Addictions*, p. 12 f.

How one longs to edit Mann's *Doctor Faustus* and *The Magic Mountain*, to render them digestible to our dainty and civilized appetites! (And yet how much of them would we dare—or even want—to throw out when we came to it, when we had actually read the books with the care required of an editor?)

The English reader of novels tends to have a high opinion of himself (fair enough, he *reads*!): he reckons he can do without the trimmings, the writer can leave a whole lot to his imagination: he has grown up into a 60,000-words man. It has been said that the distinctively German contribution to the Novel is the *Bildungs-roman*,[1] detailed, digressive, with no clearly defined terms of reference, and a long time in the building. *Doctor Faustus* was described by its English translator (a translator whose like, whatever complaints we might make of her work, we may well not see again) as a 'cathedral of a book'—an apt metaphor, if we allow that a cathedral can house the Devil as well. (A lot of little dogs have lifted their legs against *this* cathedral, too.) The British reader prefers a neat and tidy chapel of a book.

(3) The charge of humourlessness calls for closer inspection. 'What the German thinks exquisitely ludicrous, is to a Frenchman, or an Englishman, generally of mediocre mirthfulness,' wrote G. H. Lewes in 1855. 'Wit requires delicate handling; the Germans generally touch it with gloved hands. Sarcasm is with them too often a sabre not a rapier, hacking the victims where a thrust would suffice.' True, humour with the Germans tends to run to extremes, either boorish slapstick or else high rarefaction. As with the Japanese, a whole middle range of comedy seems inaccessible to them. This is indeed a sad deficiency, both in literature—if only Rilke could have laughed at himself, if only one of Rilke's ladies could have laughed at him!—and also in life, many of whose frictions are most tactfully palliated by the lubricant of an easy, natural, middle-register sort of humour.

[1] Which makes the Germans the inventors of what we now call the 'anti-hero', perhaps.

What is also sad is that the English reader, missing the sort of sense of humour to which he is accustomed and which he traditionally prizes, assumes the absence of humour of any species. Mann's stateliness, the deliberation and meticulousness with which he builds up his world, seem only pomposity to us, a laboriousness which we quickly characterize as 'Teutonic'.[1] (*Il est bête—oui, si l'on veut, mais comme l'Himalaya.*) Having made up our minds on this point with characteristic firmness, then, despite our characteristic sense of humour, we fail to sense Mann's own characteristic brand of humour, an irony too complex to attempt to analyse here, the very presence of Mann himself in his work. (Or we assume Dr Thomas Mann's presence in Dr Serenus Zeitblom, a sheep in sheep's clothing, and grow peevish when at last we are forced to admit that the two doctors don't quite agree.) We fancy we have taken *Doctor Faustus* by storm, we have simply failed to note that (in Professor Erich Heller's words) '*Doctor Faustus* is . . . its own critique, and that in the most thorough-going manner imaginable. There is no critical thought which the book does not think *about itself*'.[2]

(4) Arising out of the previous point: it would seem that in German fiction the author tends to be rather obtrusive; he orders the material around in parade-ground fashion, he deafens us with his stentorian comments on his characters and incidents. Eckermann reports Goethe as having said, 'Germans are strange people. By their profound thoughts and ideas, which they look for everywhere and which they insert into everything, they burden

[1] Hans Magnus Enzensberger's essay, 'In Search of the Lost Language' (*Encounter*, September 1963), seeks to define the English use of the word 'Teutonic': 'The wealth of associations attached to this word is considerable. They range from the primaeval forest to the study of Dr Faustus, from bearskins to Hegel's *Phenomenology of Spirit*. Castles and fortresses are Teutonic, but so are abstract terminologies. Wagner's operas and long complex sentences are Teutonic. Leather shorts, bull necks, and exaggerated studiousness are Teutonic. The Teutons are boring, have sweaty feet, and moreover are most unfairly "daemonic".' This definition is far from complete.
[2] *The Ironic German.*

their lives more than is proper.' Yet this remark ought to alert us to something in Goethe at any rate—whom *primus inter pares* we think of as inserting profundities into everything and making the reader's life a burden to him—which doesn't quite chime with our conception of him. That he is 'Godlike' we know, but there is also something oddly Mephistophelean about his interventions in his own work. Alas, we expect our rebels, our outsiders, to proclaim their dispositions, unequivocally whether by dissipation and despair, drugs and divorce, or syntactical eccentricities and misuse of commas. When Goethe misbehaves we don't notice it: we just can't believe that he isn't continuously Godlike, sublime, prudent, four-square and a bore. Our notion of German literature is certainly not baseless, but it is based on a set of lowest common factors.

(5) The German novelist does not scruple to be 'symbolic' in a way that strikes us as grossly naïve and naïvely gross.[1] An associated complaint will be that German writers are heavily aphoristic, self-appointed sages of some small provincial Weimar or other, each having an eye to the school textbook market. The English reader resents and distrusts this habit: a moral tendency should be implicit, not explicit, enacted, not announced: never trust the artist, trust the tale—and alas the artist seems to be everywhere in the tale! To make matters worse, in some of the authors more celebrated though still unread, the aphorisms appear to contradict one another and thus to cancel out. It is infuriating to have to complain, for example of *Faust*, that the work is at the same time insistently symbolic and not symbolic enough, that the poor reader is forever being got at and finally is left in the lurch. For all the heaviness and earnestness of German writers, some of them permit themselves an elusiveness and an irony which arouse grave misgivings in us. We expect the

---

[1] Cf. the verdict of the *New Yorker* in 1947 on the English translation of Elias Canetti's *Die Blending* (*Auto-da-fé*): 'Overstuffed, highly complex novel, rigid with symbolism in the best German tradition.'

monumental to stand still. There is a real difficulty here for English readers, whether of Goethe, of Thomas Mann or of Günter Grass, and unhappily no easy solution proposes itself: the only proof of these large puddings is in the eating, and sampling won't work, you may have to eat the whole thing.

(6) Another aspect of this difficulty is the frequent mingling in German literature of fantasy and realism, of the elephantine tread and the faery footstep. German scholars seem more addicted to categorization than their British colleagues—yet German writers are readier to mix categories, less embarrassed by the allegorical, than are we, with our stronger sense of humour (or more nervous one) and our greater sophistication (or more potent philistinism). Similarly disconcerting is the element of piety, reverence—'*Seid nur fromm* . . .'—seen most obviously (blatantly?) in the 'Confessions of a Beautiful Soul', which comprise Book VI of the otherwise morally ambiguous *Wilhelm Meister*, and seen in the disquisition on funeral monuments in the rather scandalous context of *Elective Affinities,* in the poet of the *Roman Elegies* tapping out hexameters on the naked back of his Roman mistress, pervasively and despite his irony, in Mann's references to great men and great works—and perhaps, for all I can tell, in Canetti's dealings with classical Chinese culture in *Auto-da-fé.* This *Frömmigkeit*, especially in association with *Gemütlichkeit*, can strike the English reader as hypocrisy (*Frömmelei* in German, incidentally), as in some contexts the very nastiest brand of sentimentality—like the commandant of a concentration camp having solemn thoughts about the sunset.[1]

The German novel has been less securely removed from poetry than the English novel. H. M. Waidson sums up the *Elective*

[1] I now read in H. M. Enzensberger (*op. cit.*): 'The S.S.-officer who carried Hölderlin in his knapsack and the concentration-camp commandant who played Schubert sonatas "*nach Feierabend*" (when "off duty") were by no means legends; these were the consequences of a "life of the mind" for which the "higher values", for which *Bildung* has always been a fig leaf to cover betrayal to those in power.'

Affinities as 'a novel by a great poet; it contains questioning and acceptance, defiance and resignation, sophistication and innocence, irony and reverence'. For a novel, we may be inclined to feel, it contains far too much. But our great poets don't usually write novels. Günter Grass on his present showing could conceivably be an English poet, but hardly an English novelist (unless perhaps a painter writing a novel). Canetti couldn't possibly be an English novelist. Kafka couldn't even be an Englishman.

Again, there is no simple test of failure or success, legitimacy or otherwise, no portable touchstone. As we know, the adjective 'poetic', applied to a novel, can as easily be a term of abuse as of praise.

(7) Scholarship is not a bed of footnotes, and what could be more painful than to be compelled by scholarly honour to complain of scholars? I allude to the paucity of stimulating criticism or commentary on the part of British Germanists. With a few honourable exceptions, our Germanists are thoroughly academic, I mean uninformative. The standard acceptable in them seems to be well below the minimum level of discourse expected from specialists in English literature (even)—as if the ability to read German literature is already so remarkable that little more is to be asked from those who have gained it. British Germanists appear to have picked up from German *Anglisten* a deep horror of literary experience and a distaste for literary judgment. The situation is exacerbated by a shortage of criticism from the German side. Where are the great German critics? Judge not— is that what *Frömmigkeit* demands?—that ye be not judged. From my own brief experience of working in a German university—it may have been quite unrepresentative—I came to understand that the literary critic was a form of life only surpassed in vulgarity and frivolity by the creative writer. Learning is *Wissenschaft* is science: which means that the only true learning is philology, and perhaps (because it can be refined upon but hardly refuted)

literary categorizing Mann didn't have to go far to find his early idea of the writer as criminal—the degenerate who commits unscientific mayhem on sweet innocent words!

(8) Granted, a few of our Germanists have written feelingly about their subject, and some have made available to us timely and inexpensive editions of German writers. But the men who have done most for German literature in our time have been chiefly amateurs, chiefly translators. Rilke and Hölderlin were especially fortunate in their translators, one of them an *Anglist*, another a Germanist (but also by some administrative error a poet). C. F. MacIntyre and Louis MacNeice did more for Goethe in England and America than all the Bi-Centennial papers of 1949 put together. True, Goethe's lyrics remain an unsolved problem—the simpler they are, the more difficult to translate—and those translators of *Faust* who are at home with the humorous, sophisticated, Mephistophelean passages will be foxed by the 'nobility' of other parts, while those who succeed with the reflective sections—has anyone really succeeded?—may be defeated by the colloquial and mischievous note. Here, as elsewhere, Goethe's diversity of tone is the great stumbling block.

But clearly we cannot blame 'translation' in this general matter. It would be base cowardice to impute the relative neglect of Thomas Mann to his translators, and ridiculous to so ascribe the absolute neglect of Franz Werfel's *The Forty Days of Musa Dagh*. And among recent efforts—I mention only those which have reached me even in far-flung Singapore, where some twenty languages and dialects are spoken, but not German—we have Grass, Uwe Johnson's *Speculations about Jakob*, Hans Hellmut Kirst's *Officer Factory* (a German *Catch-22* which gets bogged down in pious thoughts about the Good German Soldier), Goethe's *Italian Journey* in a version by W. H. Auden and Elizabeth Mayer, the poetry and plays of Hugo von Hofmannsthal and (particularly the poetry) of Brecht, and the bilingual anthology, *Modern German Poetry 1910-1960*, edited by Michael

Hamburger and Christopher Middleton.[1]

(9) We are forced to take cognizance of another distasteful possibility: that in some cases non-admiration of German literature arises out of—or *is*—non-admiration of Germans. The factors operative in this latter phenomenon do not require to be aired. In the nineteenth century things were very different. German literature was eminently respectable, French wasn't.[2] Goethe's first biographer (or almost first) was an Englishman, and the consort of George Eliot. No doubt the associations evoked by the phrase 'French novel' still vary from circle to circle, but they will always be potent: the phrase 'German novel' draws forth either a groan or nothing.

An extra factor is often at work in our reading of a foreign literature. We tend to keep an eye open for racial characteristics; we read, if we are unfavourably disposed towards the country of origin, censoriously. We do not think of Quilp or Mr B. as typical Englishmen—but in reading foreign novels we incline to attribute the villain to the race, and more readily than we attribute the hero. In a similar spirit we read our own literature 'historically', that is tolerantly—witches are being burned, but it all happened long ago, and times have changed—whereas we admit the historical element into our consideration of a foreign literature only for damnatory purposes. 'A certain gay and noisy type of life is needed to make monkeys, parrots and coloured people tolerable around us,' we read in *Elective Affinities* (H. M. Waidson's translation, *Kindred by Choice*). Monkeys, parrots and coloured people! Shades of the *Herrenvolk* indeed!

[1] '. . . two poets who are also excellent linguists, two poets who know German—can they be found again in this part of the world?' (H. M. Enzensberger, *op. cit.*).

[2] With reservations, e.g. Matthew Arnold on Edmond Scherer ('A French Critic on Goethe'): '. . . his point of view is in many respects that of an Englishman. We mean that he has the same instinctive sense rebelling against what is verbose, ponderous, roundabout, inane,—in one word, *niais* or silly,—in German literature, just as a plain Englishman has.'

But in fact the speaker—a schoolmaster as reported in Ottilie's diary—is merely proposing, fairly harmlessly, that forms of life cannot with impunity be torn from their natural context, that a zoo is disquieting because it is not nature. And Ottilie supplies the corollary: 'No one can walk unpunished among palm-trees, and one's opinions must surely change in a country where elephants and tigers are at home'. Ah yes, the Englishman running to seed under a tropical sun! Ottilie continues, 'Only the scientific investigator of nature is worthy of respect, the man who is able to describe and depict what is most strange and exotic in its own element, its locality and its surroundings. How glad I should be if I could only once hear Humboldt relating his findings!' Well said, young (1808) lady!

(10) Finally it might be noted, in extenuation of our English unresponsiveness in this matter, that a number of Germans have failed to admire German literature, or have admired it temperately. Even Herr Enzensberger admits that 'there is no denying that German literature has very often gone a long way to meet the stupidity, presumption, and arrogance of its British critics'—if this sounds a shade discourteous, remember what the man said: '*Im Deutschen lügt man, wenn man höflich ist*'—and though he speaks severely of 'the limits of Anglo-Saxon taste', Herr Enzensberger doesn't himself seem to care much for German poetry written before 1950.[1] Thomas Mann remarked in *The Genesis of a Novel,* apropos of his ignorance of *Der grüne Heinrich,* that 'my youth had been shaped far more by European literature, Russian, French, Scandinavian, and English, rather than German'. And Professor Roy Pascal (*The German Novel*) tells us that 'even for Germans, to read the great German novels is mostly a "cultural task"—infinitely rewarding, I believe, but never likely to become a dangerous passion in the reader'.

[1] '. . . Rilke, Stefan George, and von Hofmannsthal (all of whom have a place in the *bürgerliche* literary pantheon though not among the German moderns) . . .' (*op. cit.*).

Conclusion: '*Interdum vulgus rectum videt, est ubi peccat.*' It would appear from our investigations, then, that the English are right not to like certain parts of German literature and wrong not to like other parts. Further than that it would be unsafe to go. In its carefulness, impartiality, fearlessness and self-effacement, this conclusion might seem a modest exemplification of true scholarship, and *énormément caractéristique* of *Wissenschaft*, perhaps.

IV

Engmalchin

DESPITE the relative smallness of the territories concerned, the Malayan Writers' Conference held in Singapore in 1962 involved a complicated job of organization. The participants numbered 116 (with 118 observers) and were divided into four groups by language: Malay, Chinese, Tamil and English. The Malay group consisted almost entirely of Malays, the Chinese group was solely Malayan Chinese and the Tamil group solely Malayan Indian, while the English group included Chinese, Malay, Indian and Eurasian Malayans, and even a few Englishmen. It would of course be obnoxious to compare the findings of the various groups as if to deduce 'racial' or 'linguistic' characteristics from them. Obnoxious, but interesting.

Two basic questions were asked at the outset. 'Is literature an activity valuable in itself?' and 'Does literature need to have the justification of social utility?'[1] Though the Malay group answered both questions in the affirmative, its members were far from tepid in their views. They found the functions of literature in Malaya (this was before the foundation of Malaysia) to be social, ethical, religious, political and otherwise didactic, and to include 'uniting the people of Malaya', 'opposing any form of colonialism and exploitation', and 'warding off yellow culture' (which somehow or other is generally associated with the English language). No frivolous claims were made on behalf of the freedom of the writer. The image of the Malay writer deriving from the Conference represents him as a stern, edgy and even aggressive fellow.

The behaviour of the Chinese group was very different: abstract, ingenious, alternately sophisticated and naïve, and

---

[1] *Report of the Malayan Writers' Conference, Singapore.* Dewan Bahasa dan Kebudayaan Kebangsaan Singapura.

evasive. The title (in English translation) of one of its working papers was 'The Fostering of Literary Youths to Strive for the Beautiful Future of Malaya'; and to those two leading questions 'It was agreed that Malayan literature was of great value in itself and it also possessed social utility'. Other statements from this group had it that 'Malayan Chinese should try to create a Malayan type of Chinese literature', and that 'writers must be sincere'. The group was strongly opposed to any sort of State control or interference except in the eradication of yellow culture (a conventional 'must' in a country which, though it has a rather high rape-rate, is extremely respectable and, in Singapore, even puritanical). Yet the group did not display any strong aesthetic proclivity. For one thing, Malayan writers 'should promote miscegenation or intermarriage of all races in order to secure better types in the second generation as long as Mendelian doctrine proves workable'. (On the whole Chinese families, say, are still less than eager to see their children marrying Indians, say, and when it is a question of Malays intermarrying, then Islam quickly rears its resolute neck.) Likewise, 'Malayan writers should advise the citizens to form normal families. They should never possess plural consorts such as concubines or any other form of polygynous or polyandrous members as to render the house discordant and deprived of peace.' Or how could the writer attain the required serenity? And,

> Malayan writers should guide people and help them in the invention and discovery of all articles for the improvement of human culture. Never should they be instigated to invent radiological weapons such as atomic bomb, hydrogen bomb, or neutron bomb. . . . They should never make biological or bacteriological weapons such as 'Q Fever' germs, nerves, and botulin or cobalt combinations. . . . It shall be the duty of Malaya to save civilization and the human species from destruction, and it is the duty of Malayan writers to direct them.

The Tamil group was thoughtful, too, interested in translation between the four languages and in literary criticism (a subject which drew very little attention from the Malays and Chinese) and practical-minded, and its members felt that self-control and ordinary morals on the part of the writer were preferable to State control. Their working papers were studded with references to A. C. Bradley, T. S. Eliot, I. A. Richards, Plato, Richard Eberhart, Stephen Spender and Katharine Anne Porter, and in their thoroughness and recipe-manner reminiscent at times of the *Kama Sutra*. 'Writing a story in the third person is one way of writing short stories.' And 'Mixed marriages, mixed food and mixed customs should be introduced in stories, so as to facilitate the successful creation of a Malayan culture'.

The English-language group exhibited manic-depressive tendencies, at one moment towards abjection, at another towards arrogance. A whining note about outside competition (from Shakespeare, Dickens and all that lot) could be detected, and there was even an individual proposal (the most distressing moment in the whole proceedings) that 'the first requisite for the creation of a truly Malayan literature is the stopping of the import of foreign publications into this country' and foreign publishers 'should be asked to leave the country to give room to rising Malayan publishers with projects in mind for the promotion of Malayan literature'. At the same time it was this group which distinguished most firmly and thoughtfully between art and propaganda—'It was generally agreed that literature is an activity valuable in itself . . . its function is inherent in itself and literature does not exist to serve a cause'—and showed itself the most sophisticated, or Western, in contending that a writer did not necessarily set out to educate or edify and that 'there should be no limitation in the form of an ethical code, but the sensitivity of certain audiences should be respected'. Sensitivities being what they are, though, this latter reservation needed more examination than it received. Where a racial incident can be sparked off by a jostling in the street or the sight of a lump of pork, it seems hard that the writer should forever and permanently be put on his honour to write nothing which might conceivably offend anyone. One notices that pork is not banned, for instance, nor religious processions. But perhaps this appeal to his discretion and civic sense is gratifying to the writer's vanity—especially if he is a non-writing writer.

The diversity of opinion in this group was probably connected with the defensive attitude common in English-language writers. It may be the tongue of Shakespeare, but they feel (or are made to feel) that they had better apologize for using it. It seems in order for a Tamil to write in Tamil or a Chinese to write in Chinese, but how should a Malayan, whatever his racial constitution, write in *English*? Even if it happens to be his first language, even if the best education in the region is still to be had in English-medium schools and universities. . . . For the distinctiveness of Malayan English, which might render it acceptable, lies more in intonation than in idiom. And English is the colonial language, a relic of colonialism. Some members of the English group expressed the view that 'the recent harsh pronouncements against the English language have discouraged budding writers in English'. It was in the proceedings of the English and Malay groups that the political aspects of 'language' were most clearly brought out.

The organizers of the Conference ruled that there would be no moving of resolutions at the final plenary session. This was especially prudent in view of the strongly-felt contention of the Singapore Congress of Malay Language and Culture, a participating body, that

> the Malays define 'literature' as 'a work of art expressed in language'. Thus, 'Malayan Literature' is 'a work of art expressed in Malayan Language', and here Malayan Language is the National Language, that is Malay

—with its logical but ungentlemanly inference that the other three groups had no right to be present. A reading of the report, along with the dimmest recognition of the incendiary possibilities of the project, fills one with admiration for the then Director of the Dewan Bahasa dan Kebudayaan Kebangsaan (Institute of National Language and Culture), Dr Slametmuljana, an Indonesian professor seconded to Singapore, and his multi-racial staff.

'It shall be the duty of Malaya to save civilization . . . and it is the duty of Malayan writers to direct them.' It will be readily understood that the burden which Malayan writers have taken upon themselves is so grievous—to be all things to all men—as to leave them with little time or energy for writing. That some writing has been done, nevertheless, is indicated by several recent publications. *Bunga Emas*,[1] or 'Golden Flowers', offers a selection of Malayan or Malaysian writing in English and (in English versions) Chinese and Tamil. Copyright reasons are adduced for the non-inclusion of work in Malay, but this deficiency is partly (though not very reassuringly) supplied by a bilingual paperback, *Modern Malay Verse*.[2] The English-speaking Malayan, who rarely reads another local language really well, is always being told how much better (more vigorous, more enterprising, more responsible, more activist, more genuine) are the writers in Chinese and Tamil. On the evidence of *Bunga Emas* it would seem that this shame-inducing comparison needs inspection, though at the same time the anthology would hardly bear out large claims for literature written in English to date. The poetry selection indicates a preference for the Eliotic or Dylanistic, for the conception of poetry as necessarily obscure yet patently portentous. Unhappily Ee Tiang Hong and Edwin Thumboo are absent, perhaps the two poets who have best resisted this debased 'modernism' and managed to look into their hearts and write— and write even in accents discernibly (but not too contrivedly) Malayan.

[1] An Anthology of Contemporary Malaysian Literature (1930-1963). Edited by T. Wignesan.　　[2] Oxford University Press, Kuala Lumpur.

Not say I don't appreciate poetry:
But you speak of poetry which have no rhyme,
Not like the ones I sometimes quote
'What is our life so full of care
We got no time to stand and stare?'
But still I must admit
I don't like poetry
Very much. I like music.

Not jazz American stuff.
Classical music worse still too long and dull,
I like the music to be sentimental
Like at night while dim light in my room,
I turn on the radio.
O Ross Hamilton is my favourite
His words so full of meaning
'I'll go out in the night
Buy you a dream.'

But I never like painting. In school
I hated Art like anything.
And Modern Art
I cannot understand. Like Picasso—
Why he always show
A man with funny shape
Head and body all mixed up?
I think
It is all nonsensical.

(*Ee Tiang Hong, 'Song of a Young Malayan'*)

Nor is the younger generation represented, an omission which gives the anthology not merely a retrospective but even something of an obituary flavour. The poets are mainly the bright young student generation of the 1950's, the pioneers in that 'Engmalchin' idiom (English-Malay-Chinese) which was to win independence for Malayan-writing-in-English. But 'obituary' is a description from which one would certainly exempt the meaty stories of Lee Kok Liang (the most professional writer here; he has recently published a collection, *The Mutes in the Sun*) and 'Awang Kedua'. The three stories by S. Rajaratnam, at present Singapore's Minister for Culture, are neat vignettes of village life, drought, famine, poverty, sickness, in the old *New Writing* manner. If one were mischievously inclined, one might wonder what the Minister has to say about the exclusive Indianness of Mr Rajaratnam's subject-matter.

Hitherto English writing in Malaya has been left almost solely to the young, and as the young have grown up, left the university and become useful and often influential citizens, they have ceased to write. The trails are littered with promise and mostly peter out. This is understandable in a country which is itself still young. But it means that the mass of the writing is adolescent, in a timeless and universal way, it tends to the embarrassingly (and confusedly) 'personal', the apocalyptic-morbid, all too plainly betraying its origins in student frustrations and a desire for 'originality' at all costs. And this is why Malaya's most active intellectuals, the politicians, have mocked such writing with the epithet 'ivory tower'; though in these post-colonial times, when a fairly straightforward struggle has given place to a complexity of enemies, the same politicians are realizing that there are more deplorable constructions than ivory towers, worse habits than 'self-expression'—as some of the pieces in *Modern Malay Verse* serve to suggest:

> When oppression reaches deep into the bones,
> Listen to the loud cry of the peasants in the fields!
> Listen to the thunderous shout of the workers in factories!
> United, in one great rank they rise to fight.

Concurrently there has also been something of the other kind of timeless writing, the gentle, well-intentioned, sweet and over-sweet. *Sugar and Salt*, a recent novel by a twenty-year-old Malayan, Johnny Ong, is a sentimental but affecting narrative, stilted in language but rather endearingly so, which goes some way in picturing (mainly) Chinese life in Malaya, the persistence of

Chinese customs in a mixed environment which has not yet become 'Malayan' except in as far as the mixture can be called Malayan. The foreign reader will smile to see the author referring, apropos of Kuala Lumpur, to 'the inscrutable, exotic East', but he should remember that to Malayans a lot of what goes on in Malaya remains fairly exotic. That Malayan writers in English seem so often to be painstakingly describing their own surroundings as if for the benefit of English (or, let's say, foreign) eyes is not merely due to their ambition to achieve a wide foreign market. Partly it stems from their desire to explain things to Malayans of other communities. What is not 'exotic' in Malaya at present? (The Malay *kampongs*, the extremist will answer, from whence all culture must flow....) The literature of a melting-pot is bound to be heavily documentary.

The participants in the Writers' Conference were full of suggestions whereby Malayan literature could be fostered, most of them involving the government in the dispensation of largesse. But though money talks, I doubt whether it writes; and the government wisely prefers to build schools and cheap housing. The *pot-pourri* evenings arranged by the Ministry of Culture in Singapore—Malay dances or music followed by Chinese and Indian with perhaps a few English folk songs thrown in—are proving popular, but at the level of creative writing perhaps a wise passiveness is the Ministry's best policy. Except for an occasional literary competition: a recent short story contest brought in a handful of truly interesting contributions. Literature will inevitably be the last art to blossom in a small yet multi-lingual and multi-racial society: words are difficult to manage and (unlike paint and choreography and musical sounds) they are sometimes dangerous to their users. Where natural growth is concerned, there seems to be no satisfactory substitute for nature, and time is the most likely healer of literary barrenness. Even in the new countries, even in 'the inscrutable, exotic East', writers are born rather than made, and too many midwives spoil the birth.

'In states unborn and accents yet unknown': Shakespeare Overseas

No doubt it was ill temper, soured by a tropical sun, which led me recently to inveigh against what seemed a jeering reference in *The Times Literary Supplement* to a Caribbean student, a specialist in Wordsworth, who in the ecstasy of his first visit to England mistook a bank of dandelions for the famous daffodils of his master. The finger of scorn, I took it, was pointed not so much at this particular student, more sinned against than sinning, as at the old-fashioned notion that English literature could really mean something to foreigners and could properly be taught on that assumption. Now, the daffodil drama is a hoary tale: like the pieces of the true cross or like the ashes of the Buddha, this benighted student and these devilish daffodils are forever turning up all over the globe. The perenniality of the story might even be taken as an indication of Wordsworth's popularity abroad rather than as proof of the impossibility of exporting him.

Cleopatra, according to a Thai student, was bitten by an aspect; according to a Singaporean, by a wasp. . . . We teachers of literature overseas are in great part ourselves to blame for the disrepute into which our profession has fallen. We cannot resist telling our traveller's tales at London cocktail parties, at high table in Oxford or Cambridge. It was another young Singaporean Chinese, now teaching English in school, whom I interrogated in the hope of further treasure for my next leave. After some hesitation, with some shame, she confessed that there had been a time when she misread that celebrated line as 'Making the green one—red.' Even if I thought this a funny story I should be deterred from telling it by the consideration that I was considerably older than her before realizing that the line should be read 'Making the green—one red.'

England doesn't want to hear the sensible things our students have said. But do British students never commit howlers? Two suppositions seem to underly this current merriment over Eng. Lit. abroad: (1) that all Britishers read or watch Shakespeare with perfect and complete pleasure and understanding, and (2) that foreigners are tradition-bound, they have no imagination, indeed they are of a different *species* from us, they do not have hands, organs, dimensions, senses, affection, passions, if you tickle them they do not laugh, etc. A higher-minded version of this latter theory has it that we should not pervert with our literature innocent foreigners who already have their own native supply of high thoughts: this, I suspect, is related to the fallacy that the East is spiritual and the West materialistic, and therefore the latter can in the name of morality supply the former only with guns, medicine and crime stories in basic English.

* * *

It is certainly fallacious to suppose that where art is concerned people will only want more of what they already have—that, for instance, the Japanese will seize on Yeats's plays because in some vague way they resemble the native *Nō*. In fact the Japanese have seized on Shakespeare, Synge, Ibsen, Shaw, Eliot—the sorts of drama they hadn't got already, and wanted. If they want something like *Nō*, then *Nō* best fills the bill—and well they know it. Naturally it will be easier, in the early days of cultural interchange, for one country to accept from another those literary forms bearing a similarity to its own: but this sort of interest tends to fade rather soon, in fact it qualifies for the epithet 'novelty'. Japanese literary researchers may investigate the correspondences and divergences between the *Kabuki* theatre and the Elizabethan stage: Japanese readers of Shakespeare prize him for the depth of characterization and the variety of 'philosophical' generalizations and human insights which *Kabuki* does not afford.

While we are discussing fallacies, we might say a little more about the theory that English literature is irrevocably compromised because it was thrust upon subject races as a political, an imperialistic measure. One prime minister of a newly independent state, it is true, has anathematized English literature as a weakening influence, possibly because it tended to weaken the hatred of 'Britain' which at one time he was concerned to promulgate, perhaps because now it speaks out for a largeness and tolerance, a degree of individual freedom, which he feels unable to afford. (We remember what encouragement the Indians derived from English literature in their fight for independence, when—as Professor C. D. Narasimhaiah puts it—'English poets became instruments to plague their own countrymen with'.) This theory often has it that our literature, and in the nature of things Shakespeare in particular, was imposed on people already possessing an established and thriving and widely current vernacular literature, and that the imposed literature lay alongside the native one, in a state of hostility, meeting only to mar. In fact, in some cases, notably in parts of India, the vernacular literature grew up or at least was resuscitated under the direct stimulus of English literature. 'The first province wholly to come under the British sway, Bengal was also the first to experience the throes of a cultural rebirth,' writes Professor K. R. Srinivasa Iyengar in his collection, *The Adventure of Criticism*:

> When other linguistic areas—Hindi, Marathi, Tamil, Kannada, Telugu, Gujarati, Assamese, Oriya, Sindhi, Malayalam—when, early or late, they too felt the stir of returning life, they received sustenance from *two* sources, English and Bengali.

Professor Iyengar also notes that

> Of Western dramatists, Shakespeare of course was the universal favourite, and among the plays frequently translated or adapted

were *Othello*, *The Comedy of Errors*, *The Merchant of Venice*, *Cymbeline* and *Hamlet*. Gujarati, Marathi, Hindi and Assamese versions of the *Errors* appeared as early as 1865, 1878, 1879, 1889 respectively ... a Tamil adaptation of *Cymbeline* in 1898, and a Bengali edition of Shakespeare's plays in four volumes was issued between 1896 and 1902.

★   ★   ★

I shall not succeed in avoiding the old cliché about Shakespeare's 'universality'. Cliché as it is, it indicates a truth of a higher order than whatever is implied by the concept of 'Shakespeare as an Elizabethan'. Scholars may make what they can out of this latter, but Johnson's words must carry more weight:

> His characters are not modified by the customs of particular places, unpractised by the rest of the world; by the peculiarities of studies or professions, which can operate but upon small numbers; or by the accidents of transient fashions or temporary opinions: they are the genuine progeny of common humanity, such as the world will always supply, and observation will always find.

Did 'the world' mean for Johnson something much narrower than it must mean to us? I doubt it. Perhaps I may be allowed to repeat what I have said elsewhere, on the legitimacy of teaching English literature in the East. 'It is a great and varied and comprehensive literature—a humane and central literature rather than a literature of *élite* or priesthood or cult. To risk a crude generalization'—and I hope not to be irretrievably damned for my crude use throughout of such generalizations as 'abroad' and 'the 'East'—'to risk a crude generalization, we could say that on the whole Eastern art has hitherto been tied to religion or mysticism or ethics, or else it has remained pronouncedly "aesthetic"—delicate sensations for the sake of delicate sensations. English literature helps to supply a deficiency, a deficiency especially felt as the East grows more Western, more industrial, more technological, more democratic—the lack of humanistically-inspired writing, writing which explores and reports on and helps to mould the relationship between the individual and his rights and society and its demands.'

Shakespeare was the great recording genius of our Renaissance. Now Africa and Asia are experiencing their Renaissance. These regions received their industrial revolution, their scientific and medical revolution, in a lump sum, from us. All this was hardly something which could be doled out little by little: and it is an old joke that Thailand had planes before it had trains, telegraphy before roads. The arts lagged an era behind, not merely behind 'material' developments but also behind the resultant and gradual changes in social customs, in the spiritual pattern. In some countries the artists were Luddites to a degree undreamt of by Sir Charles Snow: they weren't against change so much as (in their art) wholly unaware of it. Their art was inviolate, shackled to the past. But they came to want it to yield its long-preserved virginity, to be free. They knew they couldn't go on forever producing *haiku* or *Kabuki* or variations on the *Ramayana* or paintings of goldfish and bamboo—not even to please the tourists and the foreign dons and the Christmas card makers. They are too intelligent, too lively, to *want* to do so. Naturally they would turn first to the modern literature of the West, but our current writing is too tired, too sophisticated, too blasé, sometimes too trivial, to satisfy them for long. Out of the frying-pan into the fire! What holds them, for it deals with a world which is modern (rather than mediaeval) and bursting with energy (rather than sophistication), is pre-eminently the plays of Shakespeare. Therein is a Renaissance which they can understand and feel, with its fresh challenges, fresh hopes, fresh horrors, its fresh cynicism even, the sense of discoveries being made, not just being annotated.

* * *

I would not wish to convey the impression that all Eastern students are oriental sages and the teacher's life is a bed of lotuses!

Naturally the Asian or African reader will encounter problems, some of them special problems. Ghanaians, according to Mr D. S. Baker (In *Shakespeare Survey* 16, 1963), find the tilting at romantic love in *The Taming of the Shrew* more congenial than 'the romantic world of the moonlit bank' of *The Merchant of Venice*. Does this stem from the otherness of Ghanaian attitudes towards love and marriage?—if so, what accounts for a similar preference among many British readers?—or from a shared modernity and a distinctly modern sense of humour? In *Talking of Shakespeare* (1954) Mr Norman Marshall found Indian audiences distinctly Elizabethan and thought that in evincing amusement during the balcony scene of *Romeo and Juliet* they were reacting very much as Shakespeare intended his audience should. At all events, I cannot believe that Mr Baker's explanation ('few people would attempt to sit on a bank, moonlit or otherwise, in Africa') explains very much. *Twelfth Night* is an unrewarding text to teach in the East; so is *As You Like It*—but maybe in the West too it is a difficult proposition, unless (as perhaps Mr James Smith's essay in *Scrutiny* indicates by its very tentativeness) you are prepared to thrust upon it a load of earnestness under which it totters. Often the difficulties of foreign students turn out to be our own difficulties underlined.

If a Thai student cries out that Macbeth is indeed a mere and absolute monster because he has killed a king and our Lord Buddha tells us it is wrong to kill, one may suspect a tongue in a cheek, or the traces of pretty immediate political indoctrination, or the inhibition not so much of an 'Asian' or 'traditional' education as of a non-education. If a young Thai lady denounces Lady Macbeth as equally a monster, because she scolds her husband and no good wife would do that, one may suspect a tongue deep in a cheek, or a candidate hard up for something to say (for something which will gratify her foreign teacher, with his well-known respect for native customs)—or someone at any rate taking Shakespeare seriously. . . . Incidentally, it will hardly do—

though it sometimes is done—to find Shakespeare unviable on the grounds that some or other peasant won't be able to understand him. Every country may not have its peasants, but every country has its illiterates.

The account given by Mr V. Srinivasa Rao, Reader in English in the University of Mysore, runs close to my own experience abroad:

> The puns and the verbal wit in some of the comedies are not understood by our students; when they are explained, there is understanding but no appreciation. . . . These experiences make some teachers think that our students cannot appreciate Shakespearean comedy. . . . How far are these opinions valid? It is difficult to believe that our young men are deficient in a sense of humour. They may not be able to understand or appreciate a humorous situation in some Shakespearean comedies. That is because of the difference in the social climate of our students and their consequent unfamiliarity with the comic situation. When it is explained to a class of students specializing in English literature, they evince appreciation and the proper response.
>
> With the tragedies of Shakespeare the case is different. Almost every class in the university is able to understand and enjoy a tragedy. Perhaps the theorist will conclude that we are a tragic nation, and therefore tragedy appeals to our students. Surely this cannot be so. The subject matter of tragedy appeals to our students because it is more general or universal. (*The Literary Half-Yearly*, Bangalore, January 1960).

To strive to show how Sir Toby Belch is a funny man, really, is a thankless labour. I would be falling into the error I am trying to expose if I pleaded that *King Lear* is more thoroughly understood in the East, where filial obedience means more than it does in the West. But to meet resistance in the study of a tragedy—for instance, a stern and simple-minded disapproval of Antony's unsocial behaviour, in an emergent country, where all is certainly not for love nor the world well lost over a matter which can so easily be disposed of—will often prove a fruitful experience.

★   ★   ★

But we mustn't forget the local obscurities, the difficulties of detail, the infamous daffodils. Quoting the line 'My life is fall'n into the sere, the yellow leaf', Mr Baker points out in his article on 'Shakespeare in Ghana' that the leaves in the tropics fall mainly as the dry season (the *healthier* season) is setting in. But all the same a withered leaf is a withered leaf everywhere. And Macbeth is not talking of his age in years but of his withering into spiritual death, his *'way of* life'. I allude to Mr Baker's misquotation only because it serves to remind us that we English too can err. The 'daffodil bar' can generally be overcome by means of a simple explanation given as a matter of course, I would have thought, in one's teaching. If we took seriously some of the reports of misapprehension and delusion emanating from British teachers overseas we would be forced to conclude that they ought to be sacked for arrant incompetence and dereliction of duty.

With many of these difficult points, we too need help—the show of eight kings, Polonius's windlasses and assays of bias, poor Tom's fiends, all those jokes about horns and tailors, or the operation of the sun on the mud of the Nile. And perhaps a contemporary English reader is more likely than an innocent Japanese or Indian or African to go ludicrously wrong over Antony's invitation to Cleopatra to ride on his pants triumphing. In his presidential address to the All-India English Teachers' Conference held in Baroda in 1959, Professor P. K. Guha of Jadavpur University mentioned the 'galloping method' of teaching followed by the late Professor H. M. Percival of Presidency College, Calcutta: 'He used to say to us, "I shall halt only at real difficulties and your difficulties and mine are likely to coincide".'

But Mr Baker's conclusion compels agreement, or more than agreement:

> Even if the understanding of a play is only partial or superficial, there are degrees of vitality, freshness and sheer fun in Ghanaian Shakespeare that one hopes will not be extinguished in the interests of textual criticism and purely academic study.

Indeed one hopes not! One service which overseas admirers of Shakespeare can render us is to preserve Shakespeare for the common reader.

★   ★   ★

Indian Shakespeare criticism is increasing in both quantity and quality.[1] The quality of, for example, Japanese criticism is more difficult to assess because most of it is written in the vernacular. How will Eastern interpretations of Shakespeare affect our understanding of the plays? The whole tenor of my account would suggest, I think, that such influence is likelier to be a matter of minor modifications than of radical revision. What we should expect to emerge is not an Indian Shakespeare, a Malaysian Shakespeare, a Japanese Shakespeare and so forth, but rather a contemporary Shakespeare more or less common to all countries. Except—which is more than a minor modification—that these Eastern countries may well provide an injection of enthusiasm, a more immediate recognition of Shakespeare as a living writer, concerned with living issues, not a dead classic. The special excitement which *Julius Caesar* and *Coriolanus* arouse in classes in some Asian countries is a simple and obvious instance of what I mean.

The traditional teaching of Shakespeare in India and Ceylon (and no doubt elsewhere) up until the 1940's or even later laid stress on the story, the characters, the message and the aphorisms, and on the learning by heart of great passages: it was heavily Bradleyan. However crude those classroom discussions may have been, at least Shakespeare was seen as having something to do with what (in a comprehensive gesture) I will term 'life', not as a cold abstract discipline, nor as raw material for self-aggrandizing ingenuity. (It is difficult to believe that Bradleyan teaching at its very worst could have the sterilizing and stultifying effect

---

[1] The special Shakespeare number of *The Literary Criterion* (Mysore, Winter 1963), a collection of seventeen essays of which twelve are by Indian scholars, is relevant to this discussion at many points.

of the higher symbololatry or the 'recurrent image' method mechanically applied.) Theirs was the sort of reading to which Dr John Holloway has objected on the grounds that the 'moral insights' or pieces of 'moral information' thus derived from the plays are in paraphrase so crude or banal or inaccurate that Shakespeare must have meant more, and what he meant must be sought elsewhere. But in Shakespeare these 'insights' are not *in paraphrase*: nor do we (nor, surely, did all those students) really confuse our paraphrases, or metaphors, with what is in Shakespeare. Shakespeare gives us the real thing, overpoweringly: our later descriptions are poor shadows of it, but we *have* experienced the real thing. The life in his plays is a criticism of and commentary on our lives. If we deny Shakespeare this 'informative' value, what do we leave him with? What do we leave ourselves with? We certainly would make a comic spectacle, telling simpleminded foreigners—as sometimes we seem to be doing—'Come, come, you mustn't take Shakespeare *seriously*!' Perhaps there was great virtue in that learning by heart. . . .

Much of what is said in the foregoing paragraph has already been proposed by an Indian, Mrs K. Wood, Professor of English at Elphinstone College, Bombay, in an article (in *The Indian Journal of English Studies*, 1962) touching on Dr Holloway's book, *The Story of the Night*. Mrs Wood's article ends, 'Perhaps we need . . . some shedding of our learning to remember that "His Heroes are Men".' And not exclusively Englishmen.

'As Professor Ludowyk said, "Time past in Europe after the lapse of several years becomes time present in Ceylon." It is true of India no less. As for ideas, they must have travelled at snail-pace. . . .' It is amusing that this description by Professor C. D. Narasimhaiah of the backwardness of English studies in Indian universities during the earlier part of this century should occur in *F. R. Leavis: Some Aspects of His Work*, published in Mysore in 1963—the first book to be devoted to Dr Leavis. Equally interesting, in suggesting that the time lag was not always so great, is Leavis's comment in the 'Retrospect' appended to the reprint of *Scrutiny*:

> We had a great influence—and not the less because *Scrutiny* was known to be an outlaw enterprise—on generations of Cambridge students from the Indian sub-continent who now form key *élites* in India and Pakistan. How measure the effect of such influence? And who will pronounce it negligible?

★   ★   ★

And Shakespeare—how can we measure the effect of his influence overseas? And who would dare to pronounce it negligible? Will someone, to commemorate this quater-centenary, enable the Old Vic Company to tour Africa, India, Malaysia, Japan . . .?[1] And will Britain issue a special stamp, with Shakespeare's head on it,[2] if only to assure the world of the influence he has exerted on the natives of that country?

---

[1] The New Shakespeare Company toured India, Hong Kong and Malaysia in the following year.

[2] Britain did; and also a rather tawdry Stratfordian air-letter form.

The Art and Craft of Love

1. SAUCE FOR THE GOOSE

'A SLIGHT acquaintance with the temple sculptures and painting of India gives ample proof that Indian men and women were always acutely aware of each other, and that both desired a full and sensual life.' So says Dr Edward S. Gifford in the course of a chatty book called *The Charms of Love*. Proof equally plain and even ampler is given by *The Kama Sutra of Vatsyayana*, a work composed between the first and fourth centuries A.D. by 'a religious student', translated into English by Sir Richard Burton and F. F. Arbuthnot, two oriental students, and first printed in 1883. The translation, a high-ranking item of curious literature, has been available (notably along the streets of Indian cities) in variously selective and smutty-looking avatars. It is now publicly printed—perhaps as a kind of Ranee Chatterley's Lover—for the first time in England, and brought out by Allen and Unwin.

If Burton's interest in the *Kama Sutra* was simply an interest in sex, as W. G. Archer suggests in his preface, his co-translator Arbuthnot was drawn to it by his detestation of Victorian marriage. 'Europeans and modern society generally would be greatly benefited by some such treatises,' he wrote, 'It is difficult to get Englishmen to acknowledge that matrimonial happiness may in many cases be attained by a careful study of the passions of a wife, that is to say admitting that a wife be allowed to feel passion.' Arbuthnot's enthusiasm seems apter than Burton's. The *Kama Sutra* could tend to deprave only the person who is so intent on self-depravation that he needs no outside help.

Vatsyayana begins by drawing a firm distinction between the

brute creation and mankind: from this he deduces the propriety of writing about sexual matters. At the same time he relates Kama (the life of the senses) to the other two great activities, Dharma (religious duty) and Artha (worldly welfare, acquisition), and instructs us that

> Any action which conduces to the practice of Dharma, Artha and Kama together, or of any two, or even one of them, should be performed, but an action which conduces to the practice of one of them at the expense of the remaining two should not be performed.

Despite a periodical collapse into the language of the counting-house, the *Kama Sutra* is a notably humane document. From the outset it grants women the same sexual rights it allows to men—which, in this case, is a lot.

It must be admitted that at times Vatsyayana seems to address himself to morons, or else to contortionists; and occasionally he approaches the limits of the strait and narrow, as when proposing ways of overcoming the resistance of married women or advising the elder wife how she can stir up trouble for her younger colleagues. But the sage bases himself throughout on the grand principle that the Art of Love requires two celebrants—and no sacrifice. The chapter 'On the Various Modes of Striking' distinguishes him clearly from the Marquis de Sade.

> Towards the conclusion of the congress, the breasts, the jaghana (*middle part*), and the sides of the woman should be pressed with the open palms of the hand, with some force, until the end of it, and then sounds like those of the quail or the goose should be made.

The use in love-play of sharp instruments he deplores as 'painful, barbarous, and base, and quite unworthy of imitation', and by way of discouragement he invokes the sad case of King Satakarni Satavahana of the Kuntalas who 'deprived his great Queen Malayavati of her life by a pair of scissors'. The closest he comes to standard pornography is when he expounds in detail a certain course of action and then states his disapproval of such goings-on. But in general the sage is uncensorious, and careful to remind us that his instructions and counsels are not meant to delimit our activities: 'About these things there cannot be either enumeration or any definite rule. Congress having once commenced, passion alone gives birth to all the acts of the parties.' We could welcome his comments on Warden Sparrow's agonizing reappraisal of the Connie-Mellors connection.

Such disclaiming of absolute authority is needful, for Vatsyayana is prone to enumeration and rule; he suffers from the pedagogue's common uncertainty as to where to start and when to stop. 'Nothing increases love so much as nails, and biting.' We will forget that the sage has said as much of various other phenomena, since the list of eight kinds of pressing with the nails, classified according to the marks produced, makes seductive reading. 'A peacock's foot', 'The jump of a hare', 'The leaf of a blue lotus', and the like. But sadly anti-climactic is the succeeding list of the three kinds of nails, 'according to their size: Small, Middling, Large'. In a similarly statistical spirit Vatsyayana divides men and women into three classes according to their degree of passion—Small, Middling, Intense—and works out in columns the nine kinds of union resulting from combinations and permutations of these three classes.

The comic pedanticism is aggravated by the aphoristic nature of the sutra, a sort of ticking off on the fingers which aims at exhaustiveness rather than discrimination. Yet the resultant downrightness is often engaging: 'As for the sayings that though women may fall in love, they still make no effort themselves to gain over the object of their affections, that is only a matter of idle talk.' And the sage's curtness of style averts quite admirably any suggestion of obscenity, an accident which tends to befall those tutors who choose fiction for their vehicle. The *Chin Ping Mei* of sixteenth-century China, a notably wordy piece of fiction, in its English version, *The Golden Lotus*, must resort frequently to Latin for its most didactic passages. (Its first edition, the story goes, was poisonous in a literal sense: counting on the universal malpractice of licking a finger to turn over a page, the author smeared poison on the manuscript before sending it to a personal enemy known to enjoy such literature.)

In his introduction to the *Kama Sutra* (it is compassed about with a highly respectable cloud of witnesses) K. M. Panikkar suggests that originally the sutra-form was meant to enable students to memorize the text. No doubt, when you are memorizing a list of twelve women who are 'not to be enjoyed', you might as well start off with 'A leper'. Less obvious—and alas there is no commentary—is the presence of 'A woman who is extremely white' and 'A woman who is extremely black'. If the colour bar operated then, at least it operated both ways. We can see why 'One who is formed like a male' should appear among the seventeen sorts of women not to be sought in marriage. And why the category of 'Women who are easily gained over' should include 'An immoral woman' and even 'Women who stand at the doors of their houses'. But we could wish for reason to be given why 'The wife of a jeweller' features in this company.

More disturbing than the detailed explication of the self-evident is the calculating nature of some of the advice. One section expounds the occasions on which the wives of other men may rightly be resorted to, but 'it must be distinctly understood that (this) is only allowed for special reasons, and not for mere carnal desires'. One such special reason is when a man argues: 'By being united with this woman, I shall kill her husband, and so obtain his vast riches which I covet'. Likewise the complicated balance-sheet of losses and gains, sensual and financial and religious, which the sage draws up for the courtesan. At such times we feel as the narrator of Anthony Powell's *The Kindly Ones* felt about *The Perfumed Garden of the Sheik Nefzaoui*, a sixteenth-century work issued by Burton and Arbuthnot three years after their *Kama Sutra*: 'Sincere and scholarly, there was also something more than a little oppressive about the investigation, moments when the author seemed to labour the point, to induce a feeling of surfeit in the reader'. Confusion arises because Vatsyayana is both teaching us how things ought to be (I mustn't omit to remark that much of his discourse on love-making is eminently sane) and telling us how things actually are in this imperfect world: he doesn't always make clear whether he is recommending or condoning or merely describing.

Mr Panikkar remarks that the *Kama Sutra* reflects a condition of high civilization in second-century India: peace and prosperity, education for women, freedom of social intercourse, remarriage of widows, no child marriage.... Instead of the rigid stratification of later Indian society, here we see 'a gay and happy people who worshipped their gods, performed their rituals but enjoyed life with all its refinements to the full'. True, the world of the *Kama Sutra* is free from sexual prudes, sexual tyrants and (except for eunuchs) sexual cripples. And if the sage is at times excessively business-like and even officious, he can also grow tender and lyrical, as in the section on Courtship. Yet this paradise has its pariahs. There are disparaging references to slaves and elephant drivers, and the man who makes up to female water carriers is told sternly that in this case 'external touches, kisses, and manipulation are not to be employed'. The brief account of love among the haystacks—'the superintendents of cow pens enjoy the women in the cow pens'—doesn't sound too glorious, nor does the sexual life of the inmates of the royal harems partake obviously of high civilization. Incidentally, Vatsyayana warns those who might aspire to palliate the lot of these women that it would be better not to try. If they insist, they should contrive to have themselves smuggled in and out concealed in bed coverings—a similar shift had earlier occurred to Cleopatra—or else avail themselves of a recipe which he gives for invisibility.

It is here and in the section on aphrodisiacs that the *Kama Sutra* sinks into that 'area of human foolishness, self-deceit, and pathos' of which *The Charms of Love* provides a lightning tour. Unlike Vatsyayana, Dr Gifford is a confirmed wet blanket, and the only theory he inclines to support is the one that considers tobacco an anaphrodisiac. Here perhaps is the basis for a more potent campaign against smoking. Dr Gifford's psychological explanations of the miseries and splendours of love are not always more convincing than the picturesque interpretations he rejects. Every age has its superstitions, and ours tend to be a dull lot. It is easy to poke fun at the *Kama Sutra*. We should remember that when it was written Britons were making love with clubs—and at the time it was translated, with bank balances.

2. You Too Can

The *Koka Shastra*, which occupies less than 70 pages of this book,[1] is an erotic—no, erotological—document of the twelfth century, some 900 years later than the *Kama Sutra*, upon which it is heavily dependent (or to which, W. G. Archer says, it looks back as in our day Lawrence Durrell looks back to Cavafy) and to which it adds very little. Rather, counting in the 90 pages of scholarship which act as swelling prologues to the imperial theme, it subtracts from the grateful memories one has of the *Kama Sutra* by arousing the fear that we are to be subject to a never-ending stream of erotological exhortation, with a consequent erotic erosion of our own milder shores.

The *Koka Shastra* is sensible, nonsensical, comic and pedantic by turn. The editorial foot-notes are chiefly pedantic. Since the text goes to the trouble to inform us that wily men will avoid a girl who has inverted nipples, or a beard, or flap-ears like winnowing fans, surely a foot-note might tell us why a girl called after a mountain, a tree, a river or a bird, is equally to be shunned? There may be a few new *bandhas* (coital postures) here, but they

[1] *The Koka Shastra.* And Other Mediaeval Indian Writings on Love. Translated with an Introduction and Notes by Alex Comfort. Preface by W. G. Archer.

seem largely indistinguishable and sometimes doubtfully pleasurable. To voice such reservations is to display what Alex Comfort calls 'pure Englishmanship', our national pusillanimity and defensive cynicism. Yet I note that even Dom Moraes partakes of this Englishmanship, speculating in his preface to a paperback *Kama Sutra* as to whether perhaps the ancient Indians weren't made a bit differently from the moderns.

The sage Kokkoka strikes us as a monument of good sense (good sense, perhaps, of various sorts, including the commercial) in the backwash of Dr Comfort's portentous introduction. 'One can see as good examples of nakhacchedya (erotic scratch-marks, the stock Indian love-token) in the London Underground as on any mediaeval Indian lady.' I was hoping to add my own testimony here, but on-the-spot research suggests that many Eastern scratch-marks derive from mosquito-bites. The humour lies, certainly not in scratches as such, but in our vision of the protagonist hurriedly leafing through the catalogue in search of an appropriate engraving. 'Ah, the peacock-foot this time, I think. . .'. Possibly after all Kokkoka would approve of the commodity mentioned in Dr Comfort's footnote to the classification of love-cries—'In America, one can now buy a long-playing record of these attractive sounds—they appear to have changed very little'—but strictly as an audio-aid for use in the classroom.

In order to translate these documents Dr Comfort learnt some Sanskrit, *pro bono pubico*. His interest is more than scholarly, it is all part of his energetic campaign to give English love-making a new look, to bring us 'a civilized and guilt-free view of sexuality as pleasure and fulfilment', in the teeth of the Christian tradition and such medico-moral theories as hold that sexual activity produces pimples or blindness or insanity. The question is, when we have ridded ourselves of every form of 'sexual anxiety', what are we left with? Some of us may suspect that these erotologists are proposing to liberate sex in the way aesthetes 'liberate' art, by making it a special, autonomous and unrelated activity—the

THE ART AND CRAFT OF LOVE

phantom f - - -, to adapt I. A. Richards's teminology. I am sorry
to sound so disrespectful simultaneously of the wisdom of the
East and of the biology of the West, but this mixture of unsmiling
solemnity and skin-deep airiness is a little difficult to take gracefully.

Yet Dr Comfort's intentions are kindly, he sincerely believes
that these documents will serve to 'reassure' us. And some of us I
suppose some of them will. Kokkoka shares the humaneness of
Vatsyayana's *Kama Sutra*, for him love-making requires two
makers (except in the short section on plural intercourse), and
there is absolutely no trace of the grotesque sado-masochism and
bestiality of Japanese 'pillow-art'. But some of the material (there
were giants in those days) is hardly more reassuring than Alan
Hull Walton's footnote in *The Perfumed Garden of the Shaykh
Nefzawi*: 'It must be remembered that we are here dealing with
the Arab race, in whom the genital dimensions are generally
greater than in European man'. Cold comfort indeed. Perhaps,
though, we can draw a little consolation from the comment
passed by the Shaykh himself, patently irreproachable and wholly
un-English, on certain grand Indian exploits. 'The position as you
perceive, is very fatiguing and very difficult to attain. I even
believe that the only realization of it consists in words and designs.'
Or, as Sir Richard Burton might less magisterially put it,
'C'est beau, but—is it true?'

'To be longing is better than to be satisfied,' a saying of the
Persian sage Sa'di, would seem to belong to an irreconcilable
wisdom.[1] Despite the blurb's description of its author as 'the
reverse of squeamish', despite its appearance in the Burton-
Arbuthnot series which included the *Kama Sutra* and *The Perfumed
Garden*, the *Gulistan* is a compilation of an altogether different
nature, accurately described by Professor Wickens as 'a moderate-
sized book of didactic tales, interspersed with short verses

[1] *The Gulistan or Rose Garden of Sa'di*. Translated by Edward Rehatsek.
Edited with a Preface by W. G. Archer. Introduction by G. M. Wickens.

247

summarizing and pointing the moral, and sometimes cutting and polishing new facets of pertinent wisdom'. Some of the aphorisms are neat, some of the tales telling:

> I remember, being in my childhood pious, rising in the night, addicted to devotion and abstinence. One night I was sitting with my father, remaining awake and holding the beloved Quran in my lap, whilst the people around us were asleep. I said: 'Not one of these persons lifts up his head or makes a genuflection. They are as fast asleep as if they were dead.' He replied: 'Darling of thy father, would that thou wert also asleep rather than disparaging people.'

But presumably its reputation rests more on the literary style of the Persian than on its unclothed wisdom, and unhappily Rehat-sek's translation, made in 1886, is heavy-handed and verbose and at times clumsy to the point of obfuscation.

Sir Richard Burton's prose is brisk and vivid, modulating into Latin and French as the theme requires. *Love, War and Fancy*[1] consists of part of his commentary or background-briefing to *The Arabian Nights*. Sophisticated, tolerant, shrewd, businesslike, at times coarse and (unlike the Indian sages) misogynic, this 'repertory of Eastern knowledge in its esoteric phase' includes much information, surmise and rumour concerning sexual customs, inversion, circumcision and modes of punishment— 'Impalement may be a barbarous punishment but it is highly effective, which after all is its principal object'—and should do well along Charing Cross Road. Kenneth Walker's prefatory chat about the beneficence of sexual manuals and our contemporary sexual enlightenment is difficult to account for in this context, except on the principle that 'right' sex is to be achieved through a study of perversions and superstitions. Which is as questionable as teaching literary appreciation by directing one's pupils into the sewers of the printed word.

The Arabian Nights arose out of King Shahryar's curious habit of slaying his bed-fellows after he had lain with them once. With

---

[1] Edited and Introduced by Kenneth Walker.

this in mind, some of us might be tempted to wonder whether some of the tall tales in this genre don't perhaps have their origin in sexual short-comings. Or are such speculations not only unscholarly but too too 'English' as well?

3. SEXAMETERS

Erotic Poetry, a large anthology subtitled 'The Lyrics, Ballads, Idyls and Epics of Love—Classical to Contemporary', is what, I imagine, is called a Bedside Book. No, not in *that* sense, not what the Japanese describe as 'pillow-art'. A book for browsing in, I mean, a book without much point or purpose. Useful for inducing slumber rather than waking you up.

The editor, William Cole, allows himself a very broad interpretation of the word 'erotic': it thus comprehends the anti-erotic. Indeed the anthology seems to me rich in the anti-erotic. Swift's verses about Celia, despite the final disclaimer ('Should I the Queen of Love refuse,/Because she rose from stinking ooze?'), are an obvious example. Or,

> Woman: that is to say
> A body which the birds of prey
> Distain to take away.

This latter is a piece of wisdom from the East, the Mecca of our Western erotologists and sexual reformers, the cynosure of our genuflections (one position the Anglo-Saxon has mastered!). But the West can be equally wise:

> I know but two good Houres that women have,
> One in the Bed, another in the Grave.

Or (they are said to order these matters better in France) Laforgue's petulant epitome: 'all this dirt for just three minutes' rapture!'

In time the contents of the anthology range from a Babylonian fragment of 3000 B.C. to verses written in 1963. The emotional range is rather less impressive. Spitefulness, arising out of resentment, is quite pronounced: many of these items (though they may be held to celebrate sex) hardly celebrate women. It might even seem as if the poet is intent on getting his own back: a case of the pen proving mightier than the sword. 'Epigram' is widely pertinent:

> You ask me how *Contempt* who claims to sleep
> With every woman that has ever been
> Can still maintain that women are skin deep?
> They never let him any deeper in.

The pox is what you get from women; there is no hint as to how women come by it. Women feature largely as objects, to be acquired, used and excreted. Much of the book resembles a posh butcher's shop, with a generous display of what Whitman in a characteristically happy phrase calls 'the naked meat of the body'. Thus,

> Not too lean, and not too fat—
> Choose midway between the two,
> Neither globular nor flat;
> Plump, just plump enough, will do.

The odd thing is that the majority of the female contributors (themselves a minority) look at women in much the same way as do the men. Women, we can only suppose, consider making love a man's job. Or is it rather that they consider making poetry a man's job? The book would suggest that female emancipation is by no means as far advanced as we had assumed.

But there are exceptions, honourable or dishonourable, among the frailer sex. Muriel Stuart, Charlotte Mew and Sylvia Townsend Warner contribute poems which, whether erotic or not, are good, and Edna St Vincent Millay turns the tables very neatly. Occasionally a woman's blood makes certain demands which necessitate the presence of a man, but

> let me make it plain:
> I find this frenzy insufficient reason
> For conversation when we meet again.

A thoroughly masculine attitude, to judge from elsewhere.

What is there here, besides the grudges and the whinings and the pretty plainly anti-erotic (which—don't tell me!—some people find highly erotic, but then any old thing is found erotic by somebody or other)? There is a fair spread of cheesecake, some of it agreeable, some of it disagreeably voyeuristic. George Moore has a sonnet about a lady undressing, bathing, and dressing again—it's the stockings that send him—and there is an abundance of girdles and belts and so on (and so off). Next comes the 'religious' department, with its systematic confusion between bed and altar. In his foreword Stephen Spender associates the erotic with the religious, because they both 'involve reverence for life, a sense of mystery'. Well, there is religion and religion. To me these latter-day imitations of the Song of Songs are the least appetising aspect of the anthology: wet-blanket religiosity, neither fish nor flesh. Pubic hair becomes 'moist, golden coin'. Ugh. And Whitman, the Universal Lover, sounds plain ludicrous:

> It is I, you women, I make my way,
> I am stern, acrid, large, undissuadable, but I love you,
> I do not hurt you any more than is necessary for you,
> I pour the stuff to start sons and daughters fit for these States, I press
>   with slow rude muscle,
> I brace myself effectually, I listen to no entreaties,
> I dare not withdraw till I deposit what has so long accumulated
>   within me.

No doubt it hurts him more than it hurts her. Before long the reader of this book inclines to agree with Alex Comfort (the poet, I mean, not the erotologist) that

> With better things in hand,
> No one would dip a pen. . . .

The moderns are mostly so conscious, so knowing, voyeuristic, as if they were writing for an anthology of erotic poetry—reporting back with what they knew already, for the book has little of the element of genuine surprise or discovery in it. Lawrence, though he appears here, would surely have hated it. There is little from the nineteenth century. The eighteenth century is largely coy, the seventeenth century (notably Carew) coldly ornate, and the olde-worlde ye-knowwe-whatte often tedious. My own slim selection from this anthology would include the three lady poets mentioned, Lorca, Donne, Marvell's 'Coy Mistress', Robert Graves, Cavafy, the passage from St John of the Cross, Ronald McCuaig's 'Music in the Air', Erich Kästner, Hedylos (the *Greek Anthology*), Roethke, 'She was poor but she was honest' and its counterpart, Hardy's un-Hardyesque poem 'The Ruined Maid', such frivolities (or honesties) as the anonymous assurance,

> Why blush, dear girl, pray tell me why?
>   You need not, I can prove it;
> For though your garter met my eye,
>   My thoughts were far above it,

or Matthew Prior's 'A True Maid',

> No, no; for my virginity,
>   When I lose that, says Rose, I'll die:
> Behind the elms, last night, cried Dick,
>   Rose, were you not extremely sick?

and Yeats's 'Leda and the Swan'. Characteristically, this last poem is placed in the section entitled 'By-paths and Oddities' (i.e. perversions). Most of the good poems are easily come by in the normal course of reading: they are good *poems*. As for their being 'erotic', they only make that word seem more ambiguous than ever. The epitaph on this present undertaking is supplied by Graves:

> Nothing, agreed, is alien to love
> When pure desire has overflowed its baulks,
> But why must private sportiveness be viewed
> Through public spectacles?

Index

253

INDEX